EAT UP SLIM DOWN

ANNUAL RECIPES 2005

In all Rodale cookbooks, our mission is to provide delicious and nutritious recipes. Our recipes also meet the standards of the Rodale Test Kitchen for dependability, ease, practicality, and, most of all, great taste. To give us your comments, call (800) 848-4735.

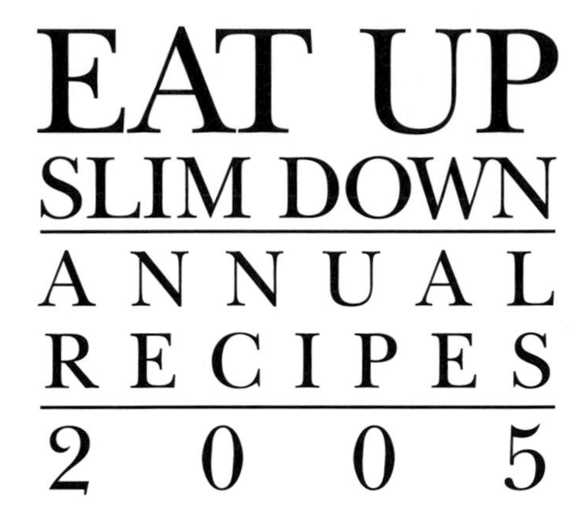

150 Simply Delicious Recipes for Permanent Weight Loss

Notice

This book is intended as a reference volume only, not as a medical manual. The foods discussed, and information and recipes given here, are designed to help you make informed decisions about your diet and health. This is not intended as a substitute for any treatment that may have been prescribed by your doctor. Keep in mind that nutritional needs vary from person to person, depending upon age, sex, health status, and total diet. If you suspect that you have a medical problem, we urge you to seek competent medical help.

Mention of specific companies, organizations, or authorities in this book does not imply endorsement by the publisher, nor does mention of specific companies, organizations, or authorities imply that they endorse this book.

Internet addresses and telephone numbers given in this book were accurate at the time it went to press.

Printed in the United States of America
Rodale Inc. makes every effort to use acid-free ♾, recycled paper ♻.

Book design by Kristen Morgan Downey
Interior and cover photography credits for this book are on page 258.

Front cover recipe: Vanilla Crisps (page 198)

ISBN-13 978-1-59486-018-8 hardcover
ISBN-10 1-59486-018-1 hardcover

2 4 6 8 10 9 7 5 3 1 hardcover

Contents

Special Thanks

In grateful appreciation to all the supporters and sponsors of the Eat Up Slim Down Recipe Sweepstakes, we would like to thank . . .

The companies that so generously provided the terrific prizes for the sweepstakes:
Capresso, Chantal, EdgeCraft, Hamilton Beach, Kuhn Rikon, Meadowsweet Kitchens, Messermeister, Smellkiller, Tilia, William Bounds

The product representatives who were so generous with their time and talents:
Val Gleason from Edgecraft, Loretta Towne from Field & Associates, and Sue Haase from Hamilton Beach

And sincere, heartfelt thanks . . .
. . . to all of the readers of eatupslimdown.com and prevention.com who were kind enough to share their delicious recipes, clever tips, and inspiring stories of weight-loss success for this book. We salute you and wish you continued success!

. . . to the nine weight-loss winners who shared their stories of success with us in personal profiles: Karyn Barczewski, Ena Bogdanowicz, Dawn D'Andria, Craig Downey, James Hoffmann, Elise Paone, Janice Saeger, and Nancy and Richard Silverman.

Acknowledgments

A very special thank you to everyone who had a hand in creating *Eat Up Slim Down Annual Recipes 2005*.

Miriam Backes
JoAnn Brader
Tara Chu
Melissa Dapkewicz
Christine Detris
Kristen Morgan Downey
Kathy Dvorsky
Kathleen Hanuschak, R.D.
Joely Johnson
Fran Kriebel
Lisa Leventer
Stacy Petrovich
Miriam Rubin
Kathy Schuessler
Eva Seibert
Kimberly Tweed
Emily Williams
Shannon Yeakel
Shea Zukowski

Contributors

This book is a compilation of the delicious and creative recipes sent to us by weight-loss winners across the United States, and even beyond. The number of recipes we received was so great, it was difficult to choose just 150. But after a careful selection process, we managed to whittle it down. Here are this year's recipe contributors. We salute their innovative efforts in the kitchen, and hope you'll enjoy eating up and slimming down with their recipes!

Name and Residence	Recipe	Page
Sheila Adams, Vancouver, British Columbia, Canada	Mediterranean Ratatouille	158
Dorie Anderson, Powell River, British Columbia, Canada	Italian Baked Fries	76
Barry Andrew, Kindersley, Saskatchewan, Canada	Barry's Summer Salad	74
Michele Barlow, Hubert, North Carolina	Corn and Bean Salad	64
Julie Baron, New York, New York	Thai Squash Soup	42
Juniper Bartlett, Grants Pass, Oregon	Tamale Pie	164
Judith Beerbaum, Pueblo West, Colorado	Steak Salad	63
Sabiha Bholat, Pinon, Arizona	Tandoori-Style Chicken with Rosemary	168
Donna Bowers, Avondale, Arizona	Grilled Salmon with Brown Rice	139
Charlene Bry, Reedsport, Oregon	Banana-Honey Muffins	246
Katie Burrage, Newfields, New Hampshire	Pumpkin Spice Bars	205
Anastasia Buyanova, Washington, D.C.	Baked Apple Oatmeal	256
Mary Cancela, Tampa, Florida	Chicken Penne	186
Kim Champion, Phoenix, Arizona	Hearty Onion Soup, 45; Fruit Omelet, 255	
Lori Clark, Goose Bay, Newfoundland and Labrador, Canada	Meatball Souvlaki	95
Teresa Cobb, Louisburg, Kansas	Beef and Pine Nut Dumplings	109
Julie Cohn, Anthem, Arizona	Sweet and Sour Meat Loaf	189
Rene Collins, Clute, Texas	Pizza Pizzazz Chicken	174
Shawna Cross, Thunder Bay, Ontario, Canada	Teriyaki Beef Wraps	91
Melissa Dapkewicz, Fogelsville, Pennsylvania	Key Lime Pie, 238; Pumpkin Pie, 240	
A. Davis, Bloomington, Illinois	Tuscan Summer Salad	59

Name and Residence	Recipe	Page
Peg Davis, Dunmore, Alberta, Canada	Cabbage Roll Casserole	161
R. E. Dawson, Arlington Heights, Virginia	Pineapple Smoothie	250
Chris Detris, Breinigsville, Pennsylvania	Peaches and Cream Pie	237
Deborah Di Stefano, Candiac, Quebec, Canada	Greek Spinach Pie Triangles	116
Dawn Eckman, Spring Lake Heights, New Jersey	Tricolor Pasta Casserole	165
Barbara Eitel, Cambridge, Ontario, Canada	Fruit Salad	213
Sharon Elzinga, Tinley Park, Illinois	Italian Chicken and Vegetables	176
Cindy Ferguson, Hampton, Prince Edward Island, Canada	Angel Hair Pasta with Chicken and Vegetables, 184; Beef and Broccoli, 191	
Dawn Fiore, Bethlehem, Pennsylvania	Summer Berry Cake	222
Agnes Forras, Seattle, Washington	Austrian Anytime Scramble	253
Jennifer Foster, Seattle, Washington	Caramel-Frosted Banana Drops	201
Liana Franceschini, Miami, Florida	Mango Salsa Grouper	130
Deanna Goodin, Pekin, Illinois	Pizza Wraps	92
Carole Grover, Baton Rouge, Louisiana	Creole Tilapia	133
Julie Harte, Gainesville, Georgia	Quick Tomato-Basil Pasta	152
Gail Hayes, Breckenridge, Minnesota	Zesty Cod Fillets	125
Mary Helmle, Utica, New York	Hot and Spicy Chili	55
JoAnn Hering, Andover, Ohio	Turkey-Stuffed Shells, 188; Raspberry Cheesecake, 225	
Marci Herman, Burnaby, British Columbia, Canada	Asian Chicken Rolls	110
Kristine Hibbs, Goulds, Newfoundland and Labrador, Canada	Thai Chicken Stir-Fry	182
Shirley Hill, Chatham, Ontario, Canada	Ham and Spinach Spread, 108; Vanilla Crisps, 198; Apple Clafouti, 209; Fruit Pizza, 211; Spinach Omelet, 254	
Sally Hines, Encino, California	Chocolate Chip Cookies	202
Melinda Huffman, Winchester, Tennessee	Spinach and Chickpea Salad	61
Cyndi Iacona, Newnan, Georgia	Broccoli and Cheese Pasta Salad	70
Cheryl Joyce, Fieldale, Virginia	Sautéed Summer Squash	84
Giovanna Kranenberg, Cambridge, Minnesota	Gianna's Pasta	151
Tammy Kuettel, Portland, Oregon	Quick Veggie Bake, 160; American Mandarin Chicken, 180	
Corinne Laboon, Pittsburgh, Pennsylvania	Incredible Crab Canapés	104
June Leas, Slayton, Minnesota	Blue Cheese Dip	107

Name and Residence	Recipe	Page
Erica Losito, St. Louis, Missouri	Tofu-Walnut Patties	142
Jennifer Magrey, Oneco, Connecticut	Skinny Scalloped Potatoes	79
Nanette Marsh, Ocala, Florida	Green Beans and Carrots Parmesan, 82; Hooked on Halibut, 126	
Marisa Martino, Mahopac, New York	Arroz con Pollo	183
Elizabeth Martlock, Jim Thorpe, Pennsylvania	Crab-Stuffed Tiger Shrimp, 122; Homemade Vanilla Pudding with Fresh Berries, 217; Carrot Cake Muffins, 245; Honey-Oatmeal Whole Wheat Rolls, 247; Spiced Pumpkin-Raisin Bread, 248	
Jennifer Maslowski, New York, New York	Hearty Veggie Stew, 54; Honey-Stuffed Peppers, 147; Breakfast Cookies, 257	
Barbara Mason, Brea, California	Mediterranean Tuna Sandwiches	88
Teresa Mattson, Ormond Beach, Florida	Applesauce Spice Cake, 226; Whole Wheat Cranberry-Orange Muffins, 242	
Mona McKinley, Dundee, Florida	Pink Stuff	214
G. C. McMillen, Hot Springs Village, Arkansas	Summer Squash Casserole	163
RoxAnn McMillian, Sunnyvale, California	Crunchy Fennel Salad	60
Eve R. Mead, Jefferson, Wisconsin	Leeks with Red Peppers	83
Terry Mehigan, Camden, Michigan	Tomato Slaw	81
Cindy Merrill, South Portland, Maine	Fruity Health Smoothie	252
Steff Metzger, Harrisburg, Pennsylvania	Steff's Salad Dressing	58
Dawn Michelsen, Freeland, Washington	Swiss Chard and Mushrooms over Rice	157
Patricia Molinari, Calgary, Alberta, Canada	Fruit and Fiber Cookies	200
Alex Mosiychuk, Kansas City, Missouri	Quick 'n' Cool Chicken Bites, 113; So Quick, So Easy Dipping Sticks, 114	
Wilmer Myers, Broadway, Virginia	Lemon Chicken	178
Christie Neal, Auburn, Washington	Lime Chicken	171
Andrea Nelson, Brampton, Ontario, Canada	Southwestern Salad	69
Barb Neri, Syracuse, New York	Balsamic Chicken	173
Rosemary Noe, Swampscott, Massachusetts	Ron's Mediterranean Chicken	179
Lori Nogler, Leominster, Massachusetts	Healthy Cheesecake	224
Richard Opiekun, Brick, New Jersey	Long Grain Rice and Lentil Soup	51
Thereza Ordacgi, Hollywood, Florida	Tropical Mahi Mahi	136
Kathy Osborne, Fort Wayne, Indiana	Spicy Chicken Tortilla Soup	48
Denise Ossello, Manhattan Beach, California	Turkey-Spinach Medley on Pitas	96

Name and Residence	Recipe	Page
Stacy Petrovich, Allentown, Pennsylvania	Banana Cream Pie	234
Peggy Pinzon, San Diego, California	Hawaiian Chicken Salad	73
Rachel Rischpater, Boulder Creek, California	Chilled Soba Noodle Salad with Ponzu Sauce	62
Jimmy Robbins, Bath, New York	Spicy Black Bean Soup	50
Jennifer Ruddock, Oshawa, Ontario, Canada	Salmon with Asparagus	138
Kim Russell, North Wales, Pennsylvania	Shrimp in Garlic-Wine Sauce	124
Karen Schlyter, Calgary, Alberta, Canada	Hot and Sour Soup, 44; Blackened Snapper, 134; Italian Vegetable Casserole, 162	
Mary Schneider, Oxnard, California	Vegetable Stir-Fry	156
Eva Seibert, Allentown, Pennsylvania	Lemon Angel Food Cake Squares, 207; Peanut Butter Pudding, 218; Lemon Pudding Cake, 228; Fudge Pudding Cake, 229; Apple Soufflé Cake, 231	
Donna Sheets, Mocksville, North Carolina	Light and Easy Cherry Cheesecake	227
Nancy Silverman, New Haven, Connecticut	Curried Fish Chowder, 53; Turkey Chili, 56; Bean Burritos, 144; Linguine with White Artichoke Sauce, 148; Frozen Strawberry Mousse, 220	
Deborah Sims, Statham, Georgia	Lemony Tuna Salad	72
Melisa Smith, Clinton, Tennessee	Creamy Baked Chicken Enchiladas	190
Gayle Socha, Parma, Ohio	Marinated Pork Tenderloin	193
Ranee Solomon, Akron, Ohio	Spinach and Mushrooms with Turkey Bacon	85
Jeffrey Stansberry, Knoxville, Tennessee	Chipotle-Grilled Turkey	167
D. Summers, Richardson, Texas	Avocado Salsa	100
Elaine Sweet, Dallas, Texas	Caramelized Onion and Sweet Potato Soup, 47; Eggplant Bruschetta, 105	
Elizabeth Templeton, Ancaster, Ontario, Canada	Lovely Barbecue Chicken	172
Leah Tews, Phoenix, Arizona	Spiced Pecans	119
Emilie Toomarian, La Canyada, California	Mango Freeze	250
Ann Trivelpiece, Hampton, Virginia	Mexican Dip	102
Michelle Tucker, Austin, Texas	Pineapple Salsa	98
Christie Turchyn, Balmoral, Manitoba, Canada	Vegetarian Tacos	145
Kathy Tweed, Cape May Court House, New Jersey	Country Cookies, 204; Peach Crisp, 208; Walnut-Pumpkin Pie, 233	
Sandy Umber, Springdale, Arizona	Easy Pita Pockets, 90; Tea Frosty, 249	
Elisa Vaillancourt, Virginia Beach, Virginia	Sun-Dried-Tomato Salmon	140

Name and Residence	Recipe	Page
Helen Velichko, Kansas City, Missouri	Simply Sensational Double-Stuffed Potatoes, 80; Turkey-Mushroom Burgers, 97; Speedy Fish Tacos, 128; Sweet 'n' Cool Peanut Bars, 203	
Vasiliy Velichko, Far Rockaway, New York	Stuffed Lamb Chops, 195; Trail-Mix Fruit Bake, 210	
Sally Waggoner, Muncie, Indiana	Onion-Grilled London Broil	192
Christine Walsh, Guysborough County, Nova Scotia, Canada	Creamy Chicken and Veggies	187
Robin Whitehurst, Annapolis, Maryland	Ahoy Soy!	252
Lori Witmer, Spring Grove, Pennsylvania	Chicken Milano	177
Renae Worsley, Clearfield, Utah	Zucchini Muffins	241
Linda Yamali, Merrick, New York	Spaghetti Squash with Stir-Fry Vegetables	153
Sheri Yarber, Troutdale, Virginia	Heart-Smart Taco Salad	66

Introduction

Here it is! The fourth installment of the cookbook created by you, the reader. As you can see, we've redesigned and updated it this year, creating a beautiful and useful new version.

While the look of the book has changed, the contents you've come to know and love have stayed the same. You'll find delicious recipes, innovative weight-loss tips, and inspiring success stories in this one-of-a-kind book.

Inside this year's edition of *Eat Up Slim Down Annual Recipes* are dozens of ideas to make cooking for weight loss easier, tastier, and more fun. We talked with food writer and cooking expert Miriam Rubin to find out the latest in weight-loss problem solving—including rundowns of the latest diet trends. Miriam also gives advice on keeping your family healthy and dining out while dieting.

To jump-start your personal weight-loss program, we have compiled 150 of the recipes submitted to us on our Web site, prevention.com, as part of the *Eat Up Slim Down* Recipe Sweepstakes. Visitors to the Web site shared their weight-loss recipes with us while entering our sweepstakes for a chance to win exciting prizes. As we tried out their dishes in our *Prevention* Test Kitchen, the creativity, presentation, and most of all, the taste of these delicious weight-loss recipes overwhelmed us.

You'll find so many dishes to please yourself and your family, including Stuffed Lamb Chops, Pizza Pizzazz Chicken, and Crab-Stuffed Tiger Shrimp. Fantastic snacks like Spiced Pecans, Greek Spinach Pie Triangles, and Blue Cheese Dip. And of course, desserts like Summer Berry Cake, Banana Cream Pie, and Fudge Pudding Cake.

And if it's motivation you're looking for, you've come to the right place. The real-life weight-loss winners featured throughout the book are truly inspiring to all of us: James, who lost weight to become a good role model for his kids; Ena, who finally stopped waiting until tomorrow to start her weight-loss plan; Dawn, whose health problems prompted her to take action; and many others whose stories will move you to get on your way to creating your own success story.

With each recipe, we've provided complete nutritional information, including both Diet Exchanges and Carb Choices for those who wish to track their intake of carbohydrates. As with any plan, be sure to consult with your doctor about the amounts that are right for you and your needs.

Congratulations on committing to this new way of eating, exercising, and living. We know this book will be just what you need to help you Eat Up and Slim Down!

Weight-Loss Problem Solver

Lose Weight the *Eat Up Slim Down* Way

Are you trying to lose weight or to keep off some recently shed pounds? Are you stuck at a weight plateau, unable to budge the scale downward? Or are you simply trying to eat more healthfully? This book can help you, in ways that are both easy and delicious. Along with appetizing recipes, the pages that follow are loaded with tools and techniques, ideas and tips—an entire workbook—that will teach you how to eat in a new and healthy way.

This book is not a diet plan, per se. It's a companion tool to aid in healthful eating and weight loss. If you're following an established plan, joining a diet group, or simply trying on your own to eat better, let our ideas and suggestions help you on your chosen path.

We'll start by defining a healthful diet and showing you the kinds of food choices that you should be making.

Eat Smaller Portions

A recent study conducted by the Centers for Disease Control and Prevention detailed what we really already knew: Food portions in the United States are too large. We're eating more than we did 30 years ago, and it's making us fat. We are simply eating too many calories on a daily basis.

What's most to blame? Large portions of

refined carbohydrates, especially cookies, pasta, and soda.

Eat More Whole Grains

"Carb" should not be a four-letter word, if it's a whole grain carb. The fiber from whole grain products instantly boosts your fiber intake, which satisfies your hunger longer so you don't overeat. What's the difference between whole grains and refined ones? Simple. Mother Nature clothed all grains in a thin, flaky shell and tucked in a nugget of germ, the tiny bud from which a new plant will sprout. But when whole grains are milled into white flour, they're stripped of these "good-for-you" garments.

Most experts advise consuming 3 to 6 servings of whole grains a day. What's in a serving?

- 1 slice of bread
- ½ small bagel
- ½ cup cooked cereal, pasta, rice, or other grain

Go for the Grain

Whole grain foods have a more complex taste and texture than refined foods—many people end up liking them better. Today's supermarkets are chock-full of healthy whole grain products, including whole wheat (flour, wheat berries, cracked wheat, and bulgur), brown rice, oats, unpearled barley, stone-ground cornmeal, quinoa, buckwheat (or kasha), and whole wheat couscous.

If you bake at home, try replacing some of the white flour with whole wheat pastry flour, which works well in muffins and quick breads.

Eat More Vegetables and Fruits

Aim for 9 servings per day: 5 vegetables and 4 fruits. What's in a serving?

For vegetables:

- ½ cup raw, chopped, or cooked
- ¾ cup vegetable juice
- 1 cup raw, leafy greens

For fruit:

- 1 small to medium piece
- 1 cup whole strawberries or melon cubes
- ½ cup canned or cut fruit
- ¾ cup fruit juice
- ¼ cup dried fruit

To get the most benefits out of the various nutrients each has to offer, including antioxidants, enjoy a wide variety of richly colored fruits and vegetables, such as orange-

LOSE WEIGHT THE RIGHT WAY

Before you begin any weight-loss plan or make a significant change in your diet, visit your doctor. This is especially important if you are pregnant, have any underlying medical conditions, or are very overweight. Be sure to have your cholesterol measured and blood pressure checked so your doctor can best advise you of any particular foods you might need to avoid.

A BETTER BREAD

On the glycemic index, which is a measure of how quickly foods digest and are absorbed into your bloodstream as sugar, white bread rates among the highest of all. Of course, if you need a sudden energy boost, white bread fits the bill. But the downside is that any sugar that isn't burned as energy gets stored as fat.

Researchers at Tufts University in Boston think that's why people in their recent study who ate the most white bread—4 to 5 daily servings—saw their waistlines widen *three times as much* as those who ate 1 serving or less, even when total calories consumed were the same.

Check the label before you buy bread to make sure it's made from whole grains and has at least 2 to 3 grams of fiber per serving. The healthy-sounding names on the loaf—such as "seven grain" or "hearty dark"—are no guarantee of whole grain content. And if the label lists "wheat flour," they are talking about plain old white flour.

Here are some breads you might want to try, along with their fiber content per serving:

- Arnold Bakery Light 100% Whole Wheat — 5 g
- Thomas's Sahara 100% Whole Wheat Pita — 5 g
- Pepperidge Farm Natural Whole Grain Oat Bran — 2 g
- Sara Lee Homestyle Wheat — 2 g

fleshed melons, sweet potatoes, and mangoes; deep red bell peppers and tomatoes; and dark green veggies such as spinach, kale, and broccoli. Vegetables and fruits also provide fiber that fills you up more (with fewer calories than many fiber-rich grains) and keeps you feeling fuller longer.

Oranges, apples, and most fruits come in their own neat traveling packages. You simply peel (or don't) and enjoy. The produce

FIBER-FULL FRUITS AND VEGGIES

FRUITS

Food	Portion	Fiber (g)
Figs, dried	2	4.6
Raspberries, red	½ cup	4.1
Blackberries	½ cup	3.8
Apple, unpeeled	1	3.7
Avocado, sliced	½ cup	3.6
Dates	5 medium	3.1
Orange	1	3.1
Banana	1	2.8
Kiwifruit	1 medium	2.5
Nectarine	1 medium	2.1
Blueberries	½ cup	1.9
Peach	1 medium	1.9
Strawberries	½ cup sliced	1.9
Dried plums (prunes)	3 medium	1.7
Pineapple, cubed	½ cup	1
Grapes, seedless	½ cup	0.8
Cantaloupe, cubed	½ cup	0.6

VEGETABLES

Food	Portion	Fiber (g)
Peas, fresh, cooked	½ cup	4.4
Sweet potato, with skin, baked	1 medium	3.4
Potato, with skin, baked	1 medium	2.3
Broccoli, cooked	½ cup	2.2
Corn, cooked	1 ear	2.1
Brussels sprouts, cooked	½ cup	2
Green beans	½ cup	2
Onion, sliced	½ cup	2
Carrot, raw	1 medium	1.8
Cabbage, shredded, cooked	½ cup	1.7
Cauliflower, cooked	½ cup	1.6
Asparagus, cooked	½ cup	1.4
Tomato	1 medium	1.3
Celery, strips	½ cup	1.0
Red bell pepper, raw, sliced	½ cup	0.9
Green bell pepper, raw, sliced	½ cup	0.8
Mushrooms, raw	½ cup	0.4

NINE EASY WAYS TO NINE A DAY

Here are nine tips for getting more fruits and vegetables into your diet.

- Add chopped fresh or frozen vegetables to your next casserole.
- Making pasta with tomato sauce? After draining the pasta, heat a little oil in the pasta cooking pot. Add a package of prewashed fresh spinach, torn kale, or arugula and cook just until wilted; toss with the pasta and sauce. Or cook fresh or frozen broccoli or cauliflower florets or baby carrots right in with the pasta, until the pasta is al dente and the veggies are crisp-tender. Drain the veggies and pasta and mix both with the sauce.
- Routinely cut up fruit for the family to spoon on their cereal. If you're serving French toast, top it with fresh fruit instead of loading on the syrup and butter. And if your family loves pancakes, add blueberries, strawberries, raspberries, sliced banana, or chopped apple to the batter. Spoon more of the fruit over the pancakes before serving, perhaps mixed with a little pancake syrup.
- Stock the fridge with crisp veggie sticks for snacking, and not just carrots and celery. Vary the mix (and the nutrients) with bell peppers, snow peas, Kirby cukes, tender green beans, and broccoli. Kids who won't eat cooked veggies often enjoy them raw.
- Don't have just an iceberg lettuce salad; jazz it up with shredded carrots and cabbage, baby spinach, tomato wedges, radishes, and sweet onion slices.
- Begin dinner or lunch with a broth-based vegetable soup. You'll start to fill up even before the main course and get a serving of veggies at the same time.
- Start your meal with a slice of ripe melon, pineapple chunks, papaya, grapefruit, or mango.
- "Extend" a tuna, salmon, or chicken salad with crunchy chopped vegetables: Try broccoli, bell pepper, fennel, radishes, cauliflower, celery, cucumber, or carrot.
- Plan a fruit snack instead of reaching for a pastry . . . you may find you have more energy.

industry has worked hard to reduce your meal prep time with prewashed salads and ready-cut veggies.

Don't forget frozen and canned fruits and vegetables, either. Opt for frozen veggies without sauces, frozen fruits without added sugar, and canned fruits packed in their own juice. That way, if the fruit needs sweetening, you are in control. And if you've got a backyard or patio, plant a garden. You'll get exercise and vitamins!

As you look through the recipes and ideas in this book you'll discover lots of ways to get more fruits and vegetables into your daily diet. And if you fill up on these, you'll have less room for more fattening, less healthy foods.

Get Plenty of Low-Fat Dairy Products

Dairy products provide essential bone-building calcium and vitamin D; aim for 3 servings a day. The minimum Recommended Dietary Allowance (RDA) for calcium is 1,000 milligrams. Women over age 50 should get 1,200 milligrams daily.

What's in a serving?

- 1 cup fat-free milk: 352 milligrams calcium
- 1 cup fat-free unsweetened yogurt: 300 milligrams calcium
- 1 cup low-fat unsweetened yogurt: 400 milligrams calcium
- ½ cup part-skim ricotta cheese or low-fat cottage cheese: 200 milligrams calcium
- ¾ cup unsweetened soy milk: 225 milligrams calcium
- 1 ounce reduced-fat hard cheese (¼ cup shredded): 117 milligrams calcium

THE ICE CREAM DIET

Here's a diet we can all scream for. Eat a nutritious breakfast, lunch, snack, and dinner, including plenty of fruits, vegetables, and fiber and a moderate amount of protein, fat, and calories. Then reward yourself with a dish of calcium-packed ice cream. And so you don't overdo it, choose an ice cream with 125 or fewer calories per serving (about ½ cup), and never, ever eat it from the container.

THE DREAM CREAMS

Flavor	Calories per ½-cup serving	Daily value of calcium*
Edy's Black Cherry Vanilla Swirl Frozen Yogurt	90	30%
Ben & Jerry's Cherry Garcia Frozen Yogurt**	170	15%
Healthy Choice Chocolate Cherry Mambo Ice Cream	120	10%
Healthy Choice Mint Chocolate Chip Ice Cream	120	10%
Healthy Choice Peanut Butter Cup Ice Cream	120	10%
TCBY soft-serve fat-free frozen yogurt	110	10%
Turkey Hill Vanilla Bean Light Ice Cream	110	10%

*Based on a 1,000-milligram Recommended Dietary Allowance
**You'll need to reduce the serving size of Ben & Jerry's frozen yogurt to approximately 125 calories if you want to eat it every day.

THE BEST WAYS TO GET CALCIUM

- Snack on low-fat flavored yogurt.
  Calcium boost: up to 350 milligrams
- Order a low-fat latte.
  Calcium boost: 150 milligrams
- Sprinkle your salad with ¼ cup shredded low-fat Cheddar cheese.
  Calcium boost: 204 milligrams
- Sip an 8-ounce glass of 1% milk (unflavored or chocolate).
  Calcium boost: 300 milligrams

Calcium Is Tops for Weight Loss

Research from the Center for Human Nutrition at the University of Colorado Health Sciences Center shows that adults who consume more calcium also burn more fat. It is suspected that calcium forces fat out of cells and into the bloodstream, where it's more quickly oxidized, or burned off. If your body doesn't get enough calcium, your fat cells retain the fat—and can grow steadily.

Other research supports calcium's role in the fight against fat—both on your hips and in your blood. University of Tennessee studies suggest that calcium blocks fat storage in the cells that plump out your tummy, hips, and thighs. And Quebec researchers have discovered that getting at least 1,000 milligrams of calcium per day improves total cholesterol levels, both "bad" LDL and "good" HDL.

Include Lean Proteins

Protein is an important part of a healthful weight-loss plan. Your daily diet should include at least 10 to 15 percent of calories from lean protein. What's in a serving? Main dishes should have about 3 to 4 ounces of cooked lean protein per serving—that's 4 to 5 ounces of uncooked skinless, boneless chicken breast, fish fillet, boneless pork chop, or trimmed, boneless sirloin steak. Remember, the visual cue for a serving is about the size of a deck of cards.

Don't count out beef. Red meat is rich in iron, zinc, and B vitamins. You can enjoy up to 3 servings of beef, lamb, or pork per week. Lean cuts of beef are tenderloin, top loin, sirloin, top round, eye of round, tip, and flank steak. For ground beef, if possible, choose a lean piece of meat and ask the butcher to grind it for you. If buying preground beef, look for the percentage lean numbers on the label. Select 90 to 95 percent lean if you're using the meat in chili or casseroles. You'll need a little more fat for burgers; look for meat at around 85 percent lean (which is 15 percent fat). Sirloin and ground round are usually your best choices.

Lamb and pork should be on the menu, too. When selecting lamb, choose leg, loin chop, trimmed blade chops, shank,

FIVE QUICK WAYS WITH CANNED BEANS

- Add chickpeas to a green salad for more protein and fiber. Sprinkle with a little crumbled low-fat feta if you like.
- Quick dip: Puree white beans in a food processor with a garlic clove, a little of the liquid from the can, and some olive oil. Season with lemon juice, salt, and pepper, and add a big handful of chopped fresh parsley.
- Add canned kidney or pink beans to sautéed spinach or escarole.
- Make a spicy black bean salsa: Mix black beans, fresh or thawed frozen corn kernels, diced tomato, red onion, and chopped cilantro, plus cumin and lime juice to taste. Spoon into avocado halves or over grilled fish or chicken.
- Prepare your next batch of chili without meat and add a combination of beans instead. Try pink, black, and kidney beans.

or sirloin roasts. Planning pork for dinner? Choose the versatile tenderloin, a loin roast, bone-in or boneless loin, sirloin or rib chops, lean boneless ham (look for reduced-sodium varieties), or Canadian bacon.

For the leanest poultry, choose cuts from the breast. Remove the skin—that's where most of the fat hides. Read the labels when buying ground turkey or chicken. Ground breast meat will have the least fat. Seven percent fat ground turkey is another good choice; it contains a little more fat, which helps keep the meat moist. Packages labeled simply "ground turkey" include the greatest portion of fatty parts.

Don't avoid eggs. A good source of protein and nutrients, eggs should be back on the menu. Enjoy up to seven per week, but reduce that number to four if you have diabetes, high cholesterol, or are very overweight.

Go fish! An essential part of any weight-loss plan, fish is packed with healthful fats that protect your heart. Include it on the menu at least twice a week. Choose fresh for best flavor, but canned tuna and salmon also count as fish meals (watch the mayo!). For best nutrition, pick oily fish such as salmon, tuna, mackerel, herring, sardines, trout, halibut, cod, and bluefish, which contain the largest amounts of healthful omega-3 fatty acids. Concerned about mercury? Stick to wild (versus farmed) Pacific salmon, as well as shrimp, summer flounder, farmed catfish, croaker, haddock, and mid-Atlantic blue crab, all of which contain omega-3s but are low in mercury. If packing your larder with frozen fish, stock only the unbreaded variety.

Consume legumes. Dried and canned beans and peas are wonderful, tasty, low-fat sources of protein and fiber. Canned are the most convenient. Use them to replace animal proteins in a meal and get 5 or more servings a week. What's in a serving? Half a cup cooked or drained canned. Reduce the sodium (and that tinny taste) in canned beans by rinsing and draining them before using.

VISUALIZE A SERVING SIZE

To get portion sizes under control, measure out your food a few times to see what a standard serving looks like on your plate. You might want to make a habit of always measuring portions of some calorie-dense foods, like pasta, oil, salad dressing, and mayonnaise, which are all too easy to overdo.

The following visual cues will help you keep portion sizes healthy.

- 1 cup = lightbulb
- ½ cup = tennis ball
- 2 tablespoons = Ping-Pong ball
- 1 teaspoon = top of thumb (from tip to joint)
- 1 ounce (of cheese, for instance) = top of thumb (from tip to joint)
- 3 ounces (of cooked meat, poultry, or fish, for instance) = deck of cards

Pick Your Fats

No all fats are equal—some are definitely better than others. But all fats are fattening, even the good ones, so keep consumption at 25 percent of daily calories or less.

Have more of these. Keep the focus on unsaturated fats, which come from plant foods and fish. Unsaturated fats include both polyunsaturated and monounsaturated types, and are easy to identify because they're liquid at room temperature. They include olive oil, canola oil, safflower oil, sesame oil, soybean oil, corn, sunflower seed oil, and peanut oil. These "good" fats do not raise levels of "bad" LDL cholesterol. According to the American Heart Association, unsaturated fats may also help lower blood cholesterol, and therefore help protect the heart, when used in place of saturated fat.

Unsaturated fats are also found in nuts and avocados. Nuts can and should make up part of a healthy diet and weight-loss plan. It is believed that the fats in nuts can help reduce blood cholesterol, blood pressure, and risk for heart disease. But nuts and nut butters should be consumed in moderation. What's in a serving? One ounce of shelled nuts or 2 tablespoons of peanut butter. Enjoy a serving five times a week.

Limit these. Saturated fats are mostly animal based and are solid at room temperature (a stick of butter). They're found in full-fat dairy products, butter, meat, and poultry skin. To reduce saturated fat, choose low-fat or fat-free dairy products, trim fat from meat, and remove skin from poultry.

Avoid these. Government and nutrition experts are advising us to limit consumption of trans fats. These man-made fats boost "bad" LDL cholesterol and blast heart-protective HDL cholesterol, thus raising your risk for

BUTTER OR MARGARINE?

If you spread butter on your toast, give light butter a try. It has less saturated fat and half the calories of regular butter. If you prefer margarine, use tub instead of stick margarine, and look for one that says "no trans fat" on the label. Whichever you choose, spread with a "light" touch.

heart disease. They show up in french fries, potato chips, cookies, and crackers, creating that crunchy texture we love—and embalming them for longer shelf life.

The good news is that trans fats can largely be avoided if you stay away from highly processed foods—foods that you should be avoiding in any case. To identify and avoid a food with trans fats, read the label to make sure it doesn't contain shortening, hydrogenated oil, or partially hydrogenated oil. Trans fats will soon become simpler to spot. In January 2006, all food labels will be required to list any trans fat content. But don't make your heart wait until then.

Roadblocks to Weight Loss

How to Steer Your Efforts toward Success

Congratulations! You're working hard; you're losing pounds. You're a hero! A slimmer, healthier you is within reach. As a bonus, losing weight is often a big boost to confidence and self-esteem.

But there's no question that losing weight can be a struggle. To help you overcome some common roadblocks, we've outlined a few strategies based on tried-and-true experience. Read on to see if some of these approaches might work for you.

Diet Slipups: They're Not the End of the World

It happens—a piece of cheesecake here, a workout not taken there. But slipups like these don't mean you've ruined your diet, and you shouldn't use them as an excuse to give up completely. Simply get back with the program, and if you stick with it, you will lose the weight. But an overly negative reaction will keep you from believing in yourself—and you'll easily reinforce diet failure. It's best to enjoy your break from the diet or gym, forgive and forget, and then get back on track.

Trick Your Cravings

The next time you find yourself reaching for a box of cookies, try doing something else. Maybe there's something else you can do that's even more enjoyable, with fewer calories.

LOOKING SHARP

As you shrink out of your clothes, donate them to a charity or have them altered. And as you reach your weight-loss goal, treat yourself to new wardrobe accessories. It's important to look your best each day: If you look good, you'll feel good about yourself.

- Change your environment: Take a walk, visit a friend, hike to a nearby park, take the dog for a run, or go to a movie, museum, lecture, or bookshop.
- Check out a new yoga or Pilates class.
- Turn the television off and have someone hide the remote.
- Brush your teeth, floss, and freshen your mouth with a swish of minty mouthwash.
- Listen to a motivational tape.
- Have a soothing cup of green or herbal tea.
- Visualize how you will look 10 or 20 pounds slimmer.

Get a New Attitude!

You've stocked the fridge with healthful foods, you've joined a gym—but even the best of intentions can be undermined by a bad attitude. Here's how to readjust negative thinking.

Old attitude: I was born to be fat. A USDA study found that women who think that their gene pool preordains their jean size were more likely to be heavy. Genes can affect your size, but it's what you eat that determines how fat you become.

New attitude: I am in control of my body. The food I eat and the lifestyle choices I make are what shape my body.

Old attitude: I won't be happy or healthy unless I lose lots of weight. Many dieters have unrealistic expectations. But doctors know that even a 10 percent weight loss feels good and can have a positive effect on your health and well-being.

New attitude: I'll be happier and healthier even if I lose just 10 or 15 pounds. If I lose more, great. But something is better than nothing.

Loved Ones Might Be Hindering Your Success

Surprisingly, the people you most count on for support could be undermining your weight-loss efforts.

Want to really bring out the worst in people? Lose weight. Ten pounds or 100, and you'll be showered with fattening food by the people who claim to love you.

Why Would They Do That?

You're in change mode. You're happy to be there, but your friends and family aren't so sure. They might be feeling guilty. Perhaps they need to lose weight too but can't get motivated. So they undermine your efforts, urging you to take a taste, just a little bite, which makes it much harder for you to reach your goal. You'll fall off the diet and prove once again that weight loss is impossible; this way, they won't have to try either.

FEELING EXHAUSTED?

Do you feel tired all the time? Are you on a diet that restricts your consumption of meat? If so, you might be suffering from iron deficiency. It's hard to get enough iron from plant sources alone. Try eating two 3-ounce servings per day of the following: shrimp, lean beef, lamb, dark-meat skinned chicken or turkey, or fish or other seafood. When meals don't include animal protein, add a food high in vitamin C, such as citrus fruit or juice, melon, berries, green leafy vegetables, bell peppers, or tomatoes. Such foods help you absorb the iron from other plant foods you're eating. Or drink a glass of water. Chronic low fluid intake is a common but overlooked cause of mild dehydration and fatigue.

They don't understand. Other folks (often spouses) who don't have a weight problem can't understand why you don't go back to eating "normally" now that you've taken off the pounds. And besides, they've suffered enough with all the changes around the house (and in the fridge).

They miss the old you (you were fine just the way you were). What they really miss are the food experiences you used to share. Sharing food is often how we express love: Baking cookies for your kids and, of course, eating them together. Happy hour with coworkers, highlighted with tasty little meatballs and bean dip. Eating a gooey triple-cheese pizza with your husband while watching the game.

How to Fight Back

Shore up your determination; recruit people to your side; get strong. First, build yourself up with regular exercise, or perhaps a vigorous evening walk with your husband or a friend, making that the shared activity instead of eating a pizza.

Strictly monitor what you eat. Plan meals, budget time for workouts. Put yourself first and be firm in your resolve. This will keep you honest, and it may also help you recognize the people and activities that do you in.

Enlist help. People can't read your mind. Tell them you need their support in staying on track, not a pan of brownies to lure you over the edge. If you need a "sponsor" to keep you "straight" when the late-night munchies hit, ask a friend if it's okay to call. Tell someone who's temping you too much that he's not being helpful. Most people are happy to help once they know what to do.

AVOID THE DANGER ZONES

Here are some healthier, lower-calorie options to consider when friends and family are enticing you.

INSTEAD OF . . .	TRY . . .
Scarfing down wings and blue cheese with friends	Going to a restaurant where your friends can get wings and you can eat something healthy
Ordering dessert	Agreeing to share dessert, then having only a forkful or two and spending lots of time marveling about how wonderful it is
A 2-hour lunch	Eating a quick, nutritious lunch, then shopping or taking a walk
Girls' night out at a restaurant or bar	Getting a manicure and pedicure with friends; you can talk your heads off and have a great time
Guys' night out at a sports bar	Playing a pickup game of basketball at the gym

Dieting in Groups

Perhaps you've noticed the diet challenges on the television news or in your local paper, or maybe you even know someone who's joined up. It's really quite simple: A group of people, most often coworkers, get together to challenge and support each other to lose weight within a set number of months. They weigh in and often set goals for the number of pounds each wishes to shed. Sometimes dieters choose different weight-loss plans and compare the results. Some form exercise groups, sharing costs to hire an instructor; others get together for a lunchtime walk and "crab" session.

Downsizing Can Be a Good Thing

Research has proven that group weight loss is a winning concept. Plus, weight-loss competitions boost morale, improve interoffice relations, and reduce sick days and health care costs. (Tell your boss this news if you want to start your own workplace diet.)

Interoffice Support

Group dieting offers a sympathetic atmosphere. A fellow dieter can be called on to talk you down from the candy machine or pastry cart. A mere cubicle away is someone to provide reassurance—someone who knows what it's like. Peer pressure may also make it less easy to give up the fight if the others are still slugging it out. And maybe, in a show of solidarity, nondieting office mates might stop bringing temptation to the lunchroom.

Broad coworker support was only one of the many positive outcomes when Rodale's accounting department challenged the human resources department to a 3-month diet duel. "We used to have tons of sweets [in the office], but not now," says Marian Schneck, Rodale's accounting director, who lost 10 pounds. "Even nonparticipants help out by keeping our work areas free of junk food."

Senior accountant Jeff Hampton jumped into the challenge and won big, dropping 20 pounds. Hampton knew it was time to take action when his mom, also overweight, suffered a heart attack.

"The group momentum gave me the motivation I needed to get serious about losing weight. Since we've begun, everyone—including those *not* competing—has helped by offering encouraging words."

Human resources coordinator Jessica Glick, who lost 6 pounds, explains that even if participants are on different diets, the obstacles are often the same. "I'm moderating my portions and my coworker is doing a low-carb diet, but we both struggle with nighttime hunger and finding time to work out. It helps to talk about it at lunch."

Mackenzie Carpenter, a staff writer and former restaurant critic for the *Pittsburgh Post-Gazette,* has joined a very public workplace take-off-the-pounds challenge with two colleagues. She's on the South Beach Diet and finds it easy to stick with. "I feel better on it than I did when I was on Atkins a year ago, when I gorged on fatty foods like Brie and bacon. It's also forced me to improve my cooking skills and to become friends with vegetables again."

Carpenter, slim most of her adult life, began her weight struggles during pregnancy. After having three children, she found herself unable to lose the extra pounds. She was inspired to get serious about dieting when her doctor informed her that she was insulin resistant, which put her at risk for diabetes and heart disease. And she was nearing age 50. "I thought the time was right to get healthy," says Carpenter. The challenge has been the impetus.

Carpenter is 5 feet 3 inches tall, and when she began the diet in January 2004, she weighed 222 pounds. Since then, she's dropped 19 pounds and credits much of her weight loss to an exercise program of walking tapes and workout videos. However, she says, "as you increase exercise intensity, especially in weight lifting, your appetite increases!"

Carpenter is determined, but she acknowledges there are challenges: "It's tough, with three kids who have very different tastes in food at dinnertime. My husband tries to participate with me, eating some of the dishes I cook, but he's never had a weight problem, so I'm not sure his heart is in it."

Carpenter also keeps a daily food journal and finds it helpful, but also a sobering wake-up call. "I'll go through the day thinking I was good, but when I tote it up at the end of the day, I'm stunned by how many calories I consumed. For even though I'm on a low-carb diet, I also watch calories."

Carpenter and her fellow dieters write a monthly progress report that's printed in the *Post-Gazette.* "So far, none of us has given up," she says.

Group dieting, especially highly publicized contests, may not be the right approach for everyone, but for some it might just provide the extra incentive to lose weight—as well as an opportunity to show it off. And even dieters who are not participating in the challenge may derive support, ideas, and solace from those who are.

The winner in the Rodale challenge? The accounting group, which lost a total of 133.2 pounds.

Diet Roundup

If you're in the market for a diet plan, it can be hard to know which to choose. There are low-carb, no-fat, calorie restricted. . . . Confused? Below is a brief description of a few of the most popular plans.

The South Beach Diet

For the first 2 weeks, this is a strict carb-limited diet. After the initial period, carbs are gradually introduced—including whole grains, vegetables, and most fruits. South Beach allows lean meats, poultry, and fish, along with moderate amounts of healthful fats, such as olive oil, and low-fat dairy products. In the maintenance phase, white sugar and flour may be consumed in limited amounts. Chocolate is not banned, but it is limited.

The Atkins Diet

This is a controlled-carb diet, strictly limiting consumption of carbohydrates from grains, fruits, and vegetables throughout all phases of the plan. The Atkins diet rates foods according to "net carbs," which is the total carbohydrate content of a food minus the sugar alcohols and fiber. The plan espouses that eating carbs is what makes you fat.

There are four phases. The first is "induction," in which you eat only 20 grams of "net carbs" a day but plenty of protein, eggs, healthy fats (olive oil and butter), plus full-fat cheeses (which are allowed in all phases of the diet). The next two phases increase the amounts of carbs, introducing fruits, some grains, vegetables, and legumes. When you have reached your goal weight and are in the maintenance phase, you may eat from 90 to 120 grams of "net carbs" per day. However, the diet cautions that some people must remain at more restricted levels.

Atkins does not feel it necessary to limit fat, except hydrogenated fat (trans fat), as long as carbohydrate intake is controlled. An extensive line of Atkins low-carb products is available in stores, online, and by mail order.

Weight Watchers

Weight Watchers is a calorie-based food plan. But instead of counting calories, you count the points that have been awarded to each food or food product, or each recipe (if it's a Weight Watchers recipe). The number of points you can eat in a day is determined by how much weight you wish to lose.

There are many facets to Weight Watchers: You may follow the diet by yourself, participate in group meetings for support and strategies, or seek help online.

Exercise is awarded "activity points," and these may be exchanged for food. You also receive 35 bonus "reserve" points each week, which you can use or not. No foods are prohibited, but healthful, nutritious choices are advocated. People on Weight Watchers are encouraged to keep track of daily points consumed and exercise performed. This is to help the dieter to understand her habits and to learn how to change them. Weight Watchers frozen entrées are widely available.

Dr. Phil's "Ultimate Weight Solution"

More motivational therapy than actual food plan, Dr. Phil's diet features seven "keys" to help you "unlock" and gain control over your eating problems. The keys address topics such as "right thinking," mastering food and impulse eating, and your support circle.

Dr. Phil pushes physical activity and positive thinking as weight-loss tools. Foods are placed in one of two groups. "High-response cost, high-yield foods" are those that take time to chew, digest, and/or prepare and that provide good nutritive values. They include whole grains, reduced- and low-fat dairy products, lean proteins, and most vegetables and fruits.

The other basic food group, "low-response cost, low-yield foods," includes full-fat cheeses and dairy products; most baked goods made with white flour and white sugar, plus pastries and the like; alcoholic beverages, sugar-sweetened sodas, and juice drinks; butter and margarine; fried foods and fast food; and many snack items—basically, foods that are high in fats and calories and low in nutrition.

Dr. Phil markets a line of vitamins, nutrition bars, and power shakes.

Five Major Eating Mistakes and Their Remedies: Advice from the Experts

We asked some of the nation's top nutrition experts to weigh in on their gripes about how the general population eats. Here's what they said:

We can't tell good fats from bad ones. Fat has been placed in an overall "bad" category, and that's just not accurate.

"You want to avoid saturated fat and trans fat, but you need *more* monounsaturated and polyunsaturated fats," says Alice Lichtenstein, D.Sc., an American Heart Association spokesperson. Try to limit any fat that comes from animals—including man-made fats like hydrogenated or partially hydrogenated vegetable oil—and you'll be in good shape. Sources of good fats are fish, nuts, avocados, and soybean and canola oils. See "Pick Your Fats" on page 9 for more about good and bad fats.

We supersize to save money. "People think that supersizing a restaurant meal is a money saver, but it's not a health bargain if it has way too many calories," says Karen Weber Cullen, Ph.D., R.D., research nutritionist at Baylor College of Medicine in Houston.

The proper serving size is about what fits

in the palm of your hand (larger for men than women, and even smaller for children). For most meals, pick one protein, one starch, one veggie, and one fruit, based on the serving that will fit into your palm.

We think that anything liquid has no calories. We drink way too much sugared soda, caloric coffee drinks, and juice. These drinks balloon calorie intake and squeeze out more nutritious foods like milk. According to a recent study published in the *Family and Consumer Sciences Research Journal*, the average American drinks 41 gallons of sugared soft drinks a year, or about a pound of pop a day, which is about 200 empty calories.

A better remedy? Make sure you get the recommended 8 glasses of water a day and make sure other beverages you consume are nutrition packed.

We don't know how "hungry" feels. "If you don't know when you're hungry, you don't know when you're full, so you won't know when to stop eating," says Elisabetta Politi, R.D., nutrition manager of the Duke University Diet & Fitness Center in Durham, North Carolina.

SIPPING SKINNY

LOSE THESE	Calories per 8 oz	CHOOSE THESE	Calories per 8 oz
Fruit smoothies	250	Diet V8 Splash	10
Juice drinks	130	Ocean Spray Light Ruby Red Grapefruit Juice	40
Sweetened iced teas	80	Diet Lemon Lipton	0
		Decaf Sugar-Free Nestea, powder	5
Sweetened soft drinks	100	Fruit-flavored seltzer	15
Flavored coffee drinks	200	Taster's Choice hazelnut, vanilla, or chocolate roast instant with 1% milk and Splenda	30
Tequila sunrise	273	1 Tbsp grenadine and 8 oz diet ginger ale	50
Gin and tonic	170	Splash balsamic vinegar in seltzer	1
Bloody Mary	130	4 oz Tabasco Bloody Mary Mix and 4 oz seltzer	30
Rosé wine	160	Inglenook alcohol-removed White Zinfandel	60

Before you eat, relax and rate your hunger from 1 (hungriest) to 7 (fullest). Then eat slowly, pausing often to note how your hunger changes. When you finish eating, rate yourself one more time. Try to stay between 2½ and 5½—not too ravenous when you start, and not completely full when you stop.

We have a microwave addiction. Many of us come home from work tired and uninspired, so the easy option is to pop a low-cal frozen dinner into the microwave.

"Eating too many heavily processed foods can leave you short on fiber and antioxidants such as vitamin C," explains Jo Ann Hatter, R.D., clinical dietitian at Stanford University Medical Center.

Complement frozen entrées with a leafy green salad, a whole wheat roll, and a piece of fruit for dessert.

Slim Down by Making Small Changes

Do you hate big life changes—moves, job switches, retirement, kids growing up and moving out (or *not* moving out)? How do you think you would feel if all the desserts were suddenly out of your life? Possibly bereft. It might be too much to handle. Maybe a better way to make a diet change is slowly, cautiously, so that it becomes something you *can* live with. Try cutting out four or five desserts or fattening snacks a week, swapping them for a piece of fruit. Does that sound more realistic? More easy switches below.

- Choose baked chips instead of fatty fried ones, and dip them in fat-free salsa—not sour cream and onion dip.
- Have your sandwich with only one slice of bread, or eat just half the sandwich.

- Order extra veggies (lettuce, tomatoes, cucumber, pickle, onion, sweet or hot peppers) on your sandwich or sub instead of more meat or cheese.
- Make your sandwich spread mustard, not mayo or salad dressing.
- Drop the fries and get a salad instead, with low-fat dressing or a squeeze of lemon.
- Change your milk from 2% to 1% or fat-free.
- Skip the butter or spread on your toast and use no-sugar-added preserves instead.
- Cut out the sugary coffee drinks at break time; instead, enjoy fruit-flavored tea, diet soda, or a small amount of juice topped off with seltzer.
- Still craving java? Order a fat-free latte or cappuccino and sprinkle it with cocoa powder, cinnamon, or vanilla powder.
- Stop eating after 7:00 or 8:00 P.M., depending on when you have dinner. Make the next meal breakfast.

Plan Your Indulgences

Try this trick: At one meal a week, enjoy something you've been avoiding. Think of it as a reward for being good the rest of the week. It may just help bring the balance and pleasure back into your life if you've been struggling with weight loss. Just be sure to stick to your diet plan and compensate by planning ahead and banking the calories, or by adding more minutes to your workout.

We polled nutritionists for their tips and personal favorite treats that allow them to have their cake—to eat it too—and still stay on course.

Dawn Jackson, R.D., of Chicago's Northwestern Memorial Wellness Institute, uses a simple equation. "I live by the 80/20 rule of moderation. If 80 percent of the time I'm eating my fruits, vegetables, lean proteins, low-fat dairy, and whole grains, then 20 percent of the time I can goof off."

"Part of a healthy diet is knowing how to fit in special treats," says dessert lover Heidi Reichenberger, R.D., of Boston.

"Determine what 'occasionally' is," cautions New York City nutritionist Julie Walsh. "I say once a week is occasional, but there are people who think that three or four times a week is occasional. That doesn't work, calorie-wise."

Tampa-based nutritionist Cynthia Sass, R.D., pairs her unhealthy indulgences with more nutritionally sound fare. "French fries are my favorite treat," she says. "I fit them in without guilt by eating them only with other foods that are low in carbs and fat to create a balance. I'll have fries with a veggie burger, skip the bun, and add a big salad tossed with vinegar and seasonings but no oil. No guilt or deprivation."

Pittsburgh nutritionist Leslie Bonci, R.D., told us, "If I want a piece of carrot cake instead of my hummus and veggie wrap, I don't sweat about it. A little slice goes a long way. A slice, not a slab! It's about substitution instead of addition."

Go for the best, the experts advise. "I make sure that every treat that's over 400 calories passes the value test," says Mary Angela Miller, R.D., a dietitian at Ohio State University Hospitals. "I just love a freshly made Dairy Queen vanilla cone dipped in chocolate. You can't keep them in the freezer, so when I'm craving one, I have to drive for it. It's a destination treat. And small is about all you can handle before it melts."

For Miller and others, the key is portion control. Instead of buying a whole container of ice cream so you're tempted to eat the whole thing, go out and purchase a small single-dip cone.

Don't Forget the Chips

"I love chips, but I don't buy big bags and keep them at my house," says Milwaukee food and nutrition consultant Laurie Meyer, R.D. "Instead, I'll buy a small bag or order them at a restaurant with a meal. That way, I eat only one serving and feel completely satisfied." Meyer plans for her splurges by eating lighter beforehand. "But I won't skip a meal or starve myself. If you starve, you binge."

Los Angeles dietitian Ruth Frechman, R.D., doesn't skip meals either. But she occasionally makes chips her main course. "I'll add a fruit and make it my meal, enjoying every bite," she says. Another chip-loving nutritionist compensates by dipping chips in low-fat cottage cheese, which gives her calcium and protein, making the meal a little more healthful.

So go ahead: Eat up without remorse, and without increasing your waist size. Just be sure to follow a personalized blueprint of

LEAST OF THREE EVILS

Knowledge is power, especially when you're choosing among equally appealing treats. If you just can't make a decision, let the calorie and fat count do it for you.

Slice of Homemade Pie

Sweet potato pie: 243 calories, 13 g fat, 5 g sat. fat

Apple pie: 411 calories, 19 g fat, 5 g sat. fat

Pecan pie: 503 calories, 27 g fat, 5 g sat. fat

Dunkin' Donuts

Boston Kreme Donut: 240 calories, 9 g fat, 2 g sat. fat

Chocolate Frosted Cake Donut: 360 calories, 20 g fat, 5 g sat. fat

Chocolate Chip Muffin: 590 calories, 23 g fat, 10 g sat. fat

Snacks

20 Lay's potato chips: 150 calories, 10 g fat, 3 g sat. fat

2 cups french fries: 590 calories, 31 g fat, 12 g sat. fat

11 onion rings: 900 calories, 64 g fat, 30 g sat. fat

Scoop of Ben & Jerry's (½ cup) Ice Cream

Cherry Garcia: 260 calories, 15 g fat, 11 g sat. fat

Chubby Hubby: 330 calories, 21 g fat, 12 g sat. fat

Peanut Butter Cup: 380 calories, 26 g fat, 13 g sat. fat

Movie Concession Treats

6 oz strawberry Twizzlers: 600 calories, 4 g fat, 0 g sat fat

3 oz Milk Duds: 340 calories, 12 g fat, 5 g sat. fat

Small popcorn with butter (popped in coconut oil): 630 calories, 50 g fat, 29 g sat. fat

portion control by planning ahead or paying the price at the gym. By wisely incorporating indulgences into your life, you'll be healthier and happier.

Emotional Eating

It's Saturday night and you don't have a date. Instead of catching a movie with a friend, you're home with a pint of premium ice cream. Are you eating it because you're hungry or because food feels like your only companion?

You drag yourself home from work exhausted. The kids are screaming, the phone is ringing, the dog is yipping, and your hand keeps reaching into a bag of potato chips. Is it because your body needs the empty calories, sodium, and fat? Or does the eating keeps you from feeling the stress?

To find out why you really eat, you have to ask yourself some questions. It's almost impossible to stop emotional eating if you aren't at least curious about the purpose it is serving. For example, have you ever said to yourself, "I eat because I am sad"?

If you honestly examine this statement, you may find that you believe that even though you'd like to lose weight, eating cookies hurts less than feeling sad. But how do you know that? When was the last time you actually let yourself feel sad without turning to a plate of cookies?

Most of us use food for emotional and spiritual sustenance that it can't possibly provide. Or we use it to keep ourselves from experiencing the full range of our feelings. But it ends up keeping us from feeling truly alive. The next time you start to reach for food for comfort, stop long enough to ask yourself, "What was going on before I wanted to eat?" You may be surprised at what you find.

And if you realize that you're eating out of frustration, sadness, anger, or even just plain boredom, stop. Pick up a pen instead of a fork. Start writing an ongoing "curiosity dialogue." Open with simple, declarative statements. What do you believe will happen if you let yourself feel these feelings? Think about how you may have come to learn that. What positive lesson can you use to replace it? Emotional eating is not about lack of willpower, and it won't be solved by dieting. While overeating (as well as undereating) can become a life-threatening concern, the roots of the problem are rarely physical. We eat when we are lonely. We eat when we are sad. We eat when we are bored, angry, grieving, frustrated, frightened. We eat because we don't know that our feelings won't destroy us—and because food is everywhere, as is the message that it will fix whatever's wrong.

Your job is to ask questions, not manufacture answers. The answers are already there, but since you haven't looked, you don't know that yet. Assume that you are extraordinarily wise and incredibly sane. Because you are.

Healthful Eating for You and Your Children

Little Changes That Can Make Big Differences

If you need to lose weight, you're hardly alone. Two out of three Americans are now overweight or obese; that's up from 50 percent just 5 years ago. And we're steadily getting fatter: The average American has gained 1 to 3 pounds every year—a whopping 10 to 30 pounds per decade—and has failed miserably at taking it off.

Even more important, if you have children and are trying to lose weight, you're not the only one who stands to benefit. Odds are your children would, too. That's because childhood obesity has tripled in the past 2 decades, with some 15 percent of school-age children weighing more than they should.

Obesity can lead to a variety of serious health consequences like type 2 diabetes and hypertension. And while we used to think that these risks only affected adults, new research shows that even some toddlers are technically obese and show signs of disease. Obese children and teens suffer emotionally and socially as well as physically. And overweight kids may also turn into chronic dieters or develop eating disorders.

So if you're on the road to weight loss, good for you! This chapter is devoted to helping you find a few more reasons to get the whole family in shape, as well as a number of helpful tips to help get the whole family back on track and on the road to better health.

Understanding the Risks of Obesity

Obese people are at risk for a number of diseases including diabetes, arthritis, heart disease, and cancer. Even so, the connection between what we eat and how we feel is difficult for many people to make. Consider the following:

The Diabetes Connection

While diabetes seems to claim a new headline every other day, one aspect of the disease has stayed the same. There is a strong connection between obesity and diabetes. In fact, the single greatest predictor of who gets type 2 diabetes and who doesn't is being overweight or obese. Research by the Centers for Disease Control and Prevention (CDC) indicates that for every kilogram (2.2 pounds) of extra weight, the risk of diabetes climbs about 9 percent. So logically, diet—what you eat, and in some cases, what you don't—is at the heart of any treatment plan. In addition to maintaining a healthy weight and getting regular exercise, eating right helps keep blood sugar and fats at steady levels, which is the key to keeping problems under control.

Obesity and Arthritis

For years doctors didn't suspect that there could possibly be a link between diet and osteoarthritis. After all, they reasoned, this condition is a "natural" result of wear and tear on the joints. What could diet possibly do? Researchers now find evidence that overweight people are at higher risk for developing osteoarthritis in non-weight-bearing joints, such as the hands, as well as weight-bearing joints like the knee. Losing weight leads to less pain and improved mobility, which can improve the odds of further weight loss.

Excess Fat and Heart Disease

Some of that spare tire around your middle is *inside* your abdomen. Eating foods high in saturated fat, such as meats and full-

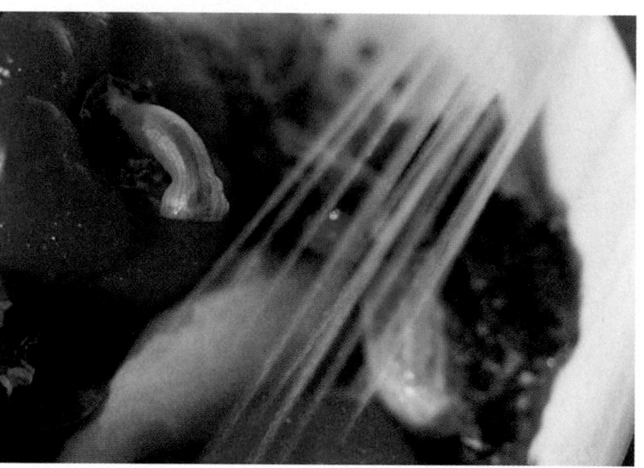

fat dairy products, increases the risk of internal belly fat, setting you up for heart disease and stroke.

According to Dr. Scott Grundy, director of the Center for Human Nutrition at the University of Texas Southwestern Medical Center in Dallas, "Fatty tissue releases fatty acids that can raise your blood sugar and triglycerides and lower your good HDL cholesterol." And being overweight raises a woman's stroke risk by 75 percent.

Plus-Size Cancer Risks

Packing on the pounds year after year means more than just plus-size clothes. Being overweight is also a known risk factor for several kinds of cancer. In fact, one in six cancer deaths is linked to extra body weight.

"Excess fat promotes the growth of cancer cells by raising blood insulin levels," says Anne McTiernan, M.D., Ph.D., researcher at the Fred Hutchinson Cancer Research Center in Seattle, and author of a book on breast health.

According to results from the 18-year Nurses' Health Study, for example, overweight women who ate diets high in added sugar and white flour (both refined carbohydrates) had a 53 percent increased risk of pancreatic cancer. And in postmenopausal women, excess fat may increase the occurrence of breast and endometrial cancers. Finally, being overweight is a known risk factor for colon cancer.

The Good News

It's not all bad news. There are a number of things you can do to fend off weight-related disease.

Improving your eating habits is a good way to start. For example, reducing the animal fats in your diet—butter, red meat, and full-fat dairy products—may help to reduce your chances of developing breast cancer, while doubling your fiber intake could reduce your risk of developing colon cancer by 40 percent. And eating a variety of colorful fruits and vegetables each day helps protect your heart.

And as we all know too well, weight loss and exercise are both keys to good health. Even losing a moderate amount of weight may help keep your blood pressure down. Lose weight and begin exercising and you'll cut your risk of both stroke and diabetes. Slim women breathe easier, too. Overweight women have twice the risk of developing asthma.

So if you and your kids improve your eating and exercise habits, you'll all live longer. Review the following good habits that can make a huge difference in how quickly you reach your weight-loss goals, and resolve to make one change a week.

Always Eat Breakfast

Breakfast, the single most important meal of the day, is not just essential for children. It fights obesity, diabetes, and heart disease all day long. Regular breakfast eaters are less

WHY NOT EGGS?

A great source of protein and B vitamins, eggs are low in saturated fat, quick and easy to prepare, and high in satisfaction. A soft-cooked egg with whole wheat toast makes a wonderful breakfast; a hard-cooked egg is a perfect snack.

HIGH-FIBER BREAKFAST FOODS

- Whole grain cereals: Look for those with at least 4 grams of fiber per serving. Even better are those with 8 or 10 grams.
- If you like hot cereals, have oatmeal, oat bran, or Wheatena. To boost the fiber even more, add ground flax seeds, dried currants, raisins, chopped dates or apricots, or a couple of tablespoons of mixed diced dried fruit.
- Whole grain breads and toast.
- Fresh fruit: It's a better source than juice for fiber and vitamins, but enjoy a glass of calcium-enriched orange juice, too. Excellent fruity fiber sources are fresh figs, raspberries, blackberries, apples with the peel, and oranges.

likely to develop insulin resistance syndrome, a common precursor of diabetes. Breakfast skippers are four and a half times more likely to be overweight. Missing your morning meal causes blood sugar to dip, leaving you overly hungry and quadrupling your chance of overeating. Coffee and pastry break, anyone?

Breakfast eaters tend to eat less fat and fewer high-calorie foods the remainder of the day because their bodies aren't running on empty. And breakfast is a great opportunity to stock up on calcium and fiber, both important weight-loss tools.

Never Skip Meals

When people cut out a meal in order to lose weight, it often backfires later in the day. Denying your hunger and skipping a meal is a bad choice. You'll overeat at the next meal.

Don't Forget to Snack

Many people are better able to control their weight if they eat every 2 to 4 hours. That way they don't get overly hungry, which—just like skipping a meal—can foster overeating later in the day. So plan for and enjoy a reasonable snack midafternoon, and you'll sail on until dinner.

What you *shouldn't* do is have bowls of snacky things within easy reach. There's too much danger of eating the whole bowl. Instead, transfer a sensible portion to a small plate, napkin, or bowl, and place the rest out of arm's reach. See our delicious smart-snacking ideas below.

Snack on nuts. They're nutritious, filling, and delicious. Measure or count out your portion because these tasty morsels can lead to nonstop munching. Rather than

FAST BREAKFASTS

- Whole grain frozen toaster waffles with sugar-free preserves and a dollop of yogurt.
- Low-fat cottage cheese with sliced tomatoes or strawberries and whole grain crispbread
- Scrambled eggs on a whole grain English muffin with salsa.
- Whole grain toast spread with low-fat ricotta cheese and a dab of sugar-free applesauce.
- A batch of Zucchini Muffins (page 241) or Whole Wheat Cranberry-Orange Muffins (page 242) frozen in a zip-top bag. Take out just what you need and defrost briefly in the microwave. Enjoy with yogurt or a smoothie.
- Cooked cereal prepared ahead of time. Check the cereal container for amounts, using half fat-free or 1% milk and half water. Add dried fruit or a cut-up apple to the cereal during the last few minutes of cooking, if you like. Spoon into a large container or individual containers and refrigerate. Zap what you need and serve hot with a little more milk and a touch of brown sugar or maple syrup. Try preparing the cereal on a weekend so you'll have it throughout the busy week.

overdo your nutty snack, extend your portion with 2 tablespoons of dried fruit; try sour cherries, cranberries, currants, or raisins.

Stuff a celery (stick). Spread with a little peanut butter or flavored low-fat cream cheese, celery sticks make an easy, satisfying, and portable snack.

Have some fruit. A few ideas for nutritious, fruity snacks: apple wedges (plain or with peanut butter or reduced-fat cheese); banana with or without yogurt; a fast-food fruit, yogurt, and granola parfait (like the one from McDonald's); seedless grapes (try them frozen); half a sliced pear and a piece of low-fat string cheese; a couple of plums; or a cup of take-out fruit salad. Citrus fruits are terrific and tote-able; enjoy grapefruit wedges, an orange, a clementine, or a tangerine.

Forget trans fat. This dangerous man-made fat—more commonly known as hydrogenated or partially hydrogenated vegetable oil—is a common ingredient in many of the foods we love to crunch and munch. How bad can it be? Trans fat can boost your risk of heart disease, diabetes, and cancer. To avoid it, snack on foods such as baked chips (read the labels) or a trans fat–free microwaveable popcorn such as Smart Balance, Newman's Own, or Bearitos. This last snack is a great nutritional bet, at 110 calories for 5 satisfying, crunchy cups.

Yes, even chocolate. Just 1 ounce of heavenly dark chocolate provides a big dose

NUTS FOR YOU

A serving of nuts is defined as 1 ounce. Those of us who don't carry scales around might want to copy this chart.

Number per Ounce	Calories per Ounce
Almonds, 22	170
Brazil nuts, 8	190
Cashews, 18	163
Chestnuts, 3½	70
Hazelnuts, 12	183
Macadamias, 12	200
Peanuts, 20	166
Pecan halves, 15	201
Pine nuts, 155	160
Pistachios, 47	160
Walnut halves, 14	185

of heart-protective antioxidants along with fabulous flavor. Does this mean that you should rush to the supermarket for a supply of medicinal chocolate bars? Sorry. However, you can consume small amounts of dark chocolate if it's wisely budgeted into your diet.

Dinnertime Strategies

Children (and husbands) learn by example. Serve them foods that are more healthful (but delicious), smaller portions, ample veggies, and fewer salty, fatty, sugary snacks and you may just start a new family tradition. Add exercise like walks or ball games and your family tradition will translate to a healthier, more energetic life for all of you.

Start Slowly

Just as with any lifestyle transformation, you need to start small, making one change at a time. Throw out all the junk food, eliminate dessert, and the whole family will rebel.

Try this instead. Serve more vegetables or salad and whole grains (such as brown rice or bulgur) and decrease the amount of protein. If no one seems to want to eat vegetables, try serving cut-up fruit like apples, melon, or even grapes to munch on.

Go meatless. Plan a vegetarian dinner once or twice a week. Have potatoes with all the fixings: low-fat sour cream or cottage cheese, shredded reduced-fat Cheddar, salsa, water-packed tuna, and mashed avocado. Or declare it soft-taco night and set out fillings of warmed fat-free refried beans, shredded lettuce or cabbage, corn kernels, avocado slices, chopped tomato, and shredded reduced-fat cheese. Or check out our wonderful Vegetarian Dishes, beginning on page 142.

Try pizza. If all anyone wants is pizza, have it made with half the usual amount of cheese and plenty of vegetable toppings instead of fatty meats. Or order it plain, leaving the kids' side unadorned (as they wish), and add chopped, steamed broccoli, scallions, and fresh tomato to the adult side at home.

Cook slimmer. Make changes to your own recipes, learning how to slim them down by using less fat and different techniques, such as oven-roasting or stove-top grilling on a ridged nonstick skillet.

THE POWER PANTRY

You'll be ready for dinner if you stock these essential staples.

- **Canned beans.** Chickpeas and white, black, and pink beans can all be strewn on salads, mixed with pasta or rice, whirled into a quick dip, or tossed together for a vegetarian chili.
- **Broth and soups.** Try the carton instead of the can; it's larger, and you don't have to decant it to store in the fridge (the can imparts a tinny flavor). Broth can be used in combination with oil to cook vegetables. And broths flavored with lemon, onion, or roasted garlic can be used as a tasty base for an easy soup dinner. Add mixed frozen vegetables, small pasta, and thinly sliced chicken or beef and simmer until tender. Use canned fat-free "cream of" type soups as the "sauce" for a casserole or bake.
- **Canned fish.** Salmon and tuna make wonderful salads and sandwiches. Mix with canned beans and reduced-fat mayo or yogurt and stuff into whole-wheat pitas for lunch or dinner. Add fresh spinach, avocado slices, tomato, cucumber, and sweet onion.
- **Canned tomatoes.** For a quick pasta sauce, soup, or an addition to a chicken dish, canned tomatoes, seasoned and plain, can't be beat. When fresh are not in season, canned have the best flavor. Avoid those with added oil, and note that some types of seasoned tomatoes and stewed tomatoes are high in sugar and, therefore, in calories.
- **Whole grains.** Choose whole wheat couscous, quick-cooking barley, quinoa, or brown rice.
- **Seasonings.** Herbs, spices, spice mixes, seasoning pastes, soy sauce, and chutney all add punch and pizzazz to simple foods such as broiled meat or fish, rice, or stews. Experiment with different flavors and ethnic seasonings to expand your family's culinary horizons, without increasing their waistlines.

Sweet treats. For dessert, offer fruit, sorbet, Fudgsicles, juice bars, or low-fat ice cream instead of higher-fat-and-calorie choices.

Leaf through our recipes. They're proven family-pleasers from the best weight-loss experts—our readers.

A Parent's Guide for Feeding Young Children

Instilling a healthy relationship with food can go a long way toward helping children grow into healthy adults. Here is some advice from the experts about the best ways to make that happen.

Eat a variety of foods. If you eat and serve a wide variety of foods, chances are your kids will learn to eat them, too. For vegetables and other foods that aren't sweet, you may need to serve the food up to 15 times before they like it. Put the broccoli or peas on the plate but don't force kids to eat it. It might just backfire.

Be a good role model. Pressuring kids to eat their vegetables is not nearly as effective as eating them yourself. This applies to everything that parents do, from the good things, such as eating healthful foods and staying active, to the not-so-good, like snacking in front of the TV. Mothers are especially important role models for their daughters.

Watch how you watch your weight. A mother's own weight concerns influence her daughter's developing weight issues, along with body satisfaction. Mothers who are overly concerned with weight and body image often have daughters who tend to be the same way, even at the age of 5.

Don't reward with food. Food used as a reward tends to be high in sugar and/or fat. Reward good deeds instead with praise or a special outing. Ask your child's teacher how good behavior is rewarded in the classroom. You might be surprised at the junk food handed out in schools.

Eat together. Convene the family at least once a day at the table. Mealtime is about more than food—it's about reviewing the day, discussing plans, and teaching good habits.

Drop out of the clean-plate club. Perhaps you remember your own parents' mealtime mantra? "Finish your dinner. Children in (fill in the country) are starving!" Avoiding food waste is admirable, but making kids finish up every bite sends the wrong message. Help your child clue in to

CHILD-FRIENDLY PORTION SIZES

Researchers at the University of North Carolina found that we're even supersizing at home, and that between 1977 and 1996, portion size for some junk foods jumped by 100 calories or more. So it should come as no surprise that parents often inadvertently serve their kids too much food. Most young children will eat only if hungry, regardless of what you put before them, but for kids over 5, as portion sizes grew, so did the amount they ate.

A good rule for preschoolers is to serve only 1 tablespoon of any given food for every year in age. One of the best ways to control portion size is to let children serve themselves from platters or bowls. Often they will take more age-appropriate portions, and serving themselves will also foster independence.

SHRINK THESE

	Typical portion	More like it
100 percent juice	8–12 ounces	4–6 ounces per day (over age 1)
Chicken nuggets	4 pieces (4–5 ounces)	2 or 3 pieces (2–3 ounces)
French fries	20–30	10
Ice cream	1½ cups	½ cup
Mac and cheese	1½ cups	1 cup
Cheese pizza	2 or 3 slices	1 slice

SERVE MORE OF THESE

	Suggested servings per day	Serving size
Fruit	2	1 medium piece; ½ cup fruit salad
Vegetables	3	7 or 8 baby carrots; 5 cherry tomatoes; ½ cup cooked peas, winter squash, or green beans
Grains	6	½ cup cereal; 1 slice whole grain bread
Milk	2 or 3	8 ounces milk or yogurt; 1½ ounces hard cheese

when he's really hungry. Serve smaller portions; your child can ask for seconds if still hungry.

Drop 100. Eating just 100 fewer calories daily of *any* food can help you lose up to 10 extra pounds in a single year.

Dessert can wait. If you must serve something sweet after dinner, do it later in the evening so it's not an expected part of the meal. This way, getting dessert isn't connected to what a child has eaten for dinner (like being a member of the clean-plate club). Instead of being a "reward" for eating up, it becomes an occasional treat.

Make the TV room a no-food zone. In a Tufts University study, researchers linked overweight children to TV viewing, not simply because of the lack of activity, but also because of the high-calorie snacks kids tend to eat while watching. When families watch TV as a regular part of meal routines, they consume fewer fruits and vegetables and more pizza, snack foods, and soda.

A Dieter's Guide to Dining Out

Go Out to Eat without Going Overboard

We're dining out more than ever before—most of us have a meal a day outside the home. If you're watching your waistline, trying to maintain weight loss, or interested in a healthy lifestyle, eating out can make it tough. Foods eaten away from home tend to be higher in calories and fat and lower in fiber. The average restaurant entrée often has between 1,000 and 2,000 calories—not counting bread, salad, appetizer, and dessert. And ubiquitous big servings invite overeating.

But today's restaurants and fast-food places are more responsive than ever to dietary needs, and they depend upon your business. As a result, the choice is yours: Load up on fat and calories, or choose carefully and enjoy a sensible meal.

Dining out includes not just fancy food enjoyed at a white-tablecloth restaurant. It's also the breakfast or lunch grabbed at the coffee shop or sandwich place, the meal on a tray from the cafeteria, the Chinese takeout ordered in on busy evenings, and the fast food munched with your kids. It's all eating out. Following is a guide that will help you make the best choices.

Sit-Down Restaurants

If you're eating out for a special occasion, kick back and enjoy yourself. Try to plan for the dinner beforehand by eating a lighter breakfast and lunch, but not by skipping a meal. If you go a little wild at dinner, eat more sensibly the next day or so, or put in a little extra time at the gym. Balance it out.

If it's a restaurant you dine at often, and you know that the delicious pork chop or steak is enough for two, have it split onto two plates to share, and order extra salad and vegetables. Or, when the meal arrives, if the portion is huge, simply ask at the outset that half be wrapped up for later. Pasta servings are often large; ask if there is a smaller portion available.

Here are a few key menu phrases to help guide your eating-out choices.

On the Menu

Avoid: deep-fried, pan-fried, crispy fried (especially in Asian restaurants), breaded, double-sautéed, melted cheese, butter sauces, cream sauces, marbled prime meats, ribs, double-thick chops, anything topped with sour cream, gravy, stuffing. . . . You get the point.

Look for: steamed, roasted, broiled, grilled, poached, light tomato sauces, broth-based soups, mussels or clams steamed in broth or tomato sauce, shrimp or seafood cocktails, fish, chicken, or lamb and vegetable kebabs, fresh fruit salsas, raitas (an Indian yogurt-cucumber condiment), tomato salsas. Menu items that sound fresh and light often are.

Ask for: Cheese to be reduced or omitted, croutons left off, sauce on the side, dressing on the side, fresh-ground pepper, a vegetable plate entrée, extra veggies instead of fries or mashed potatoes, a plain baked white or sweet potato, olive oil and balsamic vinegar or a lemon wedge to spark up salads, grilled meats, and veggies.

Additional Tricks to Try

- For an appetizer, have broth-based soup, a glass of tomato juice or a virgin Bloody Mary, a salad, or some fruit.
- Avoid the bread or ask the server to remove it.
- If you must have bread, dip it in olive oil instead of spreading it with butter, and limit yourself to one piece.

ALCOHOL CALORIES ADD UP FAST

Even if you're not overindulging, alcoholic beverages can contribute plenty of empty calories. Check this out: 12 ounces of beer = 150 calories; 5 ounces of wine = 100 calories; 1½ ounces of liquor = 100 calories. And the foods you eat while you're drinking are often high in calories—a double whammy. So simply cutting back on alcohol can do wonders for your waistline, and your determination.

- Eat only half of what is on your plate, whatever it is, and eat slowly, savoring every bite. Take the rest home for tomorrow's lunch.
- Order two appetizers instead of an appetizer and a main dish, or begin with a soup or salad and have an appetizer for your main course. Often appetizers are more highly seasoned and satisfying than big hunks of meat or piles of pasta.
- Ask how things are prepared, and don't apologize—unless you think it's going to get you what you want.
- Order a dessert to share with the table.
- Instead of having dessert, take a brisk walk after dinner and stop off for a small frozen yogurt.
- Ask for milk instead of cream for your coffee, and ask if low-fat milk is available.
- Have a cup of espresso, tea, or coffee instead of dessert, and stir in a little sugar so your meal ends on a sweet note.
- Quit the clean-plate club. Practice this useful phrase: "Take-out box, please."

Coffee Shops and Delis

At breakfast, stick with oatmeal or cold cereal with low-fat milk, perhaps with a slice of whole grain toast and fruit. Or have whole wheat toast with a slice of American cheese and tomato and a glass of fat-free milk. If cantaloupe is in season, order that with a scoop of low-fat cottage cheese. Try one egg, scrambled or fried, with sliced tomatoes and whole wheat toast. Avoid fatty meats, sausage gravy, biscuits, deep-fried, hash-browned, or home-fried potatoes, and, of course, breakfast pastries.

For breakfast to go, choose fat-free or low-fat yogurt or cottage cheese, or a hard-cooked egg and a piece of fresh fruit or cup of fruit salad. If you get a bagel, have it spread thinly with low-fat cream cheese and cut in quarters to share. One bagel equals 2 servings.

Lunch starts out right with a lentil, bean, or vegetable soup; finish up with a salad with low-fat dressing. Deli sandwiches are often piled high, so if you get one, share it. Avoid salad-type sandwiches, which are loaded with mayo; instead, go for lean white-meat turkey or chicken breast, roast beef, or ham and get extra veggies and mustard. Opt for whole wheat bread instead of a doughy roll, and fruit instead of chips or a cookie. A great munchie: baby carrots.

Cafeterias

This might be a case where you're going to have to learn to brown-bag it. Most cafeteria lines are minefields of fat and calories. But if you forgot your lunch that day, here are a few tips as you push your tray along the rails.

If the food is brown, round, or swimming in fat, keep on moving. Since the list of foods to avoid is so long, we'll focus instead on what you should choose.

Have some soup, if it's on the menu, but avoid the creamy types. Try steamed rice topped with vegetables—perhaps broccoli, green beans, or stewed tomatoes—or a small serving of pasta with tomato sauce. Or choose baked chicken and remove the skin before eating. If sandwiches are on the menu, opt for whole wheat bread and lean fillings (see above). Even grilled cheese, if it's on whole wheat bread, isn't a terrible choice;

it will be tastier with sliced tomatoes and pickle. Baked beans are a pretty good side dish instead of fries. Don't forget yogurt. Have fruit for dessert or, occasionally, Jell-O or fruit sorbet.

Often there is a salad bar, which can be a terrific option. But be picky with those tongs: What seems healthful can pack on the pounds, so choose your toppings wisely, and keep portions sensible.

Start with a base of crunchy iceberg lettuce, romaine, and spinach and add raw veggies like shredded carrots, red cabbage, cucumber and tomato slices, and cooked but undressed veggies; asparagus, beets, green beans, broccoli, and cauliflower are good choices. Add protein with hard-cooked egg, white-meat chicken or turkey, water-packed tuna, tofu, chickpeas or kidney beans, or cottage cheese. Add crunch with a few toasted nuts.

Avoid the mayo-dressed salads, sugary three-bean salad, bacon bits, chow mein noodles, and croutons. And go easy on the dressing. That innocent-looking ladle can hold plenty of calories. Use a low-fat dressing, shake on a little oil and vinegar, or bring your own favorite low-cal dressing from home (see the recipes on page 71).

Chinese Takeout

It sounds so healthy—chunks of crisp chicken with red peppers, pineapple, and cashews—but if it says double-fried, twice-cooked, or crispy fried, or if it's considered a "specialty," it's often a nutritional nightmare.

Don't avoid stir-fries, but do choose cautiously, and stay away from the sweet-and-sour preparations. Try asking for dishes to be cooked in very little oil; it might work. Order steamed (not fried) brown rice instead of white, and if the dish looks oily, drain the juices from the carton first. Make sure you order one dish that's just vegetables; especially good for you are leafy greens or broccoli. Spoon your portions onto a plate instead of eating from the container. Have about half a cup of rice and equal portions of the protein-based dish and the veggies.

A good way to go are the big, comforting brothy noodle soups with vegetables and bits of chicken or tofu—but avoid the crispy fried noodles or elaborate stuffed dumplings. These soups generally provide enough for two people or two meals.

Tea and orange wedges are perfect for dessert. And don't forget to read your fortune!

Fast Food

It's easy, cheap, the kids love it—but fast food is quickly making us fat. What can we do?

Drop the Breakfast Sandwich

It's about the worst breakfast you could eat. If you want breakfast on the go, it's just as easy to drive to a convenience store and pick up coffee, juice, and a yogurt or small container of cereal and milk—maybe even a banana.

Pizza Redux

You don't have to order a pizza with all the toppings, and you shouldn't. Pizza Hut has stepped up to the calorie challenge with Fit 'n' Delicious pizza. Made with a thinner crust and less cheese, it's got a host of more healthful toppings to choose from (you pick three). They include diced chicken, green peppers, ham, jalapeño peppers, mushrooms, pineapples, red onion, and diced tomato. Hold the pepperoni!

Is Salad the Answer?

The number of salads appearing on fast-food menu boards is certainly a good sign that we're moving in the right direction, but experts advise that you still need to weigh your options and say no to things like crunchy noodles, the whole package of roasted almonds (have just a few), bacon bits, crispy chicken (get grilled instead), and full-fat dressings.

Have It Your Own Way

Once they've been breaded and fried, the normally lean options of chicken or fish on a bun can weigh in higher than a plain burger. So order a small burger and ask them to hold the mayo.

Better yet, have a grilled chicken sandwich with lettuce, pickles, tomato, and onion and no mayo. You might also discard the top half of the bun to save even more calories.

Burger King has introduced Lite Combo Meals, which include a grilled chicken sandwich on a baguette, a side salad (dress yours with light Italian), and a large bottle of water. A fresher option, for about 430 calories.

Do You Want Fries with That?

The correct answer is "no." But if you've *got* to have fries, get a small order and share them, and only every once in a while. Never supersize.

STOP. THINK. *NOW* EAT.

Just before their mid-afternoon snack, women who paused to remember what they ate for lunch consumed 55 percent fewer calories than those who mindlessly noshed away, according to one recent study.

Taking a moment to ponder a previous meal may remind your brain (and your stomach) that you're actually still full.

Try this: Think about each food you've already eaten today and visualize what the portions looked like *before* feeding quarters into the candy machine. Doing this once a day could help you lose up to 14 pounds a year.

Other Options

At a fast-food restaurant during lunchtime, we recently noticed seniors ordering pretty sensible meals. One after the other asked for a baked potato with sour cream and chives, and some added a cup of chili. No fries, no burgers.

While the sour cream has plenty of fat calories, used judiciously, it's not so bad, and the chili is a pretty good choice, too. The ideal would be to skip the sour cream and spoon the chili into the potato. Have a glass of low-fat milk or unsweetened iced tea for a satisfying, inexpensive hot meal. Oh, and have a salad with that.

The Fast-Food Dilemma: One Mother's Solution

JoAnn Brader is test kitchen director at Rodale. For the last 24 years, she's been the person behind the testing and development of many healthful, lower-fat, calorie-sensible recipes. As a former home ec teacher, she knows her nutrition facts better than anyone.

Brader has a daughter, Jill, now 18. When Jill was much younger, Brader was confronted with the same struggles most parents face: Her child wanted fast food—just like the other kids.

Plus, McDonald's had playgrounds, which lured Jill and her mom. With Jill occupied on the playground, Brader got a break. Food was just part of the draw—often Jill didn't even finish her meal. So Brader, who (previously) hadn't eaten much fast food, scarfed down the leftovers. "They tasted good," she says, but they also made her gain weight.

When Jill was 5, fast food was it for birthday parties or the latest toys in Happy Meals. Since fast food wasn't going away, Brader decided to make some rules to control what, when, and how they ate.

"We'd make a date [for fast food]. We'd decide we'd go on a certain night, as a treat, and I'd keep the promise. I never brought fast food home, even if Jill begged. Fast food was eaten at the restaurant."

Until Jill was about 7, an order of french fries was always shared among the kids. (Brader's nieces and nephews often accompanied them.) "I never bought a full packet of fries for just one child. And Jill and I split one soda between us."

Another rule was that you must eat first, while seated—and then you could go out to play. Once the child was on the playground, any leftovers were history (tossed), and no longer did Brader find herself snacking on cold, ketchup-soaked fries.

"I'd often bring a baggie of grapes or some bananas to munch on, for me and the kids," Brader remembers. And she dropped the extra weight.

When Jill was a bit older, fast food was sometimes a meal after church, accompanied by her grandfather, but it was never purchased from the drive-thru window. "We went only if there was enough time to go in, order, sit down, and eat," says Brader.

Today, Jill Brader, like her mom, is slim, healthy, and has excellent eating habits. Jill often asks her mom to make pasta dishes for dinner, and she loves broccoli, Brussels sprouts, corn, and cauliflower. Spinach, both cooked and raw, is a favorite, as are salads.

"I advise moderation all the way," says Brader. "Don't obsess over what they won't eat. Don't deny; offer alternatives. If they like vegetables, offer those. If they don't like vegetables, they'll probably eat fruit. It's just good common sense."

Soups, Salads, and Sides

Soups

Salads

Sides

Thai Squash Soup

Julie Baron, New York, New York

Prep time: 10 minutes; Cook time: 20 minutes

5–6 shallots, unpeeled
1 can (13½ ounces) light coconut milk
2 cups reduced-sodium chicken broth
1½ pounds butternut squash, peeled and cut into ½" cubes
½ cup packed fresh cilantro + 1 tablespoon chopped, for garnish
½ teaspoon salt
2 tablespoons fish sauce
¼ cup minced scallions, green parts only
Ground black pepper

Preheat the broiler. Spray a sheet of heavy foil with cooking spray and place the shallots on top. When the broiler is ready, broil the shallots, turning occasionally, for about 5 to 7 minutes, or until softened and blackened. Remove from the broiler, let cool, then peel and halve them lengthwise.

In a large pot over medium-high heat, combine the shallots, coconut milk, broth, squash, and the ½ cup of cilantro. Cook just until the mixture begins to boil. Reduce the heat, add the salt, and simmer for about 10 minutes, or until the squash is tender. Stir in the fish sauce and cook for 2 to 3 minutes longer.

Garnish each serving with a sprinkling of the minced scallion greens and the chopped cilantro and season with pepper to taste.

Makes 6 (1-cup) servings

Per serving: *92 calories, 4 g protein, 20 g carbohydrate, 1 g fat, 1 mg cholesterol, 728 mg sodium, 2 g fiber*

Diet Exchanges: *0 milk, 3½ vegetable, 0 fruit, 0 bread, 0 meat, 0 fat*

1½ Carb Choices

Kitchen Tip

To make an edible soup bowl, cut a thin slice from the bottom of a small pumpkin or squash. Cut off the top and scoop out the insides, leaving at least ½" of shell intact. The bowl may be cooked or served raw; if it's cooked, you can eat it when you've finished the soup!

Hot and Sour Soup

Karen Schlyter, Calgary, Alberta, Canada

"This vegetable-rich soup is low in fat and carbohydrates and has lots of flavor. I find it very satisfying for lunch or a light dinner."

Prep time: 15 minutes; Cook time: 60 minutes

3 cans (14½ ounces each) reduced-sodium chicken broth
1 teaspoon grated lime zest + juice from 1 lime
2 tablespoons coarsely chopped fresh ginger + 1 tablespoon slivered
2 cloves whole garlic + 2 cloves slivered
1 jalapeño chile pepper, coarsely chopped + 1 seeded and finely chopped (wear plastic gloves when handling)
2 tablespoons olive oil
1½ pounds lean ground turkey breast
1 medium red bell pepper, chopped
2 cups sliced white mushrooms
1 bunch scallions, sliced
¼ cup soy sauce
¼ cup fish sauce
¼ cup rice wine vinegar
5 cups water
2 cups snow peas
2 cups bean sprouts
2 tablespoons toasted sesame oil

In a stockpot, combine the broth, lime zest, chopped ginger, whole garlic cloves, and chopped jalapeño pepper. Bring to a boil over medium-high heat, then cook uncovered for about 15 minutes, or until the flavors are concentrated and liquid has reduced to approximately 3 cups. Strain the broth through a sieve into a large bowl and set aside. Discard the solids and wipe out the stockpot.

In the same stockpot, warm the oil over medium heat. When hot, add the turkey and cook for about 5 minutes, or until no longer pink, stirring frequently to break the meat into small pieces. Add the bell pepper, mushrooms, scallions, and the seeded and diced jalapeño pepper and cook for 5 minutes, or until softened. Add the slivered ginger and garlic and cook for 2 minutes. Add the soy sauce, fish sauce, and vinegar and cook for 2 minutes longer. Add the reserved broth back to the stockpot as well as the water. Cover and simmer for 30 minutes, stirring occasionally. Remove the stockpot from the heat, add the snow peas and bean sprouts, and let stand uncovered for 5 minutes longer (they'll cook in the hot broth). Stir in the lime juice and sesame oil just before serving.

Makes 16 (1-cup) servings

Per serving: *138 calories, 11 g protein, 7 g carbohydrate, 8 g fat, 35 mg cholesterol, 865 mg sodium, 7 g fiber*

Diet Exchanges: *0 milk, 1 vegetable, 0 fruit, 0 bread, 1½ meat, 1 fat*

½ Carb Choice

Hearty Onion Soup

Kim Champion, Phoenix, Arizona

"If you're not on a low-carb diet, adding a stale bread heel to the bowl before serving is a wonderful way to enjoy this soup!"

Prep time: 7 minutes
Cook time: 1 hour 10 minutes

- **2 tablespoons olive oil**
- **1½ pounds sweet onions, thinly sliced**
- **3 cloves garlic, chopped**
- **1 cup white wine**
- **5 cans (14½ ounces each) reduced-fat beef broth**
- **2 sprigs thyme**
- **1 bay leaf**
- **Shredded low-fat cheese of your choice (optional)**

Warm the oil in a large pot over medium heat. When hot, add the onions and cook, stirring often, for about 30 minutes, or until brown. Add the garlic and cook, stirring, for about 3 minutes longer. Slowly add the white wine and broth and bring just to a boil, stirring constantly. Once boiling, reduce the heat to low and add the thyme sprigs and bay leaf. Simmer, uncovered, for about 30 minutes, stirring occasionally. Remove and discard the thyme sprigs and bay leaf. Top with cheese, if desired, and serve.

Makes 10 (1-cup) servings

Per serving: *79 calories, 2 g protein, 7 g carbohydrate, 3 g fat, 0 mg cholesterol, 414 mg sodium, 1 g fiber*

Diet Exchanges: *0 milk, 1 vegetable, 0 fruit, 0 bread, 0 meat, ½ fat*

½ Carb Choice

Kitchen Tip

If you're using broth that's not fat-free, store the unopened cans in the refrigerator for at least 6 hours. When you open the cans, the fat will have congealed for easy removal. If you're in a hurry, put the cans (opened or unopened) in the freezer for 15 to 30 minutes.

Caramelized Onion and Sweet Potato Soup

Elaine Sweet, Dallas, Texas

"This is a very full-bodied soup that seems almost sinful. And because it's loaded with beta-carotene and other vitamins, it makes you feel good on a damp, cool day."

Prep time: 15 minutes; Cook time: 45 minutes

- **2 tablespoons trans-free margarine or butter**
- **5 large sweet onions, thinly sliced**
- **1½ tablespoons sugar**
- **4 medium sweet potatoes, peeled and cubed**
- **2 quarts chicken broth**
- **½ teaspoon ground allspice**
- **½ teaspoon dried thyme**
- **½ teaspoon ground nutmeg**
- **½ teaspoon salt**
- **½ teaspoon ground black pepper**

In a large pot over medium-high heat, melt the margarine or butter. Add the onions and cook, stirring constantly, for 5 to 7 minutes, or until browned. Add the sugar and cook, stirring, for 3 minutes longer. Add the sweet potatoes, broth, allspice, thyme, nutmeg, salt, and pepper and bring to a boil. Quickly reduce the heat to low and continue to simmer, uncovered, for 15 to 20 minutes, or until the sweet potato pieces are fork-tender. Adjust the seasonings and serve.

Makes 14 (1-cup) servings

Per serving: *105 calories, 3 g protein, 18 g carbohydrate, 3 g fat, 2 mg cholesterol, 689 mg sodium, 3 g fiber*

Diet Exchanges: *0 milk, 1½ vegetable, 0 fruit, ½ bread, ½ meat, ½ fat*

1 Carb Choice

Kitchen Tip

For a smoother soup, transfer the ingredients to a food processor after the ingredients are fork-tender and puree in batches. Return to the pot, reheat, and serve.

Spicy Chicken Tortilla Soup

Kathy Osborne, Fort Wayne, Indiana

Prep time: 15 minutes; Cook time: 35 minutes

- **1 can (15 ounces) diced tomatoes**
- **¼ teaspoon ground black pepper**
- **1½ teaspoons chili powder**
- **1½ teaspoons ground cumin**
- **2 teaspoons Worcestershire sauce**
- **½ teaspoon hot-pepper sauce**
- **2 teaspoons olive oil**
- **1 pound boneless, skinless chicken breasts, cut into 1" pieces**
- **1 medium onion, chopped**
- **1–2 jalapeño chile peppers, chopped (wear plastic gloves when handling)**
- **2 cloves garlic, minced**
- **2 cans (14½ ounces each) reduced-sodium chicken broth**
- **¼ cup all-purpose flour**
- **½ cup water**
- **⅓ cup fat-free sour cream**
- **⅓ cup chopped fresh cilantro**
- **4 ounces reduced-fat tortilla chips, crushed**

In a food processor or blender, combine the tomatoes (with juice), black pepper, chili powder, cumin, Worcestershire sauce, and hot-pepper sauce. Process to a smooth, thick consistency and set aside.

Warm the oil in a large pot over medium-high heat. When hot, cook the chicken, onion, jalapeño pepper, and garlic, stirring frequently, for 5 minutes, or until the chicken is no longer pink and the onion is softened. Reduce the heat to low, add the tomato mixture and broth, and simmer, uncovered, for 15 minutes.

Meanwhile, in a small bowl, whisk together the flour and water until a smooth paste forms. Add to the soup and raise the temperature if necessary to keep the soup just barely boiling. Simmer for 5 minutes.

Remove from the heat, add the sour cream, and stir until well blended. Stir in the cilantro, garnish with the tortilla chips, and serve.

Makes 8 (1-cup) servings

Per serving: *197 calories, 17 g protein, 19 g carbohydrate, 6 g fat, 34 mg cholesterol, 251 mg sodium, 3 g fiber*

Diet Exchanges: *0 milk, 1 vegetable, 0 fruit, 1 bread, 2 meat, 1 fat*

1 Carb Choice

Spicy Black Bean Soup

Jimmy Robbins, Bath, New York

"For a meal that has so little fat, this soup is full of flavor. It's also a great vegetarian dish."

Prep time: 10 minutes; Cook time: 40 minutes

- **1 tablespoon olive oil**
- **2 cloves garlic, minced**
- **1 small onion, finely chopped**
- **2 cans (15 ounces each) black beans, rinsed and drained**
- **1 chipotle chile pepper in adobo sauce, finely chopped**
- **1 tablespoon chopped fresh cilantro**
- **1 can (14½ ounces) diced tomatoes**
- **1 can (14½ ounces) low-sodium chicken or vegetable broth**
- **½ teaspoon dried oregano**
- **½ teaspoon kosher salt**
- **½ teaspoon ground cumin**
- **½ teaspoon ground black pepper**
- **Juice of 1 lime**

Warm the oil in a large pot over medium-high heat. When hot, add the garlic and onion and cook for about 1 minute, or until lightly golden. Add the beans, chipotle chile pepper, cilantro, tomatoes (with juice), and broth. Reduce the heat to medium and cook for about 5 minutes. Reduce the heat to low. Add the oregano, salt, cumin, and black pepper and simmer uncovered, stirring occasionally, for about 30 minutes. Remove from the heat, add the lime juice, and serve.

Makes 4 servings

Per serving: *210 calories, 11 g protein, 30 g carbohydrate, 5 g fat, 0 mg cholesterol, 880 mg sodium, 12 g fiber*

Diet Exchanges: *0 milk, 1 vegetable, 0 fruit, 1½ bread, 1 meat, 1 fat*

2 Carb Choices

SHOPPING SAVVY

Soup's On

The famed Moosewood vegetarian restaurant has a line of organic vegetarian soups that we love, especially on busy nights. The refrigerated soups are packed in airtight pouches that are inserted into microwaveable containers. Each pouch serves two (as a first course) or makes one hearty serving. Varieties include Texas Two-Bean Chili, Creamy Broccoli & Cheese, Creamy Potato & Corn Chowder, Hearty Mushroom & Barley, Mediterranean Tomato & Rice, and Tuscan White Bean. Found at Wegmans, Whole Foods, and other grocery chains nationwide.

Photo courtesy of Fairfield Farm Kitchens

Long Grain Rice and Lentil Soup

Richard Opiekun, Brick, New Jersey

"This recipe is low in calories yet very hearty and filling. By eating dishes like this, while keeping to a strict walking program, I've been able to attain my goal weight."

Prep time: 15 minutes; Cook time: 45 minutes

- **5 cans (14½ ounces each) reduced-sodium chicken broth**
- **1½ cups lentils, rinsed and drained**
- **1 cup long grain brown rice**
- **1 can (28 ounces) diced tomatoes**
- **3 carrots, chopped**
- **1 small onion, chopped**
- **1 rib celery, chopped**
- **3 cloves garlic, minced**
- **1 teaspoon dried basil**
- **1 teaspoon dried oregano**
- **1 teaspoon dried thyme**
- **1 bay leaf**
- **2 tablespoons cider vinegar**
- **½ cup finely chopped fresh parsley**
- **Ground black pepper**

In a large pot over medium-high heat, combine the broth, lentils, rice, tomatoes (with juice), carrots, onion, celery, garlic, basil, oregano, thyme, and bay leaf. Bring to a boil, then reduce the heat to low. Simmer, covered, for 45 minutes, stirring occasionally. Remove from the heat and add the vinegar, parsley, and pepper to taste. Remove and discard the bay leaf, adjust the seasonings, and serve.

Makes 16 (1-cup) servings

Per serving: *130 calories, 7 g protein, 24 g carbohydrate, 1 g fat, 1 mg cholesterol, 34 mg sodium, 7 g fiber*

Diet Exchanges: *0 milk, 1 vegetable, 0 fruit, 1½ bread, ½ meat, 0 fat*

1½ Carb Choices

Curried Fish Chowder

Nancy Silverman, New Haven, Connecticut

Prep time: 10 minutes; Cook time: 40 minutes

2 tablespoons olive oil
1 large onion, chopped
2 ribs celery, sliced
4 carrots, sliced
2 cloves garlic, minced
1 inch-long piece of fresh ginger, peeled and finely chopped
1 teaspoon curry powder
4 cups (14½ ounces each) low-sodium vegetable broth
2 cups finely chopped potatoes
2 cups diced salt-free tomatoes
1 pound firm-fleshed whitefish fillets, such as cod or haddock
1 cup fresh or frozen peas
1 cup coarsely chopped flat-leaf parsley
Salt
Ground black pepper

Warm the oil in a large pot over medium heat. When hot, add the onion, celery, and carrots and cook for about 5 minutes, or until the vegetables start to soften. Add the garlic, ginger, and curry powder, stir, and cook for 2 to 3 minutes. Add the broth, potatoes, and tomatoes (with juice), cover, and bring to a boil. Reduce heat and simmer for about 15 minutes, or until the potatoes are tender. Add the fish and continue to simmer, uncovered, for about 12 minutes, or until the fish is cooked through. If you're using fresh peas, add them when you add the fish. If you're using frozen peas, add them about 2 minutes before the fish is done. Stir in the parsley and season to taste with salt and pepper.

Makes 8 (1-cup) servings

Per serving: *170 calories, 14 g protein, 21 g carbohydrate, 4½ g fat, 25 mg cholesterol, 400 mg sodium, 9 g fiber*

Diet Exchanges: *0 milk, 2 vegetable, 0 fruit, ½ bread, 1½ meat, 1 fat*

3 Carb Choices

Hearty Veggie Stew

Jennifer Maslowski, New York, New York

Prep time: 15 minutes

Cook time: 1 hour 10 minutes

- **3 tablespoons olive oil**
- **1 medium yellow or white onion, coarsely chopped**
- **½ teaspoon salt**
- **2 cloves garlic, minced**
- **6 russet potatoes, quartered**
- **1 pound carrots, cleaned and cut into thirds**
- **1 can (14½ ounces) low-sodium vegetable broth**
- **½ cup ketchup**
- **1 package (10 ounces) frozen green beans, thawed**
- **1 package (10 ounces) frozen green peas, thawed**
- **1 cup dried, sliced shiitake mushrooms**
- **2 tablespoons Worcestershire sauce**
- **1 tablespoon dried oregano**
- **½ teaspoon ground black pepper**
- **½ teaspoon red-pepper flakes**

Warm the oil in a large pot over medium heat. When hot, add the onion and salt and cook for 5 minutes, or until soft. Add the garlic and cook for 2 minutes longer, until lightly browned. Add the potatoes, carrots, broth, and ketchup and cook, uncovered and stirring occasionally, just until boiling. Reduce the heat to low and add the green beans, peas, mushrooms, and Worcestershire sauce. Stir in the oregano, black pepper, and red-pepper flakes and simmer, uncovered, for 30 minutes, or until the potatoes and carrots are tender.

Makes 6 (1-cup) servings

Per serving: *330 calories, 9 g protein, 62 g carbohydrate, 8 g fat, 0 mg cholesterol, 720 mg sodium, 10 g fiber*

Diet Exchanges: *0 milk, 3 vegetable, 0 fruit, 2½ bread, 0 meat, 1½ fat*

4 Carb Choices

Hot and Spicy Chili

Mary Helmle, Utica, New York

"This chili will warm you up in the winter and also provide a lot of fiber. I find that a bowl for lunch fills me up and helps me burn more calories."

Prep time: 10 minutes; Cook time: 35 minutes

2 teaspoons olive oil
1 medium onion, finely chopped
1 medium green bell pepper, finely chopped
1 package (12 ounces) soy crumbles
1 tablespoon all-purpose flour
1 teaspoon sugar
3 tablespoons chili powder
1 tablespoon cayenne pepper
¼ teaspoon ground black pepper
1 can (28 ounces) tomato sauce
1 cup water
1 can (14½ ounces) kidney beans, rinsed and drained

Warm the oil in a medium saucepan over medium-high heat. When hot, add the onion and pepper and cook for 5 to 10 minutes, or until soft. Add the soy crumbles and simmer for 5 minutes. Meanwhile, in a small bowl, mix the flour, sugar, chili powder, cayenne pepper, and black pepper. Add to the saucepan along with the tomato sauce and water. Stir gently until thoroughly mixed. Simmer, uncovered, for about 15 minutes. Add the kidney beans and simmer for 5 minutes longer, or until the beans are heated through.

Makes 4 (1-cup) servings

Per serving: *388 calories, 29 g protein, 41 g carbohydrate, 13 g fat, 90 mg cholesterol, 509 mg sodium, 7 g fiber*

Diet Exchanges: *0 milk, 2 vegetable, 0 fruit, 2 bread, 2½ meat, 1 fat*

3 Carb Choices

Turkey Chili

Nancy Silverman, New Haven, Connecticut

Prep time: 10 minutes; Cook time: 40 minutes

- **2 tablespoons vegetable oil**
- **1 large onion, chopped**
- **1 green bell pepper, chopped**
- **1 red bell pepper, chopped**
- **3 cloves garlic, minced**
- **1 teaspoon–1 tablespoon chili powder**
- **1 tablespoon ground cumin**
- **1 pound lean ground turkey breast**
- **2 cans (14½ ounces each) pinto beans, rinsed and drained**
- **1 can (28 ounces) diced tomatoes**
- **1 small bunch cilantro, stemmed and chopped**
- **Juice of ½ lime**
- **Salt**
- **Ground black pepper**

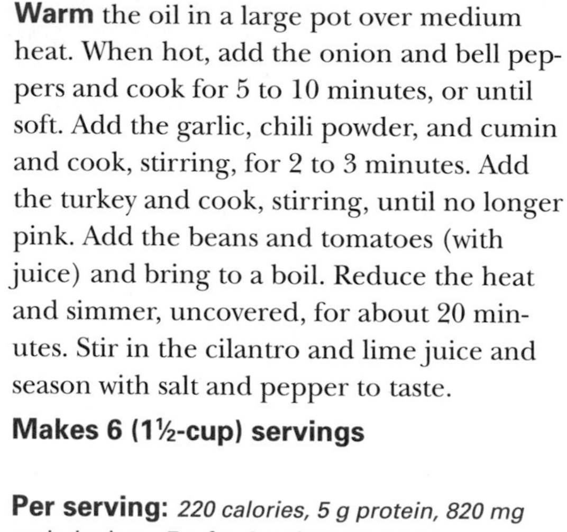

Warm the oil in a large pot over medium heat. When hot, add the onion and bell peppers and cook for 5 to 10 minutes, or until soft. Add the garlic, chili powder, and cumin and cook, stirring, for 2 to 3 minutes. Add the turkey and cook, stirring, until no longer pink. Add the beans and tomatoes (with juice) and bring to a boil. Reduce the heat and simmer, uncovered, for about 20 minutes. Stir in the cilantro and lime juice and season with salt and pepper to taste.

Makes 6 (1½-cup) servings

Per serving: *220 calories, 5 g protein, 820 mg carbohydrate, 7 g fat, 2 g cholesterol, 60 mg sodium, 21 g fiber*

Diet Exchanges: *0 milk, 1 vegetable, 0 fruit, 1½ bread, 3 meat, 0 fat*

2 Carb Choices

It Worked for Me!

Nancy and Richard Silverman

VITAL STATS

Weight lost: 30 pounds each

Time to goal: 6 years and holding

Quick tip: Join forces with a friend or spouse to make losing weight easier.

Richard and Nancy started their weight-loss efforts about 6 years ago and have worked at maintaining ever since. Despite a few ups and downs, holding on at a healthy weight remains a priority for both of them.

"My husband and I found that as we got older it became more difficult to just take off a few pounds whenever we felt the need—it's clear we are not 25 years old anymore, although we still think of ourselves as young. I also have a family history of high cholesterol and heart disease and so have always been very interested in staving off any health issues.

"In April 1998, Richard and I joined Weight Watchers at the university where he worked. By October of that year we had each lost just over 30 pounds. Richard had reached his goal weight and I wanted to lose a few more but seemed to have hit a plateau.

"Since then, he has managed to stay within 4 or 5 pounds of his goal, but I have gone up and down a bit. I joined another Weight Watchers group in 2002, this time at the humanitarian organization I work for. I stayed on the program for about 16 weeks and lost the 14 pounds that I had gained back from the previous loss.

"Losing weight through the Weight Watchers program taught us a lot about how much and what kinds of food we actually eat—I find it's like managing your money. Counting 'points' (similar to counting calories) gives you awareness of the quantities you eat. Learning to increase your fiber and eat more 'low-point-value' foods such as vegetables teaches you about food quality. And just like planning a big financial purchase, when you crave something high in calories, it's helpful to learn that you can think ahead and make smart choices that will prevent weight gain.

"We also learned to be realistic about our goals—health was the number-one priority for us rather than weight loss. I gauge my own success by a healthy BMI (body mass index) measurement and continue to strive toward that goal."

Steff's Salad Dressing

Steff Metzger, Harrisburg, Pennsylvania

"I couldn't find any decent-tasting low-calorie salad dressings, so I invented my own! Try it on your favorite greens. It'll keep in the refrigerator for up to a week."

Prep time: 5 minutes

- **1 teaspoon mustard powder**
- **¼ cup balsamic vinegar**
- **½ tablespoon Worcestershire sauce**
- **1 teaspoon lemon juice**
- **¼ teaspoon garlic salt**
- **2 tablespoons olive oil**
- **1 clove garlic, minced**

In a small bowl with a tight-fitting lid, combine the mustard powder, vinegar, Worcestershire sauce, lemon juice, garlic salt, oil, and garlic. Shake vigorously for 30 seconds.

Makes 4 servings

Per serving: *77 calories, 0 g protein, 3 g carbohydrate, 7 g fat, 0 mg cholesterol, 138 mg sodium, 0 g fiber*

Diet Exchanges: *0 milk, 0 vegetable, 0 fruit, 0 bread, 0 meat, 1½ fat*

0 Carb Choices

SHOPPING SAVVY

Rice Vinegar

A California-based company called O Olive Oil has some lovely mild rice vinegars infused with Asian flavors. Our favorites were Soy Rice Vinegar, great on steamed spinach and grilled shrimp, and Ginger Rice Vinegar, which added sparkle to broiled scallops and salmon. You can mix the vinegars with mild-flavored olive oil (or use them straight) to add Asian flair to a cucumber, scallion, and radish salad, or a mix of shredded Napa cabbage and carrots. Not bad on lettuce, either. Available at gourmet shops such as Williams-Sonoma or from ooliveoil.com.

Photo courtesy of O Olive Oil

113 Calories

Tuscan Summer Salad

A. Davis, Bloomington, Illinois

"I absolutely love *summertime vegetables, especially tomatoes and cucumbers! If I had my way, they would be the only items in the garden—besides watermelon and my husband's scallions. In order to enjoy these vegetables more, I decided to throw this concoction together instead of my traditional dinner salad."*

Prep time: 10 minutes; Chill time: 1 hour

4 tomatoes, sliced
2 cucumbers, peeled and sliced
½ medium red onion, sliced into rings
½ medium green bell pepper, sliced
2 pepperoncini, chopped
2 tablespoons sliced olives
1 tablespoon chopped fresh parsley
¼ teaspoon salt
½ teaspoon ground black pepper
½ bottle low-fat or fat-free Italian dressing

In a large bowl, combine the tomatoes, cucumbers, onion, bell pepper, pepperoncini peppers, olives, parsley, salt, and pepper. Coat with the dressing and mix. Chill for 1 hour before serving.

Makes 4 servings

Per serving: *113 calories, 3 g protein, 18 g carbohydrate, 4 g fat, 2 mg cholesterol, 413 mg sodium, 4 g fiber*

Diet Exchanges: *0 milk, 3 vegetable, 0 fruit, 0 bread, 0 meat, ½ fat*

1 Carb Choice

Kitchen Tip

Balsamic vinegar makes a great substitute for the Italian dressing called for here. And to make this salad a meal, add some cooked, rinsed, and cooled pasta.

Crunchy Fennel Salad

RoxAnn McMillian, Sunnyvale, California

Prep time: 12 minutes; Stand time: 30 minutes

- **1 small fennel bulb, sliced (see Kitchen Tip)**
- **1 cup sliced celery**
- **1 cup chopped fresh parsley**
- **¼ cup sliced red onion**
- **1 tablespoon olive oil**
- **2 tablespoons canola oil**
- **Juice of 1 lemon**
- **2 tablespoons rice vinegar**
- **Salt**
- **Ground black pepper**

In a large bowl, toss together the fennel, celery, parsley, and onion.

In a small bowl, whisk together the oils, lemon juice, and vinegar. Pour over the salad. Add salt and pepper to taste and let stand for 30 minutes before serving.

Makes 4 servings

Per serving: *130 calories, 2 g protein, 9 g carbohydrate, 11 g fat, 0 mg cholesterol, 66 mg sodium, 3 g fiber*

Diet Exchanges: *0 milk, 1½ vegetable, 0 fruit, 0 bread, 0 meat, 2 fat*

1 Carb Choice

Kitchen Tip

To slice fennel, chop off the stems and fronds just where the pale bulb turns darker green. Then cut the bulb as you would an onion, first slicing it in half lengthwise (through the bottom and stem ends). Trim and discard the bottom end. Place cut side down and slice crosswise into crescent-shaped pieces.

Spinach and Chickpea Salad

Melinda Huffman, Winchester, Tennessee

Prep time: 5 minutes

- 1 **bag (6 ounces) fresh baby spinach**
- 1 **can (14½ ounces) chickpeas, drained and rinsed**
- ¼ **cup (1 ounce) grated fat-free Parmesan cheese**
- ½ **cup alfalfa sprouts**
- 2 **tablespoons olive oil**
- ¼ **cup Champagne vinegar**

In a large bowl, toss together the spinach and chickpeas. Top with the cheese and sprouts. In a small bowl, whisk together the oil and vinegar and pour over the salad just before serving.

Makes 2 servings

Per serving: *370 calories, 14 g protein, 45 g carbohydrate, 15 g fat, 10 mg cholesterol, 620 mg sodium, 9 g fiber*

Diet Exchanges: *0 milk, ½ vegetable, 0 fruit, 2½ bread, 1 meat, 2½ fat*

3 Carb Choices

SHOPPING SAVVY

Salad Time

Bored with the same old salads? Fresh Express has a delicious and nutritious solution with their line of appetizing Everything but the Dressing salads. Look for spring greens witl crunchy walnuts and cranb baby spinach with crisp slivered almonds and cranberries, and romaine and radicchio with shredded Parmesan-Romano cheese and savory garlic croutons. All you add is the dressing. Sold in stores nationwide.

Photo courtesy of Fresh Express

Chilled Soba Noodle Salad with Ponzu Sauce

Rachel Rischpater, Boulder Creek, California

Ponzu sauce is a traditional Japanese dipping sauce.

Prep time: 15 minutes; Cook time: 15 minutes
Chill time: 1 hour

SAUCE

- **½ cup orange juice**
- **¼ cup mirin (see Kitchen Tip)**
- **2 tablespoons sugar**
- **2 tablespoons reduced-sodium soy sauce**
- **Dash of red-pepper flakes**
- **1 teaspoon cornstarch**
- **2 tablespoons water**

SALAD

- **4 ounces buckwheat soba noodles**
- **1 English cucumber**
- **1 teaspoon finely chopped fresh ginger**
- **¼ teaspoon red-pepper flakes**
- **1 scallion, sliced**
- **1 tablespoon sesame seeds**

To make the sauce: In a small saucepan, combine the juice, mirin, sugar, soy sauce, and red-pepper flakes. Bring to a boil over medium-high heat, stirring until the sugar dissolves.

Meanwhile, in a small bowl, combine the cornstarch and water, add it to the juice mixture, and boil until the mixture thickens. Set the ponzu sauce aside to cool.

To make the salad: Bring a large pot of water to a boil and cook the noodles for 5 to 6 minutes. Drain and rinse in cold water. Refrigerate for at least 1 hour before serving.

While the noodles are cooking, halve the cucumber lengthwise, seed it, and cut it into thin slices. Place in a medium bowl and toss with the cooled ponzu sauce, ginger, and red-pepper flakes. Cover and refrigerate for at least 1 hour before serving.

To assemble the salad, toss the noodles with the cucumber mixture and sprinkle with the scallions and sesame seeds.

Makes 2 servings

Per serving: *410 calories, 13 g protein, 80 g carbohydrate, 3 g fat, 0 mg cholesterol, 959 mg sodium, 3 g fiber*

Diet Exchanges: *0 milk, 1 vegetable, ½ fruit, 3½ bread, 0 meat, 2 fat*

5 Carb Choices

Kitchen Tip

Mirin is a sweet Japanese rice wine or sake (sometimes just called rice wine) that is used for cooking only, mainly in sauces and glazes. If a recipe calls for mirin or rice wine, you can substitute sherry or white wine with a little sugar.

Steak Salad

Judith Beerbaum, Pueblo West, Colorado

Prep time: 10 minutes; Marinate time: 30 minutes; Cook time: 10 minutes

2 tablespoons light soy sauce
1 clove garlic, minced
6 ounces beef tenderloin, thinly sliced
2 teaspoons toasted sesame oil
¼ cup reduced-fat beef broth
1 medium red bell pepper, sliced
½ onion, sliced into rings
½ pound mushrooms of your choice, sliced
½ head leaf lettuce, washed and torn into bite-size pieces

In a shallow glass dish, mix the soy sauce and garlic. Lay the beef slices in the sauce and turn several times to coat. Cover and refrigerate for at least 30 minutes, or overnight.

Warm the oil in a large skillet or wok over medium-high heat. When hot, add the beef and its marinade and cook, stirring constantly, for 5 minutes, or until no longer pink. Transfer the beef to a large bowl and set aside. Add the broth to the skillet and cook with the pepper, onion, and mushrooms for about 1 minute, or until the vegetables are bright and crisp-tender.

In a large bowl, toss the vegetables and beef with the lettuce and serve.

Makes 2 servings

Per serving: *303 calories, 31 g protein, 17 g carbohydrate, 13 g fat, 71 mg cholesterol, 687 mg sodium, 4 g fiber*

Diet Exchanges: *0 milk, 2½ vegetable, 0 fruit, 0 bread, 3½ meat, 2 fat*

1 Carb Choice

Corn and Bean Salad

231 Calories

Michele Barlow, Hubert, North Carolina

"This recipe is great for weight loss because it's high in fiber, which helps fill me up. It also helps me reach my daily serving of veggies, and it's got a little kick to it, too."

Prep time: 10 minutes; Chill time: 2 hours

- **1 can (14 ounces) corn kernels, drained**
- **1 can (15 ounces) kidney beans, drained and rinsed**
- **½ cup chopped red onion**
- **1 clove garlic, minced**
- **1 red bell pepper, chopped**
- **½ cup sliced black olives**
- **¼ cup finely chopped fresh cilantro**
- **¼ cup rice vinegar**
- **1 tablespoon canola oil**
- **2 teaspoons chili powder**
- **½ teaspoon salt**
- **¼ teaspoon cayenne pepper**

In a large bowl, combine the corn, beans, onion, garlic, bell pepper, olives, and cilantro.

In a small bowl, whisk together the vinegar, oil, chili powder, salt, and cayenne pepper. Pour over the salad and toss gently. Chill for at least 2 hours before serving.

Makes 4 servings

Per serving: *231 calories, 9 g protein, 39 g carbohydrate, 6 g fat, 0 mg cholesterol, 705 mg sodium, 9 g fiber*

Diet Exchanges: *0 milk, 1 vegetable, 0 fruit, 2½ bread, 0 meat, 1 fat*

2½ Carb Choices

Heart-Smart Taco Salad

Sheri Yarber, Troutdale, Virginia

Prep time: 10 minutes; Cook time: 20 minutes

- **1 pound lean ground turkey breast**
- **1 package (¾ ounce) taco seasoning**
- **⅓ cup water**
- **1 can (15 ounces) fat-free refried beans**
- **1 bag (16 ounces) baked tortilla chips**
- **2 cups diced fresh tomatoes**
- **2 cups shredded lettuce**
- **1 cup (4 ounces) shredded reduced-fat Cheddar cheese**
- **8 tablespoons fat-free sour cream**
- **1 cup taco or picante sauce**

Coat a large skillet with cooking spray and set over medium heat. Add the turkey and cook for 5 to 10 minutes, breaking up the meat with the back of a spoon, until no longer pink. Stir in the taco seasoning and water. Reduce the heat to low and simmer, covered, for 10 minutes.

Meanwhile, place the refried beans in a microwaveable bowl; cover with plastic wrap or waxed paper and microwave on high power for 1 minute. Stir and microwave again for 30 seconds longer if necessary to heat the beans evenly.

To assemble, place the tortilla chips on large serving plate and top with the beans, turkey, tomatoes, lettuce, and cheese. Garnish with sour cream and taco sauce and serve immediately.

Makes 8 servings

Per serving: *380 calories, 25 g protein, 61 g carbohydrate, 5 g fat, 30 mg cholesterol, 870 mg sodium, 7 g fiber*

Diet Exchanges: *0 milk, ½ vegetable, 0 fruit, 4 bread, 2 meat, 0 fat*

4 Carb Choices

It Worked for Me!

Janice Saeger

VITAL STATS

Weight lost: 35 pounds

Time to goal: 8 months and still losing

Quick tip: Wherever you are, always have a snack handy that fits into your chosen food plan.

Janice feels like she has always had a weight problem and believed that her heavier lower body must simply run in the family. Devising a customized meal plan that she could really live with has helped Janice shed her seemingly "hereditary" pounds.

"Since my early twenties, I've lost more than 30 pounds two different times. Both times I worked hard to keep it off, but wound up gaining back every lost pound—and then some. I used two different popular dieting approaches, but both ultimately involved weighing everything I ate, which I just didn't have the patience to do consistently. It was too tricky to plan and cook meals for myself as well as my husband and two daughters. Each time, weighing my portions became too much of a bother, and so the pounds came back.

"This time, I changed the way I ate in response to conversations that I had with my mother and her siblings, who are now in their seventies and suffer from a roster of health problems: diabetes, high blood pressure, heart disease—the whole works. I feel lucky that my blood sugar and cholesterol are at good levels, but I've already been diagnosed with high blood pressure and take medication for it. Listening to my family members' health problems really inspired me to make some changes.

"The jump start came when I borrowed a copy of *The South Beach Diet* from a friend. After reading through it, I thought that this meal plan could work for me, but there were some things about it that I just didn't like. I prefer to eat plenty of fiber and love fruit, so I was not about to cut carbs completely. Instead, I used the glycemic index food list to work out a modified form of the diet that includes high-fiber carbs, fruit, and soy. This absolutely worked like a charm for me. Without the refined sugar and white starches that I used to crave, I've lost 35 pounds and am still losing. I find all of the high-fiber cereals and grains I need at a great health food store near my home, and my husband still enjoys my cooking."

Southwestern Salad

Andrea Nelson, Brampton, Ontario, Canada

"This salad is simply great for a picnic!"

Prep time: 10 minutes; Cook time: 40 minutes
Chill time: 1 hour

- **1 cup brown rice**
- **1 can (14½ ounces) black beans, drained and rinsed**
- **2 cups frozen corn kernels, thawed**
- **1 medium red bell pepper, chopped**
- **1 small onion, chopped**
- **⅓ cup white wine vinegar**
- **¼ cup chopped fresh cilantro**
- **1 jalapeño chile pepper, finely chopped (wear plastic gloves when handling)**
- **1 teaspoon chili powder**

Cook the rice according to the package directions. Transfer to a large bowl and add the beans, corn, bell pepper, onion, vinegar, cilantro, jalapeño pepper, and chili powder. Toss gently and let stand, refrigerated or at room temperature, for 1 hour before serving.

Makes 4 servings

Per serving: *277 calories, 10 g protein, 57 g carbohydrate, 2 g fat, 0 mg cholesterol, 273 mg sodium, 10 g fiber*

Diet Exchanges: *0 milk, 1 vegetable, 0 fruit, 3 bread, ½ meat, 0 fat*

4 Carb Choices

Broccoli and Cheese Pasta Salad

Cyndi Iacona, Newnan, Georgia

Prep time: 5 minutes; Cook time: 13 minutes
Chill time: 1 hour

- **1 pound tricolor rotini**
- **1 bag (16 ounces) frozen broccoli florets**
- **1 cup (4 ounces) reduced-fat Cheddar cheese, cubed**
- **1 can (2 ounces) sliced black olives, drained**
- **½ cup light ranch dressing**
- **½ cup light zesty Italian dressing**
- **1 cup fresh cherry or grape tomatoes**
- **¼ cup Parmesan cheese (optional)**

Prepare the rotini according to the package directions. Add the frozen broccoli to the pasta water during the last 5 minutes of cooking. Drain the pasta and broccoli and rinse under cold running water to halt the cooking process. Transfer to a large bowl and add the Cheddar cheese, olives, and ranch and Italian dressings. Toss gently to combine and top with the tomatoes and Parmesan cheese. Chill for at least 1 hour or overnight.

Makes 8 servings

Per serving: *223 calories, 13 g protein, 24 g carbohydrate, 9 g fat, 10 mg cholesterol, 530 mg sodium, 3 g fiber*

Diet Exchanges: *0 milk, ½ vegetable, 0 fruit, 1½ bread, 1 meat, 1½ fat*

1½ Carb Choices

SALAD DRESSINGS

Rich, creamy, and loaded with calories is how we often view salad dressings—correctly, as they generally weigh in higher than the salad itself. If you're looking for a fresher, slimmer alternative, see the easy recipes that follow.

Vinaigrettes

Each of these quick and easy recipes has fewer than 20 calories and 2 grams of fat per tablespoon. Be sure to shake the dressing before using and store in the fridge.

Tomato Vinaigrette. Try this on a chef's salad, mixed sturdy greens, or over avocado chunks.

In a small jar, shake ½ cup low-sodium tomato-vegetable juice, ¼ cup white balsamic vinegar, 2 tablespoons extra-virgin olive oil, 2 tablespoons chopped fresh parsley or basil, 1 small crushed garlic clove, and ⅛ teaspoon ground black pepper.

Mustard Vinaigrette. Good on mixed baby greens, a pasta salad, or a seafood salad.

In a small jar, shake ⅓ cup lemon juice, 3 tablespoons water, 2 tablespoons extra-virgin olive oil, 1 tablespoon Dijon mustard, 2 tablespoons chopped fresh parsley, 1 tablespoon minced chives or scallion greens, 1 teaspoon sugar, and ⅛ teaspoon ground black pepper.

Creamy Dressings

Each recipe makes 1½ cups and should be stored in the fridge.

Low-Fat Ranch Dressing. Spoon over a romaine and roasted pepper salad, toss with a chopped salad, or serve as a dip for crisp veggies.

Whisk ¾ cup low-fat mayonnaise, ½ cup fat-free sour cream, 2 tablespoons cider vinegar, 1 tablespoon chopped fresh parsley, 1 teaspoon Dijon mustard, ½ teaspoon each sugar and celery seeds, and ¼ teaspoon each onion powder and ground black pepper. Stir in ½ cup shredded carrots.

Low-Fat Creamy Russian Dressing. Delish on an old-fashioned iceberg wedge, over sliced tomatoes and red onion, or as a sandwich spread instead of plain old mayo or mustard.

Whisk together ¾ cup low-fat mayonnaise, ½ cup fat-free sour cream, ⅓ cup bottled chili sauce, 2 tablespoons cider vinegar, 2 tablespoons chopped celery, 2 tablespoons pimiento, 2 teaspoons Worcestershire sauce, and ¼ teaspoon ground black pepper.

Lemony Tuna Salad

Deborah Sims, Statham, Georgia

"Lemon, pepper, and Parmesan cheese add lots of flavor to this low-cal tuna salad."

Prep time: 5 minutes

- **1 can (5½ ounces) water-packed tuna, drained well (see Kitchen Tip)**
- **1½ teaspoons lemon juice**
- **3 tablespoons light mayonnaise**
- **1 tablespoon grated Parmesan cheese**
- **¼ teaspoon ground black pepper**
- **¼ cup chopped onions**

Place the tuna in a medium bowl and add the lemon juice, mayonnaise, cheese, pepper, and onions. Mix thoroughly.

Makes 2 servings

Per serving: *186 calories, 21 g protein, 4 g carbohydrate, 9 g fat, 33 mg cholesterol, 490 mg sodium, 0 g fiber*

Diet Exchanges: *0 milk, ½ vegetable, 0 fruit, 0 bread, 3 meat, 1½ fat*

0 Carb Choices

Kitchen Tip

For the best taste, use a combination of solid white tuna and chunk light tuna.

282 Calories

Hawaiian Chicken Salad

Peggy Pinzon, San Diego, California

"The protein in this salad helps me feel satisfied, while its sweetness satisfies my cravings for cakes, cookies, and other sugary, fattening desserts."

Prep time: 5 minutes

- **6 leaves romaine lettuce**
- **8 ounces grilled chicken breast, cut into strips**
- **1½ cups canned or fresh pineapple chunks**
- **2 tablespoons flaked coconut**
- **2 tablespoons raisins**
- **2 tablespoons poppy seed salad dressing**

Arrange 3 lettuce leaves on each of two plates, then place the chicken slices on top.

In a small bowl, toss the pineapple chunks with the coconut, raisins, and dressing. Pour over the chicken and serve.

Makes 2 servings

Per serving: *282 calories, 27 g protein, 21 g carbohydrate, 9 g fat, 71 mg cholesterol, 190 mg sodium, 2 g fiber*

Diet Exchanges: *0 milk, 0 vegetable, 1 fruit, ½ bread, 3½ meat, 1½ fat*

1½ Carb Choices

SHOPPING SAVVY

Baby Veggies—Cute Cukes and Petite Peppers

Sweet . . . even picky eaters will enjoy these adorable veggies. Melissa's Baby Cucumbers are only 5" long, with a crunchy texture, tender skin, and no big, tough seeds. Sold in clamshell boxes, one cuke is just the right size for a salad. For a raw veggie platter, pair them with mild (never hot) Vine Sweet Mini Peppers, sold in assorted crayon-bright colors, nestled in clamshell boxes. Find both in the produce section of most supermarkets. For a store locator, go to melissas.com.

Photos courtesy of Melissa's

Barry's Summer Salad

Barry Andrew, Kindersley, Saskatchewan, Canada

Prep time: 5 minutes

SALAD

4 cups mixed salad greens

3 cups mixed fruit, such as grapes, sliced strawberries, sliced kiwi, and cubed mango, honeydew, cantaloupe, or watermelon

1 cup mandarin oranges, drained

DRESSING

½ cup orange juice

1 teaspoon orange zest

1 cup plain yogurt

½ teaspoon lemon juice

2 tablespoons mayonnaise

1 tablespoon sugar or honey

To make the salad: In a large bowl, toss the greens, fruit, and mandarin oranges.

To make the dressing: In a small bowl, combine the orange juice, orange zest, yogurt, lemon juice, mayonnaise, and sugar. Whisk together just before serving. Pour over the salad, toss gently, and serve immediately.

Makes 6 servings

Per serving: *133 calories, 3 g protein, 21 g carbohydrate, 5 g fat, 9 mg cholesterol, 61 mg sodium, 3 g fiber*

Diet Exchanges: *0 milk, 1 vegetable, 1 fruit, 0 bread, 0 meat, 1 fat*

1½ Carb Choices

Italian Baked Fries

Dorie Anderson, Powell River, British Columbia, Canada

"Everyone craves french fries—but you can enjoy these guilt-free because they're baked, not fried."

Prep time: 10 minutes; Cook time: 45 minutes

3 tablespoons olive oil
½ teaspoon Italian seasoning
½ teaspoon garlic powder
½ teaspoon salt-free spice blend
3 tablespoons Parmesan cheese
Cracked black pepper
2 large Yukon Gold potatoes, scrubbed and cut lengthwise into ½"-thick strips

Preheat the oven to 350°F. Cover a baking sheet with foil and coat with cooking spray.

In a large resealable plastic bag, combine the oil, Italian seasoning, garlic powder, spice blend, cheese, and black pepper to taste. Add the potatoes, seal the bag, and shake to coat. Spread on the prepared baking sheet.

Bake for 45 minutes, or until brown and crisp on both sides, turning halfway through cooking.

Makes 2 servings

Per serving: *255 calories, 5 g protein, 25 g carbohydrate, 15 g fat, 4 mg cholesterol, 103 mg sodium, 3 g fiber*

Diet Exchanges: *0 milk, 0 vegetable, 0 fruit, 1½ bread, ½ meat, 3 fat*

1½ Carb Choices

POTATOES

Even if you're counting carbs, don't rule out potatoes in a healthful diet. One medium potato weighs in at about 100 calories. Eaten with the skin, it provides about 3 grams of fiber, plus plenty of vitamin C and potassium. And few foods can compete with potatoes' versatility. However they're cooked, potatoes appeal to even the most vegetable-averse.

Basics

Potatoes should be firm and heavy for their size. Avoid those that are sprouting or that have a light green cast. If you find any green spots, cut them out.

For baking or mashing: Look for a high-starch potato such as a russet, Idaho, or Burbank. Low in moisture, they bake up fluffy and make light mashed potatoes.

For roasting: Look for a medium-starch, all-purpose potato with white or golden flesh, such as Ruby Gold, Yellow Finn, or Yukon Gold. Golden-fleshed potatoes also make excellent mashed potatoes with a buttery flavor.

For salads: Use a low-starch spud, such as a red-skinned potato or a white California potato. Sometimes called waxy potatoes, these hold their shape well.

To store: Keep potatoes in a cool (but not cold) dark place with good air circulation for no more than a few weeks. Don't store potatoes next to onions; they shorten each other's shelf life!

To bake: Choose potatoes that are roughly the same size so that they'll cook evenly. Scrub, then pierce several times with a fork to allow moisture to escape. Bake at 400°F directly on the oven rack for 50 to 60 minutes, or until the potatoes feel soft when gently squeezed. Avoid wrapping them in foil, which makes for dense, gummy results.

To bake several at once: Stand potatoes on end in a 6-cup or 12-cup muffin pan. This makes them easier to move in and out of the oven and provides air space around each for even cooking.

If you're looking for some new ways to cook potatoes, try the easy recipes that follow. Each makes 4 servings.

Buttermilk-Bacon Mashed Potatoes. Boil and mash 3 medium (5 to 6 ounces each) peeled, cut up russet or golden-fleshed potatoes. Stir in 6 tablespoons buttermilk, ¼ cup crumbled cooked turkey bacon, and 2 tablespoons chopped scallions. Season to taste with salt and pepper.

Barbecue Oven Fries. Cut 4 medium russet potatoes lengthwise into 5 or 6 slices. Stack the slices and cut them into ¼" strips. In a large bowl, mix 2½ tablespoons ketchup, 4 teaspoons olive oil, 2 teaspoons Worcestershire sauce, 2 teaspoons cider vinegar, and ⅛ teaspoon salt. Add the potatoes and toss. Coat a baking sheet with cooking spray; spread the potatoes evenly on the sheet and bake at 425°F for 20 minutes. Turn and bake for about 15 minutes longer, or until tender and golden.

Skinny Scalloped Potatoes

Jennifer Magrey, Oneco, Connecticut

"I believe we all need comfort food, and scalloped potatoes are one of mine. So I played around in the kitchen and created this dish, which balances my dietary needs and cravings without sacrificing flavor."

Prep time: 10 minutes; Cook time: 45 minutes

- **4 russet potatoes, scrubbed and very thinly sliced**
- **1 medium sweet onion, chopped**
- **2 cloves garlic, minced**
- **2 tablespoons all-purpose flour**
- **2 tablespoons trans-free margarine or butter**
- **1½ cups 2% milk**
- **½ teaspoon mustard powder**
- **¼ cup (1 ounce) grated Parmesan cheese**
- **Salt**
- **Ground black pepper**
- **Chives (optional)**

Preheat the oven to 350°F. Coat a 1½-quart baking dish with cooking spray.

Arrange the potatoes and onion and garlic in the prepared baking dish in alternating layers. Sprinkle the flour on top and toss lightly. Dot with the margarine or butter.

In a small saucepan over low heat, whisk together the milk and mustard powder and heat until warm. Remove from the heat, stir in the cheese, and pour over the potatoes. Season with salt and pepper to taste.

Cover and bake for 30 minutes. Uncover and bake for 15 minutes longer, or until lightly browned and bubbling. Garnish with chives, if using.

Makes 4 servings

Per serving: *263 calories, 9 g protein, 36 g carbohydrate, 9 g fat, 18 mg cholesterol, 214 mg sodium, 4 g fiber*

Diet Exchanges: *½ milk, ½ vegetable, 0 fruit, 1½ bread, ½ meat, 1½ fat*

2½ Carb Choices

Kitchen Tip

Adding chopped leftover broccoli and/or low-fat ham can transform this side dish into a meal.

Simply Sensational Double-Stuffed Potatoes

Helen Velichko, Kansas City, Missouri

Prep time: 15 minutes; Cook time: 25 minutes

- **2 large baking potatoes, scrubbed and pierced with a fork**
- **¼–½ cup 1% milk**
- **½ cup (2 ounces) grated Cheddar cheese**
- **2 tablespoons butter, at room temperature**
- **2 tablespoons bacon bits**
- **¼ teaspoon onion salt**

Preheat the oven to 375°F. Spray a baking sheet with cooking spray and set aside. Place the potatoes on a large microwaveable plate and cover with a damp paper towel. Microwave on high power for 5 minutes. Carefully turn the potatoes and microwave for 5 minutes longer, or until a fork can be inserted easily. Let stand for 5 minutes.

When the potatoes are cool enough to handle, halve them lengthwise. With a spoon, scoop out most of the insides, leaving enough potato flesh to keep the skins intact. Place the skins on the prepared baking sheet and the scooped potato into a large bowl. Add the milk, cheese, butter, bacon bits, and salt to the scooped potato and stir well to combine, then spoon equal amounts back into the skins.

Bake for 10 minutes, or until the potatoes are heated through and the cheese is melted.

Makes 4 servings

Per serving: *183 calories, 7 g protein, 14 g carbohydrate, 11 g fat, 34 mg cholesterol, 384 mg sodium, 2 g fiber*

Diet Exchanges: *0 milk, 0 vegetable, 0 fruit, 1 bread, 1 meat, 2 fat*

1 Carb Choice

Tomato Slaw

Terry Mehigan, Camden, Michigan

"This slaw is delicious as a side dish or a salsa. Use it on baked potatoes or tacos, or serve it at any barbecue."

Prep time: 8 minutes; Marinate time: overnight

- **3 tomatoes, chopped**
- **2 green bell peppers, chopped**
- **1 onion, chopped**
- **1 tablespoon white or cider vinegar**
- **2 teaspoons sugar**
- **1 teaspoon salt**

In a large bowl, combine the tomatoes, peppers, and onion. Add the vinegar, sugar, and salt and toss gently. Cover and refrigerate overnight to blend the flavors.

Makes 4 servings

Per serving: *57 calories, 2 g protein, 13 g carbohydrate, 0 g fat, 0 mg cholesterol, 591 mg sodium, 3 g fiber*

Diet Exchanges: *0 milk, 2 vegetable, 0 fruit, 0 bread, 0 meat, 0 fat*

1 Carb Choice

SECRETS OF WEIGHT-LOSS WINNERS

• Eating out? Halve it, and bag the rest. A typical restaurant entrée has 1,000 to 2,000 calories, not even counting the bread, appetizer, beverage, and dessert.

—Prevention.com

• No one said fries always have to come with your meal. Just because you're buying fast food doesn't mean you have to buy big food. Avoid entire meal combos and pair individual items, like a burger with a salad.

—Prevention.com

• Try, try again, but do not lose heart! Temporary failures should not hamper your entire program.

—Sri Tulasi Kollipara, Andhra Pradesh, India

Green Beans and Carrots Parmesan

Nanette Marsh, Ocala, Florida

"These low-calorie, good-for-you vegetables are easy and quick to prepare."

Prep time: 10 minutes; Cook time: 10 minutes

- **4 carrots, cut into 3" matchsticks**
- **1 package (8–10 ounces) frozen whole green beans**
- **1 tablespoon canola oil**
- **2 tablespoons grated Parmesan cheese**

Place a steamer basket in a large pot with 2" of water. Bring to a boil over high heat. Plate the carrots and green beans in the basket and steam for about 10 minutes, or until tender. Drain and toss with the oil. Place in a serving dish and sprinkle with the cheese.

Makes 4 servings

Per serving: *92 calories, 3 g protein, 11 g carbohydrate, 4 g fat, 2 mg cholesterol, 88 mg sodium, 3 g fiber*

Diet Exchanges: *0 milk, 2 vegetable, 0 fruit, 0 bread, 0 meat, 1 fat*

1 Carb Choice

Leeks with Red Peppers

Eve R. Mead, Jefferson, Wisconsin

"Leeks have a lot of flavor, they're very high in potassium, and they're very filling."

Prep time: 10 minutes; Cook time: 20 minutes

- **2 tablespoons olive oil**
- **1 medium onion, sliced**
- **1 red bell pepper, sliced**
- **4 leeks, white parts only, washed and sliced crosswise into thin strips (see Kitchen Tip)**
- **½ cup chicken broth**
- **Salt**
- **Ground black pepper**

Warm the oil in a large skillet over medium-high heat. When hot, add the onion and pepper and cook for 5 to 7 minutes, or until brown. Move to one side of the pan. Add the leeks in a single layer and cook for about 6 minutes. Add the broth and season with salt and pepper to taste. Cook for about 8 to 10 minutes, or until the leeks are soft. Transfer the vegetables to a serving dish and cook the liquid in the pan for a few minutes longer, or until it thickens slightly. Pour over the leeks and serve.

Makes 4 servings

Per serving: *126 calories, 2 g protein, 15 g carbohydrate, 7 g fat, 0 mg cholesterol, 140 mg sodium, 2 g fiber*

Diet Exchanges: *0 milk, 3 vegetable, 0 fruit, 0 bread, 0 meat, 1½ fat*

1 Carb Choice

Kitchen Tip

To choose the best leeks, look for those with bright, crisp leaves, and buy the smallest ones in the market, which tend to be sweetest. Leeks are often rather gritty. To clean them, halve them lengthwise down to the root ends, fan them out, and rinse well under cold running water.

Sautéed Summer Squash

Cheryl Joyce, Fieldale, Virginia

Prep time: 10 minutes; Cook time: 12 minutes

1 teaspoon olive oil
2 medium yellow squash, sliced
2 medium zucchini, sliced
1 medium onion, sliced into rings
Salt
Ground black pepper
¼– ½ cup (1–2 ounces) shredded part-skim mozzarella cheese

Warm the oil in a large skillet over medium-high heat. When hot, add the yellow squash, zucchini, and onions. Cover the skillet, reduce the heat to medium, and cook for 5 to 7 minutes, tossing once or twice. Uncover and increase the heat to medium-high once again. Cook the squash for 2 to 3 minutes longer, or until golden. Season with salt and pepper to taste, top with the cheese, and allow it to melt from the heat of the vegetables before serving.

Makes 4 servings

Per serving: *70 calories, 5 g protein, 10 g carbohydrate, 2½ g fat, 5 mg cholesterol, 190 mg sodium, 3 g fiber*

Diet Exchanges: *0 milk, ½ vegetable, 0 fruit, ½ bread, 0 meat, 0 fat*

1 Carb Choice

SECRETS OF WEIGHT-LOSS WINNERS

• Try using two water bottles as weights when you walk. That way you'll be weight training while you walk, plus you'll have water at hand when you're thirsty.

—Cynthia Watson, New Orleans, Louisiana

• Eat the low-cal items on your plate first, then graduate. Start with salads, veggies, and broth soups, and eat meats and starches last. By the time you get to the high-calorie choices, you'll be content with smaller portions.

—Prevention.com

• I always take my own salad dressing when I go out to eat to help me avoid the hidden calories in many salad dressings.

—Robert Kicinski, Valparaiso, Indiana

Spinach and Mushrooms with Turkey Bacon

90 Calories

Ranee Solomon, Akron, Ohio

Prep time: 5 minutes; Cook time: 12 minutes

3 strips turkey bacon
1 tablespoon olive oil
1 clove garlic, minced
½ pound mushrooms, sliced
1 bag (10 ounces) fresh spinach, trimmed and cleaned
Salt
Ground black pepper

In a large skillet over medium-high heat, cook the turkey bacon for about 5 minutes. Transfer to a plate and set aside.

Add the oil to the skillet and cook the garlic and mushrooms for 4 to 5 minutes. Add the spinach, reduce the heat to medium, and cook, covered, for 3 to 5 minutes longer, or until the spinach is wilted. Dice the cooled bacon and add it to the spinach mixture during the last minute of cooking time. Season with salt and pepper to taste and serve immediately.

Makes 4 servings

Per serving: *90 calories, 5 g protein, 0 g carbohydrate, 6 g fat, 10 mg cholesterol, 330 mg sodium, 2 g fiber*

Diet Exchanges: *0 milk, 1 vegetable, 0 fruit, 0 bread, ½ meat, 1 fat*

0 Carb Choice

SANDWICHES AND SNACKS

Sandwiches

Snacks

Mediterranean Tuna Sandwiches

Barbara Mason, Brea, California

"This sandwich is wonderful and easy to make! Plus, tuna is very low in the bad kind of fat and high in the healthy kind."

Prep time: 5 minutes; Chill time: 2 hours

1 can (6 ounces) water-packed tuna, drained
1 tablespoon olive oil
1 tablespoon red wine vinegar
1 clove garlic, minced
3 tablespoons chopped red onion
½ teaspoon chopped parsley
2 hard rolls, split
2 leaves lettuce
½ tomato, sliced

In a medium bowl, combine the tuna, oil, vinegar, garlic, onion, and parsley until thoroughly mixed. Cover and refrigerate for 2 hours to allow the flavors to blend.

Spread the tuna onto the bottom halves of the hard rolls. Top with lettuce and sliced tomato, close the sandwiches with the top halves of the rolls, and serve.

Makes 2 servings

Per serving: *240 calories, 19 g protein, 19 g carbohydrate, 10 g fat, 25 mg cholesterol, 400 mg sodium, 1 g fiber*

Diet Exchanges: *0 milk, ½ vegetable, 0 fruit, 1 bread, 2½ meat, 1½ fat*

1 Carb Choice

Easy Pita Pockets

Sandy Umber, Springdale, Arizona

"This tasty sandwich helps me eat vegetables. It's fast, easy, and fresh—much better than a greasy burger."

Prep time: 10 minutes

- **2 whole wheat pitas, halved**
- **½ pound turkey breast, thinly sliced**
- **1 green bell pepper, sliced**
- **1 tomato, thinly sliced**
- **¼ cup (1 ounce) shredded reduced-fat Cheddar or Monterey Jack cheese**
- **¼ cup light ranch salad dressing**

In each pita half, place one-quarter of the turkey, a few slices of pepper and tomato, and 1 tablespoon of cheese. Top with 1 tablespoon of dressing.

Makes 4 servings

Per serving: *210 calories, 15 g protein, 25 g carbohydrate, 6 g fat, 25 mg cholesterol, 860 mg sodium, 3 g fiber*

Diet Exchanges: *0 milk, ½ vegetable, 0 fruit, 1 bread, 1½ meat, 1 fat*

2 Carb Choices

SECRETS OF WEIGHT-LOSS WINNERS

• Spice up your sandwiches. I never was a fan of low-fat mayo, but I love dips. Use a package of your favorite dip mix combined with fat-free sour cream in place of mayonnaise. This will add zest to your sandwiches, leaving you feeling a lot more satisfied.

—Dinah Halterman, Harmony, North Carolina

• Use small plates when eating, like a salad plate or even a coffee cup saucer. This gives you the illusion of having a "full plate," but keeps you from eating as much. It's amazing how, psychologically, when you finish all the food on your plate, you feel full.

—Carole Bass, Wesson, Mississippi

• Never eat in front of the TV—when your eating becomes mindless, bingeing occurs.

—Prevention.com

220 Calories

Teriyaki Beef Wraps

Shawna Cross, Thunder Bay, Ontario, Canada

"I was looking for something easy and tasty to make for myself, so I decided to experiment with different and more satisfying ways to eat meat. The texture of the tortilla is fantastic. The first time I tried this, I was amazed at how filling eating just half of the wrap was."

Prep time: 7 minutes; Cook time: 8 minutes

- **2 tablespoons reduced-sodium soy sauce**
- **1 tablespoon finely chopped fresh ginger**
- **3 cloves garlic, crushed**
- **1 jalapeño chile pepper, finely chopped (wear plastic gloves when handling)**
- **¼ pound lean round steak, trimmed of excess fat and cut into strips**
- **¼ teaspoon garlic powder**
- **¼ cup 1% cottage cheese or reduced-fat sour cream**
- **1 flour tortilla (10" diameter)**
- **1 tablespoon sesame seeds**
- **2 scallions, sliced**
- **Salt**
- **Ground black pepper**

In a large resealable plastic bag, combine the soy sauce, ginger, garlic, and jalapeño pepper, then add the steak. Seal the bag and shake well. Place in the refrigerator for 8 hours or overnight, turning several times.

In a small bowl, combine the garlic powder and cottage cheese. Stir well and set aside.

Remove the meat from the bag and brush off the seasonings. Discard the marinade. In a large nonstick skillet over medium-high heat, cook the meat until just pink inside. Transfer to a plate and set aside.

In the same skillet, heat the tortilla for about 10 seconds per side (the tortilla will start to bubble). Place the tortilla on a large dinner plate and set aside.

In the same skillet, heat the sesame seeds, stirring quickly, for 10 to 20 seconds or until toasted and fragrant. Remove from the skillet and set aside. Lay the tortilla on a clean work surface. Spread the cottage cheese mixture onto the middle, top with the steak strips and scallions, season with salt and pepper to taste, and sprinkle with the toasted sesame seeds. Roll up the wrap, folding the ends toward the center as you go, slice diagonally in half, and serve.

Makes 2 servings

Per serving: *220 calories, 20 g protein, 23 g carbohydrate, 7 g fat, 25 mg cholesterol, 910 mg sodium, 2 g fiber*

Diet Exchanges: *0 milk, 0 vegetable, 0 fruit, 1½ bread, 2 meat, 1 fat*

1½ Carb Choices

Pizza Wraps

Deanna Goodin, Pekin, Illinois

These flavorful sandwiches are a tasty and filling twist on Italian-style subs.

Prep time: 5 minutes; Cook time: 8 minutes

2 teaspoons olive oil
½ medium onion, cut into rings
1 cup white mushrooms, sliced
2 ounces low-fat turkey pepperoni slices
½ cup pizza sauce
1 whole wheat or white flour tortilla (10" diameter)
¼ cup (1 ounce) shredded part-skim mozzarella
2 tablespoons grated Parmesan cheese

Warm the oil in a medium skillet over medium heat. When hot, add the onion and mushrooms and cook for 3 to 5 minutes, or until tender and slightly golden. Add the turkey pepperoni and cook for 1 to 2 minutes, or until warm.

Meanwhile, place the sauce in a microwaveable bowl and microwave on high power, stirring occasionally, for about 1 minute, or until warm.

Spread the sauce evenly over the tortilla. Top with the onion mixture, the mozzarella, and the Parmesan. Roll up the wrap, folding the ends toward the center as you go, slice diagonally in half, and serve.

Makes 2 servings

Per serving: *222 calories, 19 g protein, 21 g carbohydrate, 8 g fat, 41 mg cholesterol, 988 mg sodium, 3 g fiber*

Diet Exchanges: *0 milk, 2 vegetable, 0 fruit, ½ bread, 2 meat, 1 fat*

1½ Carb Choices

It Worked for Me!

James Hoffmann

VITAL STATS

Weight lost: 30 pounds

Time to goal: 4 months

Quick tip: Avoid eating after dinner.

James was always a gangly, skinny kid. In his twenties, though, his weight started to catch up with his height. After college, he took on a full-time career in a top financial office, and the hours seated at a desk and in meetings put on the pounds. By the time he got married, his weight was starting to become a problem.

"After my son, Ryan, was born, I realized I didn't want to be a chubby daddy. I had always hoped that I could be a role model for my son, and I definitely did not want to have any health problems that would prevent me from participating fully in his life. My wife, Jennifer, had gone on Weight Watchers after giving birth and had great success. She got her weight down to less than it was before she became pregnant, and she looked terrific.

"I knew then that I had no excuse not to lose my own extra pounds. Weight Watchers just didn't seem like the right path for me, though. I have a hard time cutting out fat and don't enjoy many of the foods that you're allowed to eat the most of on that particular plan.

"In winter of 2003 I decided it was time to try the low-carb approach that seemed to be working for so many guys. When I did, I found it was actually very easy for me to follow the basic eating style. For example, I like meat and cheese, so incorporating more of those foods into my diet was no problem. It was harder for me to change bad habits, like drinking glass after glass of full-calorie soda and eating extra meals late in the day. I used to hit the kitchen every night at around 10:00—I probably ate close to 1,000 calories and called it a 'snack.' Switching to diet soda made a big difference in the number of calories I consume. And I bought a treadmill so I can take a walk rather than making a midnight snack run.

"I'm happy to say that, in addition to my 3-year-old son, I now have a new daughter named Rebecca. Losing weight has made me feel better about my health and my ability to set a better example for both my children as they grow up."

Meatball Souvlaki

Lori Clark, Goose Bay, Newfoundland and Labrador, Canada

Prep time: 25 minutes; Cook time: 15 minutes

MEATBALLS

- 1 egg
- ¼ cup dried bread crumbs
- 1 teaspoon Dijon mustard
- ½ teaspoon dried oregano
- ¼ teaspoon salt
- ¼ teaspoon ground black pepper
- 1 pound lean ground beef

SANDWICHES

- 1 cup plain low-fat yogurt
- ½ cup grated English cucumber
- 1 clove garlic, minced
- 2 tablespoons dried mint
- Salt
- Ground black pepper
- 6 pitas, preferably whole wheat (see Kitchen Tip)
- 2 cups shredded lettuce
- 2 small tomatoes, chopped
- 6 thin slices red onion

Preheat the oven to 400°F. Line a baking sheet with foil.

To make the meatballs: In a large bowl, whisk together the egg, bread crumbs, mustard, oregano, salt, and pepper. Mix in the ground beef. Shape the mixture into 24 meatballs and place them on the baking sheet. Bake for 15 minutes, or until the meatballs are no longer pink inside.

To assemble the sandwiches: In a small bowl, combine the yogurt, cucumber, garlic, mint, and salt and pepper to taste. Lay the pitas on a clean work surface and spread ¼ cup of the yogurt mixture over each. Sprinkle equal portions of lettuce, tomatoes, and onion over each pita. Top with 4 meatballs each. Fold the pitas in half and serve.

Makes 6 servings

Per serving: *418 calories, 25 g protein, 45 g carbohydrate, 15 g fat, 91 mg cholesterol, 729 mg sodium, 6 g fiber*

Diet Exchanges: *0 milk, ½ vegetable, 0 fruit, 2½ bread, 2½ meat, 1½ fat*

3 Carb Choices

Kitchen Tip

Greek pitas do not have pockets, so ingredients can be placed on top and the pita folded over. If you prefer, use regular pitas instead and fill the pockets.

388 Calories

Turkey-Spinach Medley on Pitas

Denise Ossello, Manhattan Beach, California

"This dish is low in fat and makes a satisfying lunch or dinner. It's also easy and quick to prepare for work. Just reheat in the microwave."

Prep time: 10 minutes; Cook time: 25 minutes

- **1–2 teaspoons olive oil**
- **1–2 cloves garlic, minced**
- **½ medium onion, chopped**
- **1 pound lean ground turkey breast**
- **1 package (10 ounces) frozen chopped spinach, thawed and squeezed dry**
- **Ground black pepper**
- **4 whole wheat pitas, halved**
- **1 medium tomato, chopped**

Warm the oil in a large skillet over medium-high heat. When hot, add the garlic and onion and cook for about 5 minutes, or until tender. Add the turkey and cook, breaking up the turkey with the back of a spoon as you stir, for 15 minutes, or until no longer pink. Add the spinach and cook for 5 to 7 minutes longer.

Season with pepper to taste and spoon equal portions into the pitas. Top with tomatoes and serve.

Makes 4 servings

Per serving: *388 calories, 29 g protein, 41 g carbohydrate, 13 g fat, 90 mg cholesterol, 509 mg sodium, 7 g fiber*

Diet Exchanges: *0 milk, 2 vegetable, 0 fruit, 2 bread, 2½ meat, 1 fat*

3 Carb Choices

Turkey-Mushroom Burgers

Helen Velichko, Kansas City, Missouri

Prep time: 5 minutes; Cook time: 16 minutes

- **1 pound lean ground turkey breast**
- **2 cups sliced mushrooms**
- **¼ cup chopped fresh parsley**
- **1½ tablespoons Worcestershire sauce**
- **½ teaspoon onion salt**
- **1 tablespoon vegetable oil**
- **4 hamburger buns, split**

In a large bowl, combine the turkey, 1 cup of the mushrooms, the parsley, Worcestershire sauce, and onion salt. With clean hands, mix the ingredients until thoroughly combined and shape into equal-size patties. Set aside.

Warm the oil in a large skillet over medium heat. When hot, add the remaining 1 cup of mushrooms and cook, stirring, for 2 minutes, or until brown. Transfer the mushrooms to a plate and cover to keep warm. Place the patties in the skillet over medium heat and cook, turning occasionally, for 12 to 14 minutes, or until a thermometer inserted in the center registers 165°F and the meat is no longer pink.

Set the patties on the buns, top with the sautéed mushrooms, and serve.

Makes 4 servings

Per serving: *300 calories, 31 g protein, 24 g carbohydrate, 9 g fat, 80 mg cholesterol, 550 mg sodium, 4 g fiber*

Diet Exchanges: *0 milk, 0 vegetable, 0 fruit, 1½ bread, 4 meat, 1 fat*

1½ Carb Choices

Kitchen Tip

Wet your hands with cold water to keep meat from sticking to them.

Pineapple Salsa

Michelle Tucker, Austin, Texas

"This is a very healthy salsa that kicks up bland food."

Prep time: 5 minutes

- **1 jalapeño chile pepper, chopped (wear plastic gloves when handling)**
- **1 cup chopped pineapple**
- **2 tablespoons chopped fresh cilantro**
- **1 red onion, chopped**
- **Juice of 1 lime**

In a small bowl, combine the jalapeño pepper, pineapple, cilantro, and onion, then add the lime juice. Let stand for 30 minutes to allow the flavors to blend.

Makes 8 servings

Per serving: *16 calories, 0 g protein, 4 g carbohydrate, 0 g fat, 0 mg cholesterol, 1 mg sodium, 1 g fiber*

Diet Exchanges: *0 milk, 0 vegetable, ½ fruit, 0 bread, 0 meat, 0 fat*

0 Carb Choices

SALSA!

It's not just a dance style, it's a sassy sauce that's overtaken ketchup as our number one condiment. Salsa makes a no-fuss low-cal topping for grilled chicken, turkey, pork, fish, fried or scrambled eggs, or baked potatoes. For a super-fast side dish, stir salsa into cooked brown rice, or mix and heat with cooked corn kernels and rinsed and drained canned black beans.

Personalize jarred salsa by stirring in chopped sweet white onion, chopped fresh cilantro, chopped fresh mint, chopped avocado, chopped red bell pepper, or fresh lemon, lime, or orange juice.

Add heat to a tame jarred salsa by stirring in canned mild green chiles, sliced pickled jalapeño chiles, hot-pepper sauce, chopped fresh serrano chiles, canned chipotle chiles, chili powder, cayenne, or red-pepper flakes. Or, in tomato season, why not make your own?

Fresh Tomato Salsa. In a bowl, combine 4 large seeded and chopped summer tomatoes, ⅔ cup finely chopped sweet onion (or 4 finely chopped scallions), ⅓ cup finely chopped fresh cilantro, 1–2 seeded and finely chopped fresh jalapeño or serrano chile peppers (leave in some seeds in for more heat), 2 teaspoons lime juice, and 1 teaspoon salt. Toss, let sit for 1 hour at room temperature, and serve. Makes about 13 (¼-cup) servings.

Avocado Salsa

D. Summers, Richardson, Texas

"This salsa is great on a salad, with chips, or on top of any kind of grilled meat. It really helps perk up a low-carb diet with lots of flavor."

Prep time: 5 minutes

1 ripe avocado, coarsely chopped
1 tablespoon finely chopped red onion
1 tablespoon finely chopped jalapeño chile pepper (wear plastic gloves when handling)
1 tablespoon lime juice
1 tablespoon coarsely chopped fresh cilantro
1 tablespoon seeded and chopped ripe tomato
Salt
Ground black pepper

In a large bowl, add the avocado, onion, jalapeño pepper, lime juice, cilantro, and tomato. Stir carefully, trying not to break up the avocado. Season with salt and pepper to taste.

Makes 4 servings

Per serving: *80 calories, 1 g protein, 5 g carbohydrate, 7 g fat, 0 mg cholesterol, 40 mg sodium, 3 g fiber*

Diet Exchanges: *0 milk, 0 vegetable, ½ fruit, 0 bread, 0 meat, 1½ fat*

0 Carb Choices

THE HEALTHY AVOCADO

Despite their high fat content, avocados are healthy fruits, containing oleic acid, which helps lower cholesterol. Most of the fat in the avocado is the health-friendly monounsaturated kind, and avocados are cholesterol-free. Just one packs more cancer-fighting fiber than a typical bran muffin and more potassium than two bananas.

Avocados originated in Mexico, where the average person enjoys 22 pounds a year, much of it mashed into guacamole.

Hass avocados—the ones with dark, pebble-textured skin, buttery flavor, and ultra-rich, creamy flesh—are grown year-round in Mexico and shipped to the United States. They're also grown in California.

Florida Fuerte avocados have smooth green skin and firmer flesh. Fuerte avocados contain about half the fat of Hass avocados but lack their luscious flavor.

Avocados are ready to use when they yield to gentle pressure; they shouldn't be mushy. Firm avocados will ripen in a day or two on the kitchen counter; once ripe, refrigerate and enjoy as soon as possible. Here are seven ways to use an avocado.

1. For quick guacamole, mash an avocado with 2 to 3 tablespoons salsa and lime juice.
2. Add avocado slices and shredded chicken to hot chicken broth; sprinkle with chopped cilantro and a squeeze of lime juice.
3. Alternate avocado slices, ripe tomato, and sweet onion slices. Drizzle with olive oil and lemon or lime juice, then sprinkle with ground cumin.
4. Strew avocado chunks and halved cherry tomatoes over scrambled eggs.
5. Dump the yolks and mayo from your next batch of deviled eggs and fill the whites with mashed avocado seasoned with lemon juice and hot-pepper sauce.
6. Rebuild the BLT: Spread light mayo on a slice of whole grain toast, then spread salsa on another. Fill the sandwich with arugula, crisp turkey bacon, and avocado and tomato slices.
7. For brunch, make a platter of smoked salmon, sliced cucumbers, sweet onion, and thin-sliced pumpernickel bread. Instead of cream cheese, provide mashed avocado to spread on the bread.

Mexican Dip

Ann Trivelpiece, Hampton, Virginia

"This dip is low in fat but still tasty for snacking—which we all do so much! We love it served with baked corn chips."

Prep time: 5 minutes; Cook time: 6 minutes

- **8 ounces fat-free cream cheese, at room temperature**
- **1 small onion, finely chopped**
- **1 can (16 ounces) vegetarian chili, with beans**
- **1 can (2 ounces) chopped mild green chiles, drained**
- **½ cup (2 ounces) shredded reduced-fat Monterey Jack cheese**

In a 9" glass pie pan, layer the cream cheese, onion, chili, chopped chiles, and cheese. Microwave on high power for 6 minutes or until heated through.

Makes 8 servings

Per serving: *120 calories, 10 g protein, 12 g carbohydrate, 3½ g fat, 10 mg cholesterol, 460 mg sodium, 2 g fiber*

Diet Exchanges: *0 milk, 0 vegetable, 0 fruit, ½ bread, 1 meat, ½ fat*

1 Carb Choice

Incredible Crab Canapés

Corinne Laboon, Pittsburgh, Pennsylvania

"These tasty low-cal canapés make a great snack. Serve them on your favorite reduced-fat crackers."

Prep time: 10 minutes; Chill time: 2 hours

2 cans (5½ ounces each) flaked crabmeat, drained
2 tablespoons light mayonnaise
8 ounces fat-free cream cheese, at room temperature
¼ teaspoon garlic powder
¼ teaspoon salt
Fresh parsley, chopped

In a medium bowl, combine the crabmeat, mayonnaise, cream cheese, garlic powder, and salt. Stir gently until thoroughly mixed. Line a small plate with a piece of plastic wrap and place the crab mixture in the center. Gently shape the mixture into a log, roll in the plastic wrap, and twist the ends to secure. Refrigerate for 2 hours.

Unwrap the cheese log, roll it in the parsley, and serve.

Makes 8 servings

Per serving: *67 calories, 10 g protein, 2 g carbohydrate, 2 g fat, 24 mg cholesterol, 360 mg sodium, 0 g fiber*

Diet Exchanges: *0 milk, 0 vegetable, 0 fruit, 0 bread, 1½ meat, ½ fat*

0 Carb Choices

Eggplant Bruschetta

Elaine Sweet, Dallas, Texas

"I cut the fat in this family favorite to make it healthy. It's a fun way to get children to try eggplant!"

Prep time: 10 minutes; Cook time: 40 minutes
Bake time: 8 minutes; Chill time: 2 hours

EGGPLANT

1 eggplant (about 1½ pounds)
1 tablespoon extra-virgin olive oil
1 small yellow onion, finely chopped
2 tablespoons tomato paste
1 tablespoon white wine vinegar
1 tablespoon water
2 tablespoons lemon juice
1 teaspoon salt
½ teaspoon red-pepper flakes
½ teaspoon garam masala (see Kitchen Tip)

BRUSCHETTA

3 pitas, cut into wedges
1½ teaspoons garlic powder

To make the eggplant: In a large pot of boiling water, cook the eggplant whole for 30 minutes. Carefully remove from the boiling water and set aside. When the eggplant has cooled, remove the stem and peel, then coarsely chop. Set aside.

Warm the oil in a large skillet over medium heat. When hot, cook the onion for 6 minutes. Add the tomato paste, vinegar, and water and cook, stirring constantly, until the liquids have evaporated. Add the eggplant, lemon juice, salt, red-pepper flakes, and garam masala and stir well. Cook for 5 minutes longer to allow the eggplant to cook through. Transfer to a serving dish, cover, and refrigerate for at least 2 hours before serving.

To make the bruschetta: Preheat the oven to 350°F.

Spread the pitas on a baking sheet, coat lightly with cooking spray, and sprinkle with garlic powder.

Bake the pitas for 5 minutes, turn them, and bake for 3 minutes longer, or until golden brown. Serve immediately with the eggplant dip.

Makes 4 servings

Per serving: *220 calories, 7 g protein, 41 g carbohydrate, 5 g fat, 0 mg cholesterol, 848 mg sodium, 8 g fiber*

Diet Exchanges: *0 milk, 2½ vegetable, 0 fruit, 1½ bread, 0 meat, 1 fat*

3 Carb Choices

Kitchen Tip

To make garam masala, place 2 tablespoons *each* cumin seeds, coriander seeds, cardamom seeds, and black peppercorns; 1 cinnamon stick (3") broken into pieces; and 1 teaspoon whole cloves in a skillet over medium-high heat. Toast the spices until they give off a sweet, smoky aroma. Cool completely. Transfer the mixture in batches to a spice mill and grind to a powder. Stir in 1 teaspoon nutmeg and ½ teaspoon saffron. Use immediately or store in an airtight container in a cool, dry place for up to 3 months. Makes about ½ cup.

Blue Cheese Dip

June Leas, Slayton, Minnesota

"Whenever I crave something fattening, I remember how good this dip is and make a batch. It's good with baby carrots."

Prep time: 5 minutes; Chill time: 1 hour

- **4 ounces blue cheese, crumbled**
- **1 cup low-fat sour cream**
- **1 packet (1 ounce) dry ranch salad dressing mix**

In a small bowl, combine the blue cheese, sour cream, and dressing mix. Stir gently until thoroughly blended. Cover and refrigerate for at least 1 hour before serving.

Makes 12 servings, 2 tablespoons each

Per serving: *80 calories, 3 g protein, 3 g carbohydrate, 5 g fat, 15 mg cholesterol, 300 mg sodium, 0 g fiber*

Diet Exchanges: *0 milk, 0 vegetable, 0 fruit, 0 bread, ½ meat, 1 fat*

0 Carb Choices

SECRETS OF WEIGHT-LOSS WINNERS

• Eating peanut butter twice a day keeps me from snacking on other less healthy foods. Because it's filling, I eat smaller meals. Best of all, it tastes good and is good for you. It's the simple things in life that make you happy and satisfied.

—Robin Whitehurst, Annapolis, Maryland

• Put on some upbeat music or turn on the TV and march in place swinging your arms for 20 to 30 minutes. In the summer when it's humid, you can do this with the fan blowing on you!

—Rhonda Taylor, Bradford, Pennsylvania

• Candy bowl at work or home got you down? Want to share candy with your friends, family, and coworkers, but not be tempted yourself? Try stocking it with candy that you don't like. This way you won't be tempted to eat the whole bowl and you'll have the satisfaction of sharing with others. This works great at Halloween, too!

—Jill Cummings, Bellevue, Washington

• Ounce for ounce, juice has as many calories as soda. Set a limit of one 8-ounce glass of fruit juice a day.

—Prevention.com

Ham and Spinach Spread

Shirley Hill, Chatham, Ontario, Canada

"This recipe has given me another light lunch or supper to add to my repertoire. It satisfies me and helps me lose weight. It's great on garlic toast." **(see Kitchen Tip)**

Prep time: 10 minutes; Cook time: 14 minutes

- **1 pound fresh spinach, washed and trimmed**
- **1 tablespoon olive oil**
- **3 ounces sliced cooked ham, finely chopped**
- **2 cloves garlic, minced**
- **Salt**
- **Ground black pepper**
- **2 hard-cooked eggs, coarsely chopped**

Bring a large pot of lightly salted water to a boil over high heat. Cook the spinach for about 3 minutes, or until bright green. Remove from the heat, rinse under cold water, and drain thoroughly. Chop coarsely and set aside.

Warm the oil in a large skillet over medium-high heat. When hot, add the ham and garlic and cook for 3 to 4 minutes. Stir in the spinach, season with salt and pepper, and cook for about 5 minutes longer, stirring occasionally. Add the chopped eggs and cook 1 minute longer.

Makes 6 servings

Per serving: *105 calories, 9 g protein, 6 g carbohydrate, 6 g fat, 79 mg cholesterol, 327 mg sodium, 4 g fiber*

Diet Exchanges: *0 milk, 1 vegetable, 0 fruit, 0 bread, 1 meat, 1 fat*

½ Carb Choice

Kitchen Tip

To make garlic toast, simply toast 8 slices of white, wheat, Italian, or whole grain bread, then rub with split garlic cloves and butter.

Beef and Pine Nut Dumplings

Teresa Cobb, Louisburg, Kansas

Prep time: 25 minutes; Cook time: 12 minutes

- **1 pound lean ground beef**
- **1 cup green chili salsa**
- **¼ cup chopped fresh cilantro**
- **⅓ cup finely chopped toasted pine nuts**
- **⅓ cup chopped scallions**
- **1 egg**
- **1 clove garlic, minced**
- **40 wonton wrappers, trimmed to 3" squares**

In a large bowl, combine the beef, ½ cup of the salsa, the cilantro, pine nuts, scallions, egg, and garlic. With clean hands, mix the ingredients until thoroughly combined.

On a clean work surface, place 1 teaspoon of the mixture in the center of a wonton wrapper. Moisten the edges with water, bring the corners together over the filling, and press the edges together to seal. Repeat with the remaining filling and wrappers.

Place a steamer basket in a large pot with ½" of water. Coat the rack with cooking spray and bring the water to a simmer. Working in batches, place the dumplings on the rack (make sure they don't touch each other), cover, and steam for 10 to 12 minutes, or until cooked through. Serve with the remaining salsa.

Makes 40 dumplings

Per dumpling: *60 calories, 3 g protein, 5 g carbohydrate, 3 g fat, 14 mg cholesterol, 83 mg sodium, 0 g fiber*

Diet Exchanges: *0 milk, 0 vegetable, 0 fruit, ½ bread, ½ meat, ½ fat*

½ Carb Choice

Kitchen Tip

To prevent dumplings from sticking to the steamer, line the steamer rack with cabbage leaves. Just be sure to leave openings so the steam can escape.

332 Calories

Asian Chicken Rolls

Marci Herman, Burnaby, British Columbia, Canada

"These low-fat chicken rolls are very filling and versatile. You can add different veggies or use lean beef if you want. They're very attractive and can be served as a main course or an hors d'oeuvre if you're having company."

Marinate time: 30 minutes; Prep time: 10 minutes
Cook time: 25 minutes; Stand time: 10 minutes

2 small boneless, skinless chicken breast halves, butterflied and pounded to ¼" (see Kitchen Tip)
2 spears asparagus
1 carrot, cut into thin strips (¼" thick)
2 scallions, cut into thin strips
½ red or green bell pepper, cut into thin strips
½ small zucchini, cut into thin strips
½ teaspoon grated fresh ginger
½ teaspoon minced garlic
Ground black pepper
3 tablespoons reduced-sodium soy sauce
½ cup reduced-sodium chicken broth
Prepared dipping sauce (optional)

Working with one chicken breast at a time, lay half of the asparagus, carrot, scallions, pepper, and zucchini along one edge of each breast, trimming the vegetables as necessary to the same length as the breast. Sprinkle with ginger, garlic, and pepper. Roll up the chicken, enclosing the ingredients as you go. Secure each end with kitchen string and transfer to a small bowl. Cover with the soy sauce and refrigerate for 30 minutes. Coat a medium skillet with cooking spray and warm over medium-high heat. When hot, cook the chicken for 10 to 15 minutes, turning to ensure both sides are evenly browned. Add the broth, lower the heat, and simmer for about 15 minutes, or until the chicken is cooked through. Allow the chicken to rest for about 10 minutes, then remove the string and slice. If desired, serve with dipping sauce of your choice.

Makes 2 servings

Per serving: *332 calories, 59 g protein, 14 g carbohydrate, 3 g fat, 137 mg cholesterol, 932 mg sodium, 3 g fiber*

Diet Exchanges: *0 milk, 1½ vegetable, 0 fruit, ½ bread, 8 meat, 0 fat*

1 Carb Choice

Kitchen Tip

To butterfly a boneless chicken breast, start at the thickest side of the breast and slice it crosswise through the side, almost in half. Open the breast up like a book and press to flatten. To pound it thin, place the chicken between 2 pieces of plastic wrap and pound it with a meat mallet to the desired thickness, being careful not to tear the plastic.

Quick 'n' Cool Chicken Bites

Alex Mosiychuk, Kansas City, Missouri

Prep time: 10 minutes; Cook time: 14 minutes

SAUCE

- **½ cup plum preserves**
- **2 tablespoons lime juice**
- **1 tablespoon soy sauce**
- **1 tablespoon Dijon mustard**
- **3 teaspoons prepared chopped ginger**

CHICKEN

- **¼ cup sesame seeds**
- **6 cups toasted rice cereal**
- **3 tablespoons vegetable oil**
- **¾ teaspoon salt**
- **½ teaspoon garlic powder**
- **½ cup buttermilk**
- **2 large eggs**
- **2 pounds boneless, skinless chicken breast halves, cut into 1" pieces**

To make the sauce: In a medium bowl, combine the preserves, lime juice, soy sauce, Dijon mustard, and ginger. Set aside until ready to serve.

To make the chicken: Place a rack in the upper third of the oven and preheat to 450°F.

Spread the sesame seeds on a baking sheet and toast for 2 to 4 minutes, or until golden. Transfer to a plate to cool slightly. Coat the same baking sheet and another one with cooking spray and set aside.

In a food processor, combine the cereal, oil, salt, and garlic powder. Add the cooled sesame seeds and process to fine crumbs. Transfer to a large bowl.

In another bowl, whisk together the buttermilk and eggs until well combined. With one hand, dip each piece of chicken in the buttermilk mixture, then drop into the crumb mixture. With the other hand, roll the chicken firmly in the crumbs and place on the baking sheets.

Bake for 8 to 10 minutes, or until golden. Serve with the plum dipping sauce.

Makes 36 pieces

Per piece: *78 calories, 7 g protein, 7 g carbohydrate, 2 g fat, 26 mg cholesterol, 148 mg sodium, 0 g fiber*

Diet Exchanges: *0 milk, 0 vegetable, 0 fruit, ½ bread, 1 meat, ½ fat*

½ Carb Choice

So Quick, So Easy Dipping Sticks

Alex Mosiychuk, Kansas City, Missouri

Prep time: 2 minutes; Cook time: 8 minutes

- **2 mini pizza crusts (8 ounces each)**
- **2 tablespoons grated Parmesan cheese**
- **½–1 teaspoon dried Italian seasoning**
- **1 cup marinara sauce**

Preheat the oven to 350°F.

With a sharp knife or pizza cutter, slice each pizza crust into 6 strips. Transfer to a baking sheet and arrange so that the strips touch each other. Coat with cooking spray and sprinkle evenly with cheese and Italian seasoning. Rearrange so there is a bit of space between the strips.

Bake for 8 minutes, or until golden.

While the pizza sticks are baking, pour the marinara sauce into a medium microwaveable bowl. Microwave on high power for 1 minute, or until warm, stirring once. Serve the breadsticks immediately with the warm sauce.

Makes 2 servings

Per serving: *405 calories, 14 g protein, 69 g carbohydrate, 7 g fat, 4 mg cholesterol, 969 mg sodium, 5 g fiber*

Diet Exchanges: *0 milk, 0 vegetable, 0 fruit, 4½ bread, ½ meat, 1 fat*

4½ Carb Choices

Greek Spinach Pie Triangles

Deborah Di Stefano, Candiac, Quebec, Canada

"This is an authentic Greek recipe, passed down in my family. The triangles are very simple to make and really impress people, as they look like they're professionally made!"

Prep time: 35 minutes; Cook time: 10 minutes

1½ cups chopped fresh spinach
⅓ cup finely chopped onion
1 tablespoon chopped fresh parsley
1 tablespoon chopped fresh dill
1 scallion, coarsely chopped
1–2 tablespoons 1% milk
⅓ cup reduced-fat feta cheese, crumbled
2 tablespoons liquid egg substitute
1 tablespoon olive oil
½ package phyllo dough
3 tablespoons trans-free margarine or butter, melted

Preheat the oven to 350°F. Coat a baking sheet with cooking spray.

In a medium bowl, combine the spinach, onion, parsley, dill, and scallion.

In another bowl, combine the milk, feta cheese, egg substitute, and oil. Lightly mix with a wooden spoon just enough to wet all of the ingredients, then add to the spinach mixture. Mix thoroughly, making sure all of the spinach mixture is coated with the cheese mixture. Set aside.

Working quickly, take a sheet of the phyllo dough, brush with the melted margarine, then layer with a second sheet of phyllo dough. Cut the sheet into 4 equal strips. At the bottom of the strip, add 1 tablespoon of the spinach mixture. Fold as you would a flag: First fold the bottom right corner up to meet the left edge to form a triangle (the right angle will be on the top left). Press gently to seal the edges, then fold the triangle up so that the right angle is now on the bottom left. Continue folding until you reach the end of the strip. Place the triangle on the baking sheet and coat lightly with cooking spray. Repeat with the remaining filling and 3 strips of phyllo.

Bake for about 10 minutes, or until golden.

Makes 36 triangles

Per triangle: *40 calories, 1 g protein, 0 g carbohydrate, 2 g fat, 0 mg cholesterol, 70 mg sodium, 0 g fiber*

Diet Exchanges: *0 milk, 0 vegetable, 0 fruit, ½ bread, 0 meat, ½ fat*

0 Carb Choices

Kitchen Tip

Don't worry about getting the triangles perfect. As long as they're wrapped securely so the filling stays inside, they'll look irresistible after baking!

It Worked for Me!

Dawn D'Andria

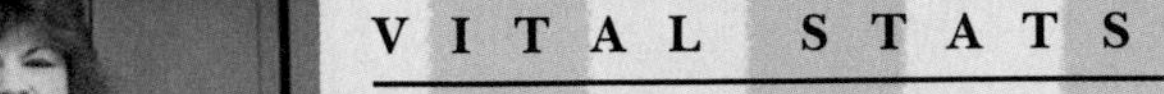

VITAL STATS

Weight lost: 50 pounds

Time to goal: 7 months

Quick tip: If you are cutting carbs, don't be afraid to expand your menu options by asking for a meal served without the roll, or a sandwich minus the bread.

At age 37, Dawn found herself battling a number of health conditions, including high cholesterol, high blood pressure, and colitis. The medications she needed to take added pounds; losing weight eased her symptoms and allowed her to lower her dosages—a win-win situation!

"I reached a point in my life where I just wanted to start feeling better about myself. I had always been a skinny, athletic kid growing up, but had gained weight in my thirties. I was also concerned about the amount of prescription medication I was taking. Drug prices were going up, and I thought if I lost some weight I could improve my health enough to at least lower my dosages.

"Like so many other people, I turned to the Atkins diet. I pretty much followed it religiously, although as I started losing weight, I would give myself 1 day off each week to cheat and eat something I craved, like fried chicken wings and a beer. The diet was not hard for me to follow, because I let myself get creative when it came to cooking. You can adapt just about any recipe using the Atkins products that are on the market now: You can buy low-carb flour, or make your own bread crumbs from low-carb bread.

"My doctor fully supported me in following Atkins. In fact, my gastroenterologist was the person who recommended the diet to me in the first place. He said it was a good choice for someone dealing with colitis because, unfortunately, we can't eat a large amount of fruits and vegetables.

"Since losing weight, I'm happy to say that my cholesterol has improved and taking the stairs at work is so much easier for me. I'm scheduled to see my doctor again soon and I'm looking forward to another good report. My ability to work out was restricted due to surgery that I had to have in January, but now I'm looking forward to making exercise a part of my life. I've been able to maintain my weight loss for the past 5 months but would still like to lose another 25 pounds."

Spiced Pecans

Leah Tews, Phoenix, Arizona

"These tasty treats allow you to watch your carbs and satisfy your sweet tooth."

Prep time: 2 minutes; Cook time: 20 minutes

4 cups pecan halves
1 teaspoon hot-pepper sauce
2 tablespoons sugar
1 teaspoon ground cinnamon
1 teaspoon vanilla extract

Preheat the oven to 275°F.

In a large bowl, combine the pecans, hot-pepper sauce, sugar, cinnamon, and vanilla extract. Stir until the nuts are completely coated, then spread on a baking sheet and heat for 20 minutes.

Makes 24 servings

Per serving: *139 calories, 2 g protein, 4 g carbohydrate, 14 g fat, 0 mg cholesterol, 1 mg sodium, 1 g fiber*

Diet Exchanges: *0 milk, 0 vegetable, 0 fruit, ½ bread, ½ meat, 2½ fat*

½ Carb Choice

MAIN DISHES

Crab-Stuffed Tiger Shrimp

Elizabeth Martlock, Jim Thorpe, Pennsylvania

"This elegant main dish makes just as impressive an appetizer."

Prep time: 25 minutes; Cook time: 35 minutes

SAUCE

- **1 teaspoon olive oil**
- **2 cloves garlic, minced**
- **2 medium shallots, finely chopped**
- **Salt**
- **Ground black pepper**
- **¼ cup finely chopped roasted red peppers**
- **1 cup fat-free half-and-half**
- **1 cup 2% milk**
- **¼ cup grated Parmesan cheese**

STUFFING

- **1 can (6 ounces) special or lump crabmeat**
- **1 tablespoon light mayonnaise**
- **1 cup fresh whole wheat bread crumbs**
- **½ teaspoon crab-boil seasoning, such as Old Bay**
- **¼ cup finely chopped roasted red peppers**
- **Salt**
- **Ground black pepper**

SHRIMP

- **1 pound large shrimp**
- **1 tablespoon olive oil**
- **Paprika**
- **2 tablespoons chopped fresh parsley**
- **2 tablespoons finely chopped roasted red peppers**

To make the sauce: Warm the oil in a medium saucepan over medium heat. When hot, add the garlic and shallots and cook for 1 minute, or until fragrant. Season with salt and black pepper, then add the roasted red peppers, half-and-half, and milk. Whisking constantly, bring the mixture almost to a boil, then add the cheese. Continue to whisk until thickened. Cover to keep warm and set aside.

To make the stuffing: In a medium bowl, combine the crabmeat, mayonnaise, bread crumbs, crab-boil seasoning, roasted red peppers, and salt and pepper to taste. Mix carefully and set aside.

Preheat the oven to 350°F.

To make the shrimp: Coat a baking sheet with cooking spray. Peel and devein the shrimp, cutting along the back of each shrimp to make a flat surface for the stuffing. Arrange the shrimp on the prepared baking sheet about 2" or 3" apart. On each shrimp, place about 1 tablespoon of stuffing, then drizzle with oil and dust with paprika.

Bake for about 20 minutes, or until the shrimp turn pink and opaque. Transfer to a serving plate, drizzle with sauce, top with fresh parsley and red peppers, and serve.

Makes 4 servings

Per serving: *371 calories, 39 g protein, 17 g carbohydrate, 15 g fat, 238 mg cholesterol, 604 mg sodium, 1 g fiber*

Diet Exchanges: *½ milk, ½ vegetable, 0 fruit, ½ bread, 5 meat, 2½ fat*

1 Carb Choice

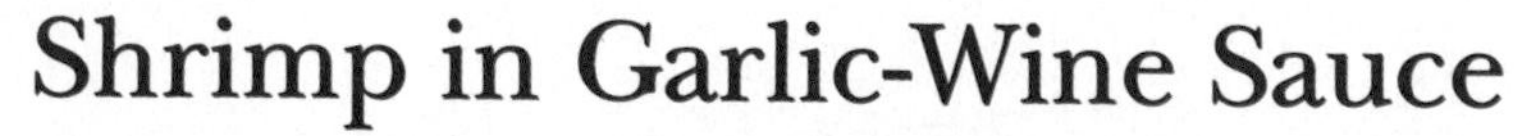

Shrimp in Garlic-Wine Sauce

193 Calories

Kim Russell, North Wales, Pennsylvania

"This meal takes only about 20 minutes to prepare. It's healthy, low in fat, and delicious. I keep a bag of shrimp in my freezer at all times so I can whip this up whenever the mood strikes."

Prep time: 10 minutes; Cook time: 9 minutes

- **2 tablespoons olive oil**
- **½ teaspoon red-pepper flakes**
- **4 cloves garlic, minced**
- **1 pound large shrimp, peeled and deveined**
- **2 tablespoons dry white wine**
- **2 tablespoons lemon juice**
- **½ teaspoon paprika**
- **2 tablespoons finely chopped fresh parsley**
- **Salt**
- **Ground black pepper**

Warm the oil in a large nonstick skillet over medium-high heat. When hot, add the red-pepper flakes and cook for about 30 seconds. Add the garlic and cook for about 1 minute, or until fragrant. Add the shrimp, wine, lemon juice, and paprika. Cook, stirring occasionally, for 4 to 6 minutes, or until the shrimp turn pink and opaque. Sprinkle with the parsley, season with salt and pepper, and serve.

Makes 4 servings

Per serving: *193 calories, 23 g protein, 3 g carbohydrate, 9 g fat, 172 mg cholesterol, 171 mg sodium, 0 g fiber*

Diet Exchanges: *0 milk, 0 vegetable, 0 fruit, 0 bread, 3 meat, 1½ fat*

0 Carb Choices

Zesty Cod Fillets

Gail Hayes, Breckenridge, Minnesota

Prep time: 5 minutes; Cook time: 25 minutes

- **4 cod fillets (4 to 6 ounces each)**
- **2 teaspoons Dijon mustard**
- **½ cup whole wheat bread crumbs**
- **1 teaspoon lemon-pepper seasoning**
- **2 tablespoons freshly grated Parmesan or Asiago cheese**
- **2 teaspoons olive oil**

Preheat the oven to 375°F. Coat a 13" × 9" glass baking dish with cooking spray.

Spread one side of each fillet with ½ teaspoon of the mustard and arrange in the baking dish, mustard side up.

In a small bowl, combine the bread crumbs, lemon pepper, and cheese. Sprinkle evenly over the fillets, then drizzle with oil.

Bake for 20 to 25 minutes, or until the fish flakes easily.

Makes 4 servings

Per serving: *140 calories, 22 g protein, 3 g carbohydrate, 4 g fat, 50 mg cholesterol, 250 mg sodium, 0 g fiber*

Diet Exchanges: *0 milk, 0 vegetable, 0 fruit, 0 bread, 3 meat, ½ fat*

0 Carb Choices

SAVORY FISH MARINADES

Use any of these marinades to add moisture and great flavor to 1½ pounds salmon, swordfish, bluefish, or mahi mahi. Marinate the fish in the refrigerator for up to 1 hour, then drain off the marinade. Place on a lightly oiled rimmed baking sheet and bake at 425°F for 10 to 15 minutes (depending on thickness). Fish is done when it is just opaque in the thickest part.

Herb-Mustard Marinade. Mix ¼ cup chopped fresh dill, 3 tablespoons *each* Dijon mustard and extra-virgin olive oil, 2 tablespoons white wine vinegar, 2 minced garlic cloves, ½ teaspoon salt, and ¼ teaspoon ground black pepper.

Provençal Marinade. Mix ½ cup *each* white wine and canned crushed tomatoes, 2 tablespoons extra-virgin olive oil, the juice and grated zest of ½ orange, 3 minced garlic cloves, a pinch of red-pepper flakes, ½ teaspoon salt, and ¼ teaspoon ground black pepper.

Garlic and Mint Yogurt Marinade. Mix ½ cup plain low-fat yogurt, 2 tablespoons extra-virgin olive oil, 1 tablespoon lemon juice, 2 minced garlic cloves, 1¼ teaspoons dried mint leaves, ¼ teaspoon hot-pepper sauce, ¼ teaspoon salt, and ⅛ teaspoon ground black pepper.

Hooked on Halibut

Nanette Marsh, Ocala, Florida

"This is a healthy way to enjoy a guilt-free, easy-to-make meal."

Prep time: 5 minutes; Cook time: 20 minutes
Chill time: 1 hour

3 tablespoons lemon juice
1 teaspoon salt
½ teaspoon paprika
6 halibut steaks (5 to 6 ounces each)
2 tablespoons trans-free margarine
½ cup chopped onion
1 large bell pepper, cut into strips

In a shallow bowl, combine the lemon juice, salt, and paprika. Add the fish, cover, and refrigerate for 1 hour, turning once.

Preheat the oven to 450°F. Coat a 13" × 9" baking dish with cooking spray.

Melt the margarine in a medium skillet over medium-high heat and cook the onion for 5 to 10 minutes, or until brown. Place the fish in the prepared baking dish and top with the onion and bell pepper strips.

Bake for 10 minutes, or until the fish is just opaque.

Makes 6 servings

Per serving: *171 calories, 24 g protein, 3 g carbohydrate, 6 g fat, 40 mg cholesterol, 492 mg sodium, 1 g fiber*

Diet Exchanges: *0 milk, ½ vegetable, 0 fruit, 0 bread, 3½ meat, 1 fat*

0 Carb Choices

Speedy Fish Tacos

Helen Velichko, Kansas City, Missouri

Prep time: 15 minutes; Cook time: 6 minutes

2 cups sliced green cabbage
½ cup chopped scallions
½ cup reduced-fat sour cream
2 tablespoons taco seasoning
1 tablespoon lime juice
1 tablespoon orange juice
1 tablespoon oil
1 pound firm whitefish fillets, cut into bite-size pieces
8 whole wheat flour tortillas (8" diameter)
8 lime wedges

In a medium bowl, combine the cabbage, scallions, and sour cream.

In another medium bowl, combine the taco seasoning, lime juice, and orange juice. Add the fish pieces and toss to coat.

Warm the oil in a large nonstick skillet over medium-high heat. When hot, add the fish and cook for 5 minutes, or until the fish flakes easily. Warm the tortillas according to package directions.

To assemble the tacos, spoon about ¼ cup of the cabbage mixture down the center of each tortilla. Divide the fish evenly among the tortillas and fold in half. Serve with lime wedges.

Makes 4 servings

Per serving: *490 calories, 31 g protein, 54 g carbohydrate, 4 g fat, 60 mg cholesterol, 770 mg sodium, 5 g fiber*

Diet Exchanges: *0 milk, ½ vegetable, 0 fruit, 3 bread, 3 meat, 2½ fat*

3½ Carb Choices

Mango Salsa Grouper

Liana Franceschini, Miami, Florida

Prep time: 15 minutes; Cook time: 10 minutes
Chill time: 2 hours

1 mango, finely chopped
½ cup chopped fresh cilantro
½ cup chopped red bell pepper
½ cup chopped poblano or green bell pepper
½ cup chopped red onion
¼ cup rice wine vinegar
Salt
Ground black pepper
1–2 teaspoons olive oil
4 grouper fillets (5 to 6 ounces each)

In a medium bowl, combine the mango, cilantro, red bell pepper, poblano or green bell pepper, onion, and vinegar. Toss well and season with salt and pepper to taste. Cover and refrigerate the mango salsa for at least 2 hours. Preheat the grill to medium-high. Coat a piece of foil with cooking spray and lay on a grill rack.

Rub the oil on the fish and place on the foil over the coolest part of the grill. Grill for 8 to 10 minutes, or until the fish flakes easily. Serve with the mango salsa.

Makes 4 servings

Per serving: *286 calories, 51 g protein, 12 g carbohydrate, 3 g fat, 0 mg cholesterol, 140 mg sodium, 2 g fiber*

Diet Exchanges: *0 milk, ½ vegetable, ½ fruit, 0 bread, 7 meat, 0 fat*

1 Carb Choice

LEMONS AND LIMES

Prized for their sweet, acidic juice and flavorful zest, lemons and limes have a wide range of uses in the kitchen, especially in lower-calorie dishes. Limes are more aromatic and slightly more acidic than lemons, and, of course, the flavor is different, but they can often be used interchangeably. A bit of fresh lemon or a spritz of lime juice is often all that is needed to enliven a dull-tasting dish, especially chicken, seafood, salads, and vegetables.

Basics

To choose: Look for plump, firm (but not hard) fruit that is heavy for its size, with smooth, brightly colored rinds.

To store: Refrigerate for 2 to 3 weeks.

To remove zest: Be sure to remove the zest before squeezing the juice, or it will be a nearly impossible task. To avoid a bitter taste, remove only the outer brightly colored layer, or zest, and not the inner white pith. Use a microplane rasp-style grater for fastest results. One medium lemon yields 2 to 3 teaspoons of zest; 1 medium lime yields 1 to 2 teaspoons of zest.

To squeeze maximum juice: Bring fruit to room temperature and roll under the firm pressure of your palm to soften it and get the juices flowing. Or, pierce with a fork and microwave on medium power for 10 to 20 seconds. A medium lemon yields 2 to 4 tablespoons of juice; a medium lime yields 1 to 2 tablespoons juice.

Salmon Grilled on a Lemon Bed. Preheat the barbecue grill to medium-high. Tear off 4 large sheets of heavy-duty foil. For each packet, fold a piece of foil in half like a book. Open up the foil and coat one half with cooking spray. On the sprayed half, arrange 4 thin lemon slices, slightly overlapping, then place a 6-ounce skinned salmon fillet on top. Brush the salmon with 1 teaspoon olive oil and sprinkle with salt and freshly ground pepper to taste. If desired, sprinkle with 1 teaspoon snipped fresh dill. Place 2 rings of sweet onion on top. Fold the foil over and secure the edges. Repeat, making 4 packets in all. Transfer the packets to the grill. Grill for about 15 minutes, or until the fish is just opaque in the thickest part.

310 Calories

Creole Tilapia

Carole Grover, Baton Rouge, Louisiana

"This simple, inexpensive meal can be prepared in less than 10 minutes if you make the rice ahead of time. You can store the cooked rice in ½-cup portions."

Prep time: 5 minutes; Cook time: 10 minutes

½ cup quick-cooking brown rice
1 onion, sliced
2 ribs celery, sliced
2 large carrots, sliced
2 tilapia fillets (5 to 6 ounces each)
1 cup canned diced tomatoes
2 tablespoons chopped fresh cilantro, parsley, or basil
Seasoning salt
Ground black pepper

Prepare the rice according to package directions.

Meanwhile, coat a large skillet with cooking spray. Over medium-high heat, cook the onion, celery, and carrot for 5 minutes, or until tender. Add the tilapia and cook for 3 minutes. Carefully turn the fish and add the tomatoes and herbs. Season with salt and pepper to taste. Simmer for 2 minutes, or until the fish flakes easily. Serve over the rice.

Makes 2 servings

Per serving: *310 calories, 31 g protein, 42 g carbohydrate, 2½ g fat, 70 mg cholesterol, 580 mg sodium, 6 g fiber*

Diet Exchanges: *0 milk, 3 vegetable, 0 fruit, 1½ bread, 4 meat, 0 fat*

3 Carb Choices

Kitchen Tip

To remove the stubborn odor of fish from a pan, boil equal parts vinegar and water in it for 10 minutes.

Blackened Snapper

Karen Schlyter, Calgary, Alberta, Canada

"I created this recipe to spice things up a bit and to get myself to eat more fish. I love it, and it's good for high-protein diets."

Marinate time: overnight; Prep time: 5 minutes
Cook time: 7 minutes

SPICE MIX

- **¼ cup chili powder**
- **2 teaspoons salt**
- **2 teaspoons ground black pepper**
- **2 teaspoons paprika**
- **2 tablespoons dried basil**
- **2 teaspoons cayenne pepper**
- **¼ cup dried parsley**
- **2 tablespoons ground cumin**

SNAPPER

- **1 cup low-fat milk**
- **4 snapper fillets (5 to 6 ounces each)**
- **2 tablespoons olive oil**
- **Tartar sauce (optional)**

To make the spice mix: In a small bowl, combine the chili powder, salt, black pepper, paprika, basil, cayenne pepper, parsley, and cumin. Mix well and transfer to a small covered container. (This makes about 1 cup, so you'll have some left over.)

To make the snapper: In a shallow dish, pour the milk over the snapper fillets, cover, and refrigerate overnight.

Remove the fillets from the milk, pat dry with a paper towel, and rub ⅓ cup of the spice mixture onto the fish.

Warm the oil in a large skillet over medium-high heat. When hot, add the fish and cook for 2 to 3 minutes per side, or until the fish flakes easily. Serve with tartar sauce, if desired.

Makes 4 servings

Per serving: *260 calories, 31 g protein, 6 g carbohydrate, 10 g fat, 60 mg cholesterol, 710 mg sodium, 3 g fiber*

Diet Exchanges: *0 milk, 1 vegetable, 0 fruit, 0 bread, 4 meat, 1½ fat*

½ Carb Choice

Ena Bogdanowicz

VITAL STATS

Weight lost: 50 pounds

Time to goal: 3 months

Quick tip: Don't be afraid to make healthy changes to traditional family recipes.

Ena had always wanted to lose weight but didn't know how to start. Her family turned out to be the support system she needed to make lasting life changes.

"My weight has always been a problem for me, and although I had always wanted to go on a diet, I just didn't know how to do it. I would say to myself, 'Tomorrow I will start a diet,' and I would eat some salad and hard-boiled eggs for a day or two before getting too hungry and just giving up.

"About a year ago, I noticed that many of my coworkers were suddenly losing weight and looking terrific. I heard that they were 'doing Atkins,' so I asked my daughter about it. She told me that the South Beach Diet was really the newest way to lose weight. I bought that book the very next day and found it was easy to follow. The book tells you exactly what to eat every day, including snacks.

"The biggest change was avoiding all sugars. For many years I had been snacking on sweets between meals without even realizing it. I would eat only one or two cookies at a time, but then grab two more every 2 hours. I never really realized how much sugar I was eating.

"When I started the diet, I was cooking only for myself, because I was the only overweight person in the house. My daughter helped me by often putting a full, diet-friendly breakfast out for me in the mornings so I wouldn't be tempted to eat the wrong foods. Eventually, I introduced some of the South Beach meals to my family. For example, my husband loves fish; when I cook seafood now, he has his meal with rice and I have a salad on the side instead. I am a native of Central America and cook a lot of traditional food, so I've also added new cooking techniques to favorite family dishes.

"In addition to changing my eating style, I started exercising as well—another new thing for me. I worried that a treadmill would be terribly boring, but my son put a TV in my workout room to help me stick with it. Now I walk while I watch my soap operas for an hour and enjoy every minute."

366 Calories

Tropical Mahi Mahi

Thereza Ordacgi, Hollywood, Florida

"This delicious dish is the perfect combination for a complete healthy meal that family and friends can enjoy with you. Try it and wait for the compliments!"

Marinate time: 30 minutes
Cook time: 30 minutes

2 tablespoons reduced-sodium soy sauce
1 can (8 ounces) pineapple chunks, drained, juice reserved
2 cloves garlic, minced
4 mahi mahi fillets (about 6 ounces each)
1 tablespoon olive oil
1 medium tomato, finely chopped
½ medium yellow onion, finely chopped
½ medium red bell pepper, finely chopped
½ medium yellow bell pepper, finely chopped
1 cup brown basmati rice
2½ cups water
2 scallions, sliced

In a large, shallow baking dish, combine the soy sauce, reserved pineapple juice, and garlic. Add the fish and turn to coat. Cover and refrigerate for 30 minutes.

Meanwhile, warm the oil in a medium skillet over medium-high heat. When hot, add the tomato, onion, and bell peppers and cook for 2 to 3 minutes, or until softened. Add the rice and cook, stirring, for about 5 minutes, or until fragrant. Add the water, bring to a boil, then cover and reduce the heat. Simmer for 45 minutes, or until the rice is tender.

Preheat the oven to 450°F. Bake the fish for 10 to 15 minutes, or until it flakes easily. Serve with the rice and garnish with the pineapple chunks and scallions.

Makes 4 servings

Per serving: *366 calories, 30 g protein, 37 g carbohydrate, 10 g fat, 53 mg cholesterol, 141 mg sodium, 5 g fiber*

Diet Exchanges: *0 milk, 1½ vegetable, ½ fruit, 1½ bread, 4 meat, 1½ fat*

2½ Carb Choices

Kitchen Tip

If mahi mahi is not available, swordfish makes a great substitute.

Salmon with Asparagus

Jennifer Ruddock, Oshawa, Ontario, Canada

Prep time: 10 minutes; Cook time: 10 minutes
Bake time: 25 minutes

- **2 salmon steaks (6 to 8 ounces each)**
- **2 teaspoons olive oil**
- **1 tablespoon trans-free margarine or butter**
- **1 tablespoon finely chopped onion**
- **1 clove garlic, minced**
- **1 tablespoon unbleached or all-purpose flour**
- **1 cup 1% milk**
- **6–8 thin spears asparagus, cut into 1"pieces**

Preheat the oven to 350°F. Coat a baking sheet with cooking spray.

Place the salmon steaks on the prepared baking sheet and drizzle with 1 teaspoon of the oil. Bake for 20 to 25 minutes, or until the fish is opaque.

Meanwhile, warm the margarine or butter in a medium saucepan over medium heat. When hot, add the onion and garlic and cook for 2 to 3 minutes, or until golden. Whisk in the flour and cook for 1 to 2 minutes longer, or until the flour becomes a pale nutty color. Slowly add the milk and cook, whisking constantly, for 1 minute longer, or until the sauce becomes smooth and thick. Remove from the heat and set aside.

In a medium skillet over medium-high heat, cook the asparagus in the remaining 1 teaspoon of oil for 2 to 3 minutes, or until crisp-tender. Add to the sauce and cover until the salmon is done.

Top the salmon with the asparagus sauce and serve.

Makes 2 servings

Per serving: *380 calories, 36 g protein, 11 g carbohydrate, 20 g fat, 90 mg cholesterol, 180 mg sodium, 1 g fiber*

Diet Exchanges: *½ milk, ½ vegetable, 0 fruit, 0 bread, 4 meat, 2½ fat*

1 Carb Choice

Grilled Salmon with Brown Rice

380 Calories

Donna Bowers, Avondale, Arizona

"I eat fish at least three times a week and exercise five times a week, and I've gone from a size 12 to a size 6. This dish is great served with fresh steamed green beans."

Prep time: 5 minutes; Cook time: 30 minutes

- **½ cup brown rice**
- **2 salmon fillets (5–6 ounces each)**
- **2 sprigs rosemary**
- **¼ cup lemon juice**
- **Salt**
- **Ground black pepper**

Cook the rice according to package directions.

Meanwhile, preheat the barbecue or gas grill to high.

Place each salmon fillet on a piece of foil, then sprinkle with equal parts rosemary and lemon juice and season with salt and pepper to taste. Fold the foil over the fish and wrap tightly, crimping the sides as you go to form a packet. Place the fish on the grill and cook for 9 to 12 minutes. Turn the packets over, then grill for 5 minutes longer. Remove from the grill and very carefully open the packets—they will release a lot of steam.

The fish is done when it is opaque. Serve over the rice.

Makes 2 servings

Per serving: *380 calories, 32 g protein, 39 g carbohydrate, 10 g fat, 80 mg cholesterol, 360 mg sodium, 2 g fiber*

Diet Exchanges: *0 milk, 1½ vegetable, 0 fruit, 2½ bread, 4 meat, 1 fat*

2½ Carb Choices

Sun-Dried-Tomato Salmon

Elisa Vaillancourt, Virginia Beach, Virginia

"This dish is so easy to prepare and tastes so good that I don't mind having salmon every week."

Prep time: 5 minutes; Cook time: 10 minutes

- **¼ cup sun-dried tomatoes**
- **1–2 cloves garlic**
- **Salt**
- **Ground black pepper**
- **1½ pounds salmon steak, with skin**
- **1–2 teaspoons olive oil**

Preheat a grill to high.

In a small food processor, combine the sun-dried tomatoes, garlic, salt, and pepper. Pulse until a smooth paste forms.

Rub the salmon on both sides with the oil.

Coat a piece of foil with cooking spray and lay on a grill rack. Place the salmon on the foil, cover, and cook for 10 minutes, or until the fish is opaque. Top with the sun-dried-tomato mixture and serve.

Makes 4 servings

Per serving: *240 calories, 31 g protein, 2 g carbohydrate, 11 g fat, 85 mg cholesterol, 280 mg sodium, 0 g fiber*

Diet Exchanges: *0 milk, ½ vegetable, 0 fruit, 0 bread, 4 meat, ½ fat*

0 Carb Choices

Kitchen Tip

Whenever you cook salmon, make extra. Leftovers chill well for a day or two and can be quickly tossed into pasta or salads.

Tofu-Walnut Patties

Erica Losito, St. Louis, Missouri

Prep time: 25 minutes; Cook time: 10 minutes

- **½ pound firm tofu**
- **¾ cup rolled oats**
- **1 cup fresh whole wheat bread crumbs (from about 2 slices)**
- **¼ cup whole wheat flour**
- **1 onion, chopped**
- **½ cup walnuts, finely chopped**
- **1½ teaspoons beef bouillon powder**
- **¼– ½ teaspoon garlic powder**
- **¼ teaspoon salt**
- **2 teaspoons dried savory or 1 teaspoon dried sage**
- **½–1 cup water**

With the back of a fork, finely crumble the tofu into a large bowl. Add the oats, bread crumbs, and whole wheat flour and mix gently, then add the onion, walnuts, bouillon powder, garlic powder, salt, and savory and mix again. Slowly add enough water so that you can shape the tofu mixture into 6 patties.

Coat a large skillet with cooking spray and cook the patties over medium-high heat for 3 to 5 minutes, or until golden. Flip the patties and continue cooking until browned on the other side.

Makes 6 servings

Per serving: *170 calories, 7 g protein, 19 g carbohydrate, 8 g fat, 0 mg cholesterol, 350 mg sodium, 3 g fiber*

Diet Exchanges: *0 milk, ½ vegetable, 0 fruit, 1 bread, ½ meat, ½ fat*

1 Carb Choice

Kitchen Tip

This recipe is also great baked! Place the patties on a baking sheet lightly coated with cooking spray and bake in a 350°F oven for 20 minutes, turning after 10 minutes. You can also use this mixture to make meatballs.

FIVE RULES OF FOOD SAFETY

Good food-safety habits are perhaps the most important foundation of cooking, ensuring a clean environment and helping to stave off foodborne illness.

Here are five steps to ensure that your food is safe to eat.

Shop smart. In the store, buy perishable items last. Don't buy cans or glass jars with dents, cracks, or bulging lids. If you spot something questionable after you get home, follow this cardinal rule: When in doubt, throw it out.

If you have a long drive home from the store, or if it's a hot day, bring along a cooler for perishables. Bags of ice are readily available in the store.

Keep foods chilled. Set your refrigerator to no higher than 40°F and your freezer to 0°F. If you won't be using meat, poultry, or fish within a few days, freeze it. When refrigerating raw meats, poultry, or fish, leave them in the store's packaging (when possible) and place in a shallow pan so that the food's juices are contained. When defrosting and marinating, do so in the refrigerator rather than on countertops.

Clean often. Wash your hands with hot, soapy water before and after handling food, and especially after using the restroom, changing diapers, and playing with pets. Use hot, soapy water on all dishes, utensils, and work surfaces as well. Don't bother with special "antibacterial soap." It's not an effective product. Dish soap and hot water are all you need.

Wood or plastic cutting boards? It doesn't matter, as long as they're cleaned with hot water and soap after use. Plastic may be more convenient because it can go in the dishwasher. Replace cutting boards that have deep cuts, which could harbor bacteria. Kitchen towels should be washed in the hot cycle of your washing machine, and sponges should be washed in hot water or put in the dishwasher daily to kill bacteria.

Avoid cross-contamination. Keep raw meat, poultry, seafood, and eggs away from ready-to-eat foods. When prepping food, cut vegetables and salad ingredients first, then raw meats and poultry. After preparing raw meat, wash all cutting boards, utensils, and work surfaces with hot, soapy water. Be careful to avoid placing cooked food on a plate that previously held raw meat, poultry, eggs, or seafood (unless the plate has been cleaned). When soaking up meat and poultry juices, use disposable towels instead of sponges. Discard all unused marinades or, if using as a baste or sauce, bring to a boil first to kill bacteria.

Use a thermometer. To be certain that food has cooked to a safe temperature, use an instant-read thermometer to check for doneness (wash it after use), along with visual checks. Avoid eating uncooked meat, poultry, seafood, and eggs. When reheating leftovers, make sure that they reach a temperature of at least 165°F.

Bean Burritos

Nancy Silverman, New Haven, Connecticut

Prep time: 15 minutes; Cook time: 15 minutes

- **2 cans (16 ounces each) fat-free refried beans**
- **10 low-fat flour tortillas (10" diameter)**
- **1¼ cups salsa + ¾ cup for garnish**
- **5 slices Cheddar-flavored soy cheese**
- **Chili powder**

Preheat the oven to 375°F. Coat a 10" × 13" baking dish with cooking spray.

In a small saucepan over medium heat, cook the beans until heated through. Remove from the heat and set aside.

Working in batches, soften the tortillas a few at a time according to package directions. Spread each with about ⅓ cup of the beans, followed by 2 tablespoons of salsa and ½ slice of cheese. Roll up the tortilla and place it seam side down in the prepared baking dish; repeat until all of the tortillas are filled. Coat the burritos with cooking spray and sprinkle with chili powder.

Bake, uncovered, for about 15 minutes, or until heated through and browned on top. Garnish with additional salsa and serve.

Makes 10 servings

Per serving: *151 calories, 7 g protein, 28 g carbohydrate, 2 g fat, 6 mg cholesterol, 504 mg sodium, 6 g fiber*

Diet Exchanges: *0 milk, ½ vegetable, 0 fruit, 1½ bread, ½ meat, 0 fat*

2 Carb Choices

Vegetarian Tacos

Christie Turchyn, Balmoral, Manitoba, Canada

Prep time: 5 minutes; Cook time: 40 minutes

- **1 cup brown rice**
- **4 cloves garlic, minced**
- **2 small onions, finely chopped**
- **1 can (14½ ounces) Mexican-style diced tomatoes**
- **1 can (4 ounces) chopped mild green chiles**
- **¼ cup water**
- **1 package (¾ ounce) taco seasoning**
- **6 corn tortillas (6" diameter)**

Prepare the rice according to package directions.

Meanwhile, in a small skillet, cook the garlic and onions in a little water and cooking spray. When the onions are slightly translucent, add the tomatoes and chiles and cook for about 3 minutes. Add the water and taco seasoning and mix well. Cook for another 3 minutes, then stir into the rice.

Warm the tortillas according to package directions, top with the rice mixture, and serve.

Makes 6 servings

Per serving: *210 calories, 4 g protein, 46 g carbohydrate, 1.5 g fat, 0 mg cholesterol, 830 mg sodium, 5 g fiber*

Diet Exchanges: *0 milk, 1 vegetable, 0 fruit, 2½ bread, 0 meat, 0 fat*

3 Carb Choices

Kitchen Tip

These tacos are great served with toppings like lettuce, tomatoes, salsa, or low-fat cheese. Or be creative and add your own favorites!

Honey-Stuffed Peppers

Jennifer Maslowski, New York, New York

Prep time: 10 minutes; Cook time: 30 minutes
Stand time: 5 minutes

- **1¼ cups brown rice**
- **4 large green bell peppers, cored and seeded**
- **½ cup slivered almonds**
- **1 tablespoon olive oil**
- **¼ teaspoon ground cinnamon**
- **½ teaspoon salt**
- **¼ teaspoon ground ginger**
- **¼ cup honey**
- **1 can (14½ ounces) chickpeas, rinsed and drained**
- **¼ cup raisins (optional)**

Preheat the oven to 400°F. Prepare the rice according to package instructions.

Meanwhile, coat an 8" microwaveable baking dish with cooking spray. Set the bell peppers upright in the dish, cover with plastic wrap, and microwave on high power for 2 to 3 minutes, or until soft. Set aside.

Place the almonds on a baking sheet and toast for 5 minutes, shaking frequently. Set aside.

In a small saucepan over low heat, combine the oil, cinnamon, salt, ginger, and honey. Cook, stirring constantly, for about 2 minutes, or until well blended (do not let it come to a boil). Set aside 2 tablespoons of this honey mixture.

In a bowl, combine the cooked rice, chickpeas, toasted almonds, and raisins, if using. Add the honey mixture from the saucepan. Evenly divide the honey-rice mixture and fill the bell peppers.

Drizzle with the reserved 2 tablespoons of honey mixture, cover with foil, and bake for 15 minutes, or until heated through.

Uncover and let stand for 5 minutes before serving.

Makes 4 servings

Per serving: *390 calories, 11 g protein, 65 g carbohydrate, 12 g fat, 0 mg cholesterol, 510 mg sodium, 9 g fiber*

Diet Exchanges: *0 milk, 1½ vegetable, 0 fruit, 3½ bread,1 meat, 2 fat*

4 Carb Choices

Kitchen Tip

To keep stuffed peppers from collapsing while baking, place them in small ovenproof bowls, ramekins, or muffin-pan cups.

Linguine with White Artichoke Sauce

Nancy Silverman, New Haven, Connecticut

Prep time: 8 minutes; Cook time: 20 minutes

- **2 tablespoons olive oil**
- **1 tablespoon unbleached or all-purpose flour**
- **½ cup dry white wine**
- **2 cups chicken broth**
- **½ cup finely chopped celery heart, with leaves**
- **3 cloves garlic, minced**
- **Juice of ½ lemon**
- **1 can (16 ounces) water-packed artichoke hearts, drained and quartered**
- **Salt**
- **Ground black pepper**
- **1 pound whole wheat linguine**
- **½ cup (2 ounces) freshly grated Parmesan cheese**

Warm the oil in a large saucepan over medium heat. When hot, stir in the flour and cook, stirring, for 1 to 2 minutes, or until golden brown. Add the wine, broth, celery, and garlic. Bring to a boil, then reduce the heat and simmer uncovered for 10 minutes. Add the lemon juice and artichoke hearts and simmer for 5 minutes longer. Remove from the heat and season with salt and pepper to taste.

Meanwhile, cook the pasta according to package directions, drain, and return to the pot. Add the artichoke sauce and toss gently to combine over low heat for 1 to 2 minutes.

Place in a large serving bowl, stir in the cheese, and serve immediately.

Makes 6 servings

Per serving: *400 calories, 17 g protein, 66 g carbohydrate, 8 g fat, 5 mg cholesterol, 590 mg sodium, 12 g fiber*

Diet Exchanges: *0 milk, 1½ vegetable, 0 fruit, 4 bread, ½ meat, 1 fat*

4 Carb Choices

Kitchen Tip

Instead of artichoke hearts, you can also try one of the following: fresh asparagus, broccoli, or broccoli rabe, lightly steamed and chopped; 1 can water-packed tuna, drained and flaked; or 2 cups cooked cannellini beans. You can also add olive slices or a handful of fresh chopped tomatoes to any of the variations.

GREAT LOW-FAT COOKING STYLES: ITALIAN

You can add Italian zest to just about any cut of meat, poultry, or fish by brushing on this savory herbed oil before broiling or pan-grilling. One recipe flavors about 1¼ pounds of meat or fish. It's especially good on chicken, thin boneless pork chops, and swordfish slices.

Herbed Oil. In a cup, mix 1½ tablespoons extra-virgin olive oil, 2 crushed garlic cloves (use a press), 1½ teaspoons dried rosemary (or 1 tablespoon fresh), ¼ teaspoon salt, and ⅛ teaspoon ground black pepper.

Italian food needs a sauce, and this super-easy marinara will become a favorite. It makes enough to coat 1 pound of pasta (serving 4 to 6), and it's also delicious on grilled chicken or pork. For a heartier meal, add your favorite meatballs, broiled sliced turkey sausage, or sliced portobello mushrooms.

Marinara Sauce. In a large, heavy saucepan, cook 4 large peeled and smashed garlic cloves (smash with the side of a chef's knife) in 2 tablespoons extra-virgin olive oil over medium heat, stirring and pressing down on the garlic, for 4 minutes, or until it just turns golden.

Carefully (the pan is hot!) stir in a 28-ounce can whole tomatoes in puree (crush them with your hands first), ¼ teaspoon each dried oregano and salt, and ⅛ to ¼ teaspoon red-pepper flakes. Bring to a boil. Reduce the heat and simmer, partially covered, mashing the tomatoes with the side of a spoon, for 15 minutes, or until lightly thickened. If you like, stir in a handful of slivered fresh basil.

Gianna's Pasta

Giovanna Kranenberg, Cambridge, Minnesota

"So very quick, easy, and delicious!"

Prep time: 10 minutes; Cook time: 20 minutes

2 tablespoons olive oil
1½ cups mixed finely chopped red, yellow, and orange bell peppers
½ medium onion, finely chopped
1 small clove garlic, minced
8 ounces white mushrooms, sliced
4 cups fresh broccoli florets
½ cup Marsala wine
1½ cups penne
½ cup grated Parmesan cheese
Salt
Ground black pepper

Warm the oil in a large nonstick skillet over medium heat. When hot, add the bell peppers, onion, and garlic and cook, stirring occasionally, for about 2 minutes, or until crisp-tender. Add the mushrooms and cook for about 2 minutes longer. Add the broccoli and stir to combine. Add the wine, partially cover the pan, and cook for about 10 minutes longer, or until the broccoli is bright green and tender.

Meanwhile, in a large pot, cook the penne according to package directions, drain, and place in a large bowl. Add the broccoli mixture and toss gently to combine. Sprinkle with cheese, season with salt and pepper to taste, and serve.

Makes 4 servings

Per serving: *268 calories, 10 g protein, 28 g carbohydrate, 10 g fat, 8 mg cholesterol, 453 mg sodium, 7 g fiber*

Diet Exchanges: *0 milk, 2 vegetable, 0 fruit, 1 bread, 1 meat, 2½ fat*

2 Carb Choices

Quick Tomato-Basil Pasta

Julie Harte, Gainesville, Georgia

Prep time: 10 minutes; Cook time: 13 minutes

- **½ pound angel hair pasta**
- **1 tablespoon olive oil**
- **2 tablespoons minced garlic**
- **1 pound plum tomatoes, chopped**
- **Salt**
- **Ground black pepper**
- **¾ cup (3 ounces) freshly grated Parmesan cheese**

Cook the pasta according to package directions. Drain and place in a large bowl.

Meanwhile, warm the oil in a medium skillet over medium-high heat. When hot, add the garlic and cook, stirring, for 1 minute, or until fragrant. Add the tomatoes and cook for about 10 minutes longer. Season with salt and pepper and pour over the cooked pasta. Top with the cheese, toss gently, and serve.

Makes 4 servings

Per serving: *270 calories, 12 g protein, 37 g carbohydrate, 9 g fat, 11 mg cholesterol, 365 mg sodium, 3 g fiber*

Diet Exchanges: *0 milk, 1 vegetable, 0 fruit, 2 bread, 0 meat, 1 fat*

2½ Carb Choices

SECRETS OF WEIGHT-LOSS WINNERS

• Give it away! After company leaves, give away leftover food to neighbors, doormen, or delivery people, or take it to work the next day.

—Prevention.com

• When I was overweight, I developed the habit of wearing oversized clothing to hide my weight gain. As I began to lose weight, I forced myself to wear tighter fitting clothes as an incentive to continue to lose. When I felt the clothes loosen on my body over time, wearing tighter clothes motivated me to lose more. Sometimes it's easy to hide inside oversized clothes rather than confront the weight problem.

—Charissa Bosch, Fox Valley, Saskatchewan, Canada

• Get calories from foods you chew, not beverages. Have fresh fruit instead of fruit juice.

—Prevention.com

Spaghetti Squash with Stir-Fry Vegetables

Linda Yamali, Merrick, New York

Prep time: 5 minutes; Cook time: 24 minutes
Stand time: 10 minutes

- **1 medium spaghetti squash (2½–3 pounds)**
- **1 teaspoon olive oil**
- **1 bag (10 ounces) fresh or frozen Asian vegetable mix**
- **¼ cup prepared stir-fry sauce**

With a fork, pierce the skin of the spaghetti squash and place on a microwaveable dish. Cover with wax paper and microwave on high power for 5 to 7 minutes, rotate, and microwave for 3 to 5 minutes longer, or until tender. Let stand for 10 minutes, then cut in half and scrape the squash strands into a large serving bowl.

Meanwhile, warm the oil in a large skillet over medium-high heat and add the vegetable mix. Cook, tossing, for 5 to 7 minutes, or until the vegetables are crisp-tender. Add the stir-fry sauce and turn the vegetables to coat. Cook for 5 minutes longer. Add to the spaghetti squash, toss gently, and serve.

Makes 4 servings

Per serving: *178 calories, 5 g protein, 32 g carbohydrate, 4 g fat, 0 mg cholesterol, 1,020 mg sodium, 5 g fiber*

Diet Exchanges: *0 milk, 5½ vegetable, 0 fruit, 0 bread, 0 meat, ½ fat*

2 Carb Choices

GRAINS COOKING SCHOOL

Good carbohydrates such as fiber-rich grains can play an important role in low-calorie eating. They are a great addition to many meals, including salads, soups, sautés, and meat dishes. Just be sure to watch portion sizes.

Basics

To choose: Freshness is an important consideration when buying grains. Whole grains, which have a higher fat content and a greater tendency to turn rancid, are more perishable than refined grains. Shop where there is a large turnover of grains and buy them in small quantities. If possible, sniff them: They should smell clean, never stale or musty.

To store: Store grains in tightly covered jars either at room temperature or in the refrigerator or freezer. Always refrigerate grains with a high oil content, such as wheat germ.

To cook fluffy grains: Use a wide pan like a Dutch oven or a deep skillet; a heavy bottom or nonstick coating makes cleanup easier.

To reheat cooked grains: Put the grains in a saucepan with a thin layer of water. Cover and simmer until heated through. Or place in a microwaveable dish, drizzle with water, cover with a lid or waxed paper, and microwave on high power until steamy.

Flavor Tips

To boost flavor: Before cooking grains, toast them in a skillet over medium heat, just until fragrant. You can also cook grains in canned broth instead of water, or use half broth and half water. Reduce or eliminate the salt.

To add flavor to cooked grains: Stir in sliced scallions, diced tomato, chopped fresh parsley, chives, or fresh leafy herbs, such as basil, mint, or cilantro. Or drizzle with a small amount of fruity olive oil, or sprinkle with freshly grated Parmesan cheese.

Cooking times for grains: Most grains are incredibly easy to cook. For those listed below, measure the water into a heavy-bottomed saucepan and bring to a boil (unless otherwise indicated). Add ¼ teaspoon salt. Then, stir in the grain and return to a boil. Reduce the heat to medium-low, cover, and simmer until tender. If necessary, drain off any excess liquid.

Grain	Amount of Grain (cups)	Water (cups)	Cooking Directions	Yield (cups)
Barley, quick-cooking	1¼	2	Simmer 10–12 min	3
Buckwheat groats (kasha)	⅔	1½	Add to cold water; bring to a boil; cover and simmer 10–12 min, or follow directions on package for toasting dry in a skillet and stirring in an egg, to keep the kernels separate	2
Bulgur	1	2	Add to cold water; bring to a boil; cover and simmer 12–15 min or, if using in a salad, soak in warm water to cover for 12 to 30 min; drain	3
Cornmeal	1	2¾	Combine cornmeal and 1 cup cold water; add to the 2¾ cups boiling water; cover and simmer 10 min, stirring often	3½
Farina, quick-cooking	¾	3½	Simmer 2–3 min; stir constantly	3
Hominy grits, quick-cooking	¾	3	Simmer 5 min	3
Millet	¾	2	Simmer 15–20 min; let stand, covered, 5 min	3
Oats, rolled, quick-cooking	1½	3	Simmer 1 min; let stand, covered, 3 min	3
Quinoa	¾	1½	Rinse thoroughly for 2 minutes; simmer 12–15 min	2¾
Rice, brown	1	2¼	Simmer 35–45 min; let stand, covered, 5 min	3
Rice, white	1	2	Simmer 15 min; let stand, covered, 5 min	3
Rye berries	¾	2½	Soak overnight in the 2½ cups water; do not drain; bring to a boil, reduce heat, cover, and simmer 30 min	2
Wheat, cracked	⅔	1½	Add to cold water; bring to a boil, cover, and simmer 12–15 min; let stand, covered, 5 min	2
Wheat berries	¾	2½	Soak overnight in the 2½ cups water; do not drain; bring to a boil, reduce heat, cover, and simmer 30 min	2
Wild rice	1	2	Simmer 45–55 min	2⅔

Vegetable Stir-Fry

Mary Schneider, Oxnard, California

Prep time: 10 minutes; Cook time: 25 minutes

- **1 box (16 ounces) red beans and long-grain rice mix**
- **2 tablespoons olive oil**
- **1 small sweet onion, cut into wedges**
- **1 large red or yellow bell pepper, cut into strips**
- **4 ribs celery, sliced on the diagonal**
- **3 medium zucchini, sliced**
- **½ cup white mushrooms (optional)**
- **½ teaspoon ground black pepper**

Prepare the rice mix according to package directions.

Meanwhile, warm the oil in a large skillet or wok over medium-high heat. When hot, add the onion, bell pepper, celery, zucchini, mushrooms (if using), and black pepper. Cook, stirring frequently, for about 10 minutes, or until the onions are soft and translucent. Serve over the red beans and rice.

Makes 4 servings

Per serving: *288 calories, 10 g protein, 48 g carbohydrate, 8 g fat, 0 mg cholesterol, 715 mg sodium, 7 g fiber*

Diet Exchanges: *0 milk, 1 vegetable, 0 fruit, 2½ bread, 0 meat, 1½ fat*

3 Carb Choices

Swiss Chard and Mushrooms over Rice

Dawn Michelsen, Freeland, Washington

"This delicious dish is light enough to allow you to enjoy dessert—completely guilt-free!"

Prep time: 10 minutes; Cook time: 45 minutes

1½ cups brown rice
1 tablespoon olive oil
½ large onion, chopped
1 clove garlic, sliced
½ cup chopped red bell pepper
1 bunch Swiss chard, coarsely chopped
½ pound cremini mushrooms, sliced
Salt
Ground black pepper
1 teaspoon balsamic vinegar

Prepare the rice according to package directions.

Meanwhile, warm the olive oil in a large saucepan over medium-high heat. When hot, add the onion, garlic, and bell pepper and cook for 2 to 3 minutes, or until tender. Add the Swiss chard and mushrooms and cook for 3 to 5 minutes, or until the chard is wilted and the mushrooms are soft. Season with the salt, pepper, and balsamic vinegar. Spoon over the rice and serve.

Makes 4 servings

Per serving: *230 calories, 7 g protein, 41 g carbohydrate, 5 g fat, 0 mg cholesterol, 50 mg sodium, 5 g fiber*

Diet Exchanges: *0 milk, 1½ vegetable, 0 fruit, 2 bread, 0 meat, 1 fat*

3 Carb Choices

Mediterranean Ratatouille

Sheila Adams, Vancouver, British Columbia, Canada

Prep time: 20 minutes; Cook time: 45 minutes

¼ cup olive oil
2 large onions, finely chopped
2–4 cloves garlic
1 large eggplant, cut into 1" cubes
3–4 medium green bell peppers, cut into 1" chunks
4–6 small zucchini, cut into ¼" slices
5–6 large ripe tomatoes, finely chopped, or 1 can (28 ounces) diced tomatoes
1 teaspoon salt
1 teaspoon sugar
2 teaspoons dried oregano

Warm the oil in a large pot over medium-high heat. When hot, add the onions and garlic and cook for about 10 minutes, or until tender. Add the eggplant and bell peppers and cook for 5 minutes longer, stirring frequently. Add the zucchini, tomatoes (with juice), salt, sugar, and oregano and simmer, uncovered, for about 30 minutes, or until the vegetables are tender. Adjust the seasonings and serve hot or cold.

Makes 4 servings

Per serving: *268 calories, 6 g protein, 34 g carbohydrate, 14 g fat, 0 mg cholesterol, 855 mg sodium, 11 g fiber*

Diet Exchanges: *0 milk, 5 vegetable, 0 fruit, ½ bread, 0 meat, 2½ fat*

2 Carb Choices

Quick Veggie Bake

Tammy Kuettel, Portland, Oregon

Prep time: 20 minutes
Cook time: 1 hour 15 minutes

- **½ cup vegetable or chicken broth**
- **2 tablespoons olive oil**
- **2 yams or sweet potatoes (about 1½ pounds), cubed**
- **1 large sweet onion, sliced into rings**
- **2 carrots, sliced**
- **8 ounces white mushrooms, sliced**
- **1–2 cloves garlic, thinly sliced**
- **2 cups fresh green beans, cut into 2" pieces**
- **1 can (15 ounces) kidney beans, rinsed and drained**
- **1 teaspoon dried Italian seasoning**
- **¼ teaspoon celery seeds**
- **½ teaspoon dried thyme**
- **½ teaspoon dried sage**
- **½ teaspoon paprika**
- **4 scallions, sliced**

Preheat the oven to 425°F. In a small saucepan, bring the broth to a boil.

Meanwhile, in a 3-quart baking dish, toss the oil with the yams, onion, carrots, mushrooms, garlic, green beans, and kidney beans. Add the Italian seasoning, celery seeds, thyme, sage, and paprika and mix. Pour the hot broth over the dish and cover with foil.

Bake for 1 hour, or until tender, tossing the vegetables every 15 minutes. Bake for 10 to 15 minutes longer if necessary. Garnish with the scallions and serve.

Makes 4 servings

Per serving: *277 calories, 10 g protein, 45 g carbohydrate, 7 g fat, 0 mg cholesterol, 412 mg sodium, 11 g fiber*

Diet Exchanges: *0 milk, 3 vegetable, 0 fruit, 2 bread, 0 meat, 1½ fat*

3 Carb Choices

Cabbage Roll Casserole

Peg Davis, Dunmore, Alberta, Canada

"This dish is hearty yet very low in calories and fat."

Prep time: 15 minutes
Cook time: 1 hour 30 minutes

- **½ large onion, chopped**
- **1 clove garlic, minced**
- **½ small head cabbage, chopped (about 10 cups)**
- **2 carrots, thinly sliced**
- **1 green bell pepper, chopped**
- **1 cup rice**
- **2 cans (28 ounces each) diced tomatoes**
- **2 tablespoons packed brown sugar**
- **¼ cup white vinegar**
- **1 teaspoon dried thyme**
- **¼ teaspoon salt**
- **1 teaspoon Dijon mustard**

Preheat the oven to 350°F. Coat a 13" × 9" baking dish with cooking spray.

In a large bowl, combine the onion, garlic, cabbage, carrots, and bell pepper. Add the rice and mix well.

In another large bowl, combine the tomatoes (with juice), sugar, vinegar, thyme, salt, and mustard. Stir into the cabbage mixture until blended, then turn into the prepared baking dish. Do not stir.

Bake, covered, stirring well every 30 minutes, for 1½ hours, or until the cabbage is soft and the rice is cooked.

Makes 8 servings

Per serving: *162 calories, 4 g protein, 35 g carbohydrate, 1 g fat, 0 mg cholesterol, 239 mg sodium, 5 g fiber*

Diet Exchanges: *0 milk, 2 vegetable, 0 fruit, 1½ bread, 0 meat, 0 fat*

2 Carb Choices

Kitchen Tip

Add 8 ounces of cooked beef, soy crumbles, or lean ground turkey to the cabbage mixture and bake for a great protein boost!

Italian Vegetable Casserole

Karen Schlyter, Calgary, Alberta, Canada

"My biggest problem when trying to lose weight is getting my daily dose of vegetables. I quickly get sick of salads, so I came up with this way of making veggies that I love."

Prep time: 10 minutes; Cook time: 35 minutes

1 small fennel bulb, sliced
1 medium onion, sliced
2 cloves garlic, minced
2 tablespoons olive oil
2 medium zucchini, sliced (about 2 cups)
1 cup sliced white mushrooms
½ teaspoon salt
1 teaspoon ground black pepper
1 tablespoon dried oregano
2 tablespoons dried parsley
1 tablespoon dried basil
1 can (8 ounces) no-sodium tomato sauce
1 can (14½ ounces) diced tomatoes
1 cup (4 ounces) shredded part-skim mozzarella cheese
¼ cup grated Parmesan cheese

Preheat the oven to 400°F.

In a 13" × 9" baking dish, combine the fennel, onion, garlic, and oil. Place in the oven and bake, uncovered, for 5 minutes, or until slightly softened. Add the zucchini, mushrooms, salt, pepper, oregano, parsley, and basil, stir well, and return to the oven for 15 minutes. Stir in the tomato sauce and diced tomatoes (with juice) and top with the mozzarella and Parmesan cheeses. Bake for 15 minutes longer, or until the sauce is bubbling and the cheese is melted.

Makes 4 servings

Per serving: *250 calories, 13 g protein, 23 g carbohydrate, 13 g fat, 20 mg cholesterol, 690 mg sodium, 7 g fiber*

Diet Exchanges: *0 milk, 3½ vegetable, 0 fruit, 0 bread, 1½ meat, 2 fat*

2 Carb Choices

Summer Squash Casserole

G. C. McMillen, Hot Springs Village, Arkansas

"I love veggie casseroles, but they're often high in calories and fat. This one is tasty and low in fat, too!"

Prep time: 10 minutes; Cook time: 40 minutes

6 medium summer squash or zucchini (about 2 pounds), sliced
½ cup chopped onion
½ cup chopped bell pepper
½ cup shredded reduced-fat Cheddar cheese
½ cup part-skim ricotta cheese
salt
Ground black pepper
1 egg, beaten
2 tablespoons chopped fresh parsley
½ cup crumbled reduced-fat crackers

Preheat the oven to 350°F. Coat a 1½-quart baking dish with cooking spray.

Place a steamer basket in a large pot with 2" of water. Bring to a boil over high heat. Place the squash in the basket and steam for 3 to 5 minutes, or until tender. Drain and place in a large bowl.

Coat a medium skillet with cooking spray and set over medium-high heat. Add the onion and bell pepper and cook for 5 minutes, or until soft. Fold into the bowl with the squash along with the Cheddar and ricotta cheeses. Season with salt and pepper to taste. Fold in the beaten egg and spread the mixture evenly in the prepared baking dish. Top with the parsley and crackers.

Bake, uncovered, for 30 minutes.

Makes 2 servings

Per serving: *370 calories, 25 g protein, 40 g carbohydrate, 15 g fat, 145 mg cholesterol, 640 mg sodium, 7 g fiber*

Diet Exchanges: *0 milk, 4 vegetable, 0 fruit, 1 bread, 2½ meat, 1½ fat*

2 Carb Choices

To choose summer squash, look for a firm squash with glossy, brightly colored skin. Small to medium-size squash always have the best texture and flavor. Larger ones tend to be watery and have more seeds.

Tamale Pie

Juniper Bartlett, Grants Pass, Oregon

"This low-fat, low-calorie dish is packed with nutrition and very filling. I don't feel deprived after eating it."

Prep time: 15 minutes; Cook time: 30 minutes
Stand time: 2 hours

- **2 cups water**
- **¾ cup cornmeal**
- **½ cup chopped onion**
- **1 can (15 ounces) black beans, rinsed and drained**
- **1 can (4 ounces) diced green mild chiles, drained**
- **½ cup shredded reduced-fat Cheddar cheese**
- **¾ cup fat-free sour cream**
- **1 cup mild or hot salsa**

Coat two 9" × 9" baking pans with cooking spray.

Place the water in a 4- to 6-quart saucepan and bring to a boil over medium-high heat. When boiling, add the cornmeal in a slow, steady stream, whisking constantly. When the mixture returns to a boil, reduce the heat and simmer, stirring frequently, for 15 to 20 minutes, or until thick. Remove from the heat, spread equally into the prepared pans, and let cool for several hours at room temperature.

Preheat the oven to 350°F.

Spread the onion, beans, chiles, ¼ cup of the cheese, the sour cream, and the salsa over the cornmeal in one of the baking pans. Remove the cornmeal from the other pan and place it on top, followed by the remaining ¼ cup of cheese.

Bake, uncovered, for 15 to 20 minutes.

Makes 4 servings

Per serving: *282 calories, 18 g protein, 43 carbohydrate, 4 fat, 6 g cholesterol, 891 sodium, 9 g fiber*

Diet Exchanges: *½ milk, 1½ vegetable, 0 fruit, 2 bread, 1½ meat, ½ fat*

3 Carb Choices

Kitchen Tip

You can substitute shredded chicken or ground beef for the beans in this recipe.

Tricolor Pasta Casserole

Dawn Eckman, Spring Lake Heights, New Jersey

Prep time: 15 minutes; Cook time: 58 minutes

16 ounces tricolor pasta
1 tablespoon olive oil
3 cloves garlic, minced
1 small onion, finely chopped
½ cup chopped green or red bell pepper
1 (15-ounce) container fat-free or part-skim ricotta cheese
2 cups (8 ounces) shredded fat-free mozzarella
2 cups fresh or frozen broccoli florets
1 package (10 ounces) frozen chopped spinach, thawed and squeezed dry
¼ cup grated reduced-fat Parmesan cheese
1 jar (26 ounces) marinara sauce

Preheat the oven to 350°F. Spray a 13" × 9" baking dish with cooking spray.

Cook the pasta according to package instructions and drain.

Meanwhile, warm the oil in a large skillet over medium-high heat. When hot, add the garlic, onion, and pepper and cook for about 5 minutes, or until soft. Set aside.

In a large bowl, combine the cooked pasta with the ricotta cheese, 1 cup of the mozzarella cheese, the broccoli, spinach, Parmesan cheese, and marinara sauce. Add the cooked garlic, onion, and pepper. Transfer to the prepared baking dish and top with the remaining 1 cup of mozzarella cheese.

Bake, covered, for 30 minutes, then uncover and bake for 15 minutes longer, until bubbling.

Makes 12 servings

Per serving: *246 calories, 14 g protein, 21 g carbohydrate, 12 g fat, 23 mg cholesterol, 453 mg sodium, 3 g fiber*

Diet Exchanges: *0 milk, 1 vegetable, 0 fruit, 1 bread, 1½ meat, 2 fat*

1½ Carb Choices

Chipotle-Grilled Turkey

Jeffrey Stansberry, Knoxville, Tennessee

"This low-carb dish is amazingly satisfying. For a change of pace, serve with baked tortilla strips and your favorite fixings."

Prep time: 10 minutes; Marinate time: 2 hours
Cook time: 35 minutes

RELISH

- 1 cup coarsely chopped tomatillos
- Juice and grated zest from ½ lime
- 3 tablespoons olive oil
- 1 tablespoon chopped fresh cilantro
- 2 cloves garlic, minced
- ¼ teaspoon salt
- ¼ teaspoon ground black pepper
- Pinch of sugar

TURKEY

- ½ cup chipotle salsa
- ⅓ cup lime juice
- ⅛ teaspoon ground cumin
- Ground black pepper
- 1 teaspoon sugar
- 1 pound turkey breast cutlet, lightly pounded to 1" thick
- 1 cup pickled jalapeño chile peppers, drained
- 1 tablespoon cider vinegar
- 2 tablespoons chopped fresh cilantro
- Baked tortilla chips

To make the relish: In a food processor, combine the tomatillos, lime juice, lime zest, oil, cilantro, garlic, salt, pepper, and sugar. Pulse until chunky. Transfer to a small bowl, cover, and refrigerate until ready to serve.

To make the turkey: In a small glass bowl, combine the salsa, lime juice, cumin, pepper, and sugar. Spread evenly onto the turkey and refrigerate in a resealable plastic bag for no more than 2 to 3 hours.

Preheat the oven to 400°F.

Remove the turkey from the marinade (reserve 3 tablespoons) and pat dry. On a heat-proof grill pan set over high heat, cook the turkey for 4 minutes per side. Transfer to a plate and set aside.

Spread the chiles on the grill pan. Pour the vinegar over the chiles, followed by the reserved marinade. Lay the turkey breast over the chiles. Cover loosely with foil and bake for 15 to 20 minutes. Bake uncovered for 5 minutes longer, or until the juices run clear.

Let the turkey rest for about 5 minutes, then slice against the grain into ¼" strips. Top with tomatillo relish and cilantro and serve with tortilla chips.

Makes 4 servings

Per serving: *233 calories, 28 g protein, 4 g carbohydrate, 11 g fat, 70 mg cholesterol, 202 mg sodium, 1 g fiber*

Diet Exchanges: *0 milk, ½ vegetable, 0 fruit, 0 bread, 3½ meat, 2 fat*

0 Carb Choices

Tandoori-Style Chicken with Rosemary

Sabiha Bholat, Pinon, Arizona

"This low-fat recipe is very filling and deliciously fragrant."

Prep time: 5 minutes; Marinate time: 1 to 8 hours; Cook time: 15 minutes

- **1 whole chicken, cut into 4 pieces, skin removed**
- **1 cup yogurt**
- **2 tablespoons garlic powder**
- **2 tablespoons ground ginger**
- **2 tablespoons ground cumin**
- **1 tablespoon olive oil**
- **2 teaspoons chili powder**
- **1 teaspoon ground cinnamon**
- **1 teaspoon ground nutmeg**
- **1 teaspoon salt**
- **1 teaspoon ground black pepper**
- **1 tablespoon dried rosemary leaves, crumbled**

Cut several shallow slits into each piece of chicken (this will help the flavors soak into the chicken as it marinates). Set aside.

In a large bowl, combine the yogurt, garlic powder, ginger, cumin, oil, chili powder, cinnamon, nutmeg, salt, pepper, and rosemary. Stir well and add the chicken pieces, turning to coat. Cover and refrigerate for at least 1 hour, but preferably overnight, turning the pieces occasionally.

Preheat the grill to high.

Remove the chicken from the yogurt mixture and drain off the excess.

Grill for about 10 to 15 minutes per side, or until a thermometer inserted in the thickest portion registers 170°F and the juices run clear.

Makes 4 servings

Per serving: *112 calories, 14 g protein, 3 g carbohydrate, 5 g fat, 45 mg cholesterol, 656 mg sodium, 0 g fiber*

Diet Exchanges: *0 milk, 0 vegetable, ½ fruit, 0 bread, 0 meat, ½ fat*

0 Carb Choices

Craig Downey

VITAL STATS

Weight lost: A total of 120 pounds

Time to goal: Six months for the first 70 pounds, 3 years and holding for the remaining 50 pounds

Quick tip: Use the "one handful" rule: Eat no more than a handful of any food type at one time (a handful of carbs, a handful of protein, and so on).

In high school, Craig Downey had relied on exercise to keep him fit despite his imposing size. When his activity level dropped, so did his lean muscle mass—and the pounds went from solid to soft.

"In the summer before my junior year of college, I weighed 330 pounds and was finding it harder and harder to move around quickly. I knew I would have to get fit before school started in order to play football. So my brother and I went on what we called our 'Spartan' diet. I ate minimal amounts of food and worked out like a dog—and I wound up losing 70 pounds in about 6 months. I know now that this approach is far from healthy, but I was young and looking for a quick fix.

"In the years after graduating college, I found that I would gain 20 pounds, drop them, and gain them back again. By the time I got tired of the yo-yo cycle, I was hovering at around 270 pounds—and it wasn't muscle weight. My clothes no longer fit.

"The turning point came when my wife and I went out to celebrate our anniversary. After a huge meal, we decided to visit an old college friend. When he answered the door, my jaw dropped. My old 'eating buddy' (who had matched me pound for pound) was in such amazing shape that I barely recognized him. We talked about what had changed for him and he told me about a program called Body for Life. I decided immediately to make the same changes that my friend had.

"I started the 12-week program, stuck to it religiously, and never felt better. The changes I made were really very basic: I ate more often (up to six meals a day) but took much smaller portions. Also, I moved my exercise regimen to the morning so I wouldn't skip it.

"I have stuck with this program for 3 years now, and my weight is down to a trim 210. Getting started really felt like a 'program,' and it was a challenge for me to stick with it. But now it's just the way I live my life, and my family and friends know it. I also feel like a positive role model for my two children, and that makes it totally worthwhile to me."

Lime Chicken

Christie Neal, Auburn, Washington

"Lots of flavor without the fat!"

Marinate time: 2 hours; Cook time: 20 minutes

- **½ cup lime juice**
- **¼ cup chopped fresh cilantro**
- **Salt**
- **Ground black pepper**
- **2 boneless, skinless chicken breasts (about 12 ounces)**
- **1 tablespoon olive oil**

In a resealable plastic bag, combine the lime juice and cilantro, then season with salt and pepper to taste. Rub the chicken with the oil and place in the bag. Refrigerate for 2 hours.

Preheat the grill to medium-high and cook the chicken for about 10 minutes per side, or until a thermometer inserted in the thickest portion registers 160°F and the juices run clear.

Makes 4 servings

Per serving: *130 calories, 20 g protein, 3 g carbohydrate, 4½ g fat, 50 mg cholesterol, 130 mg sodium, 0 g fiber*

Diet Exchanges: *0 milk, 0 vegetable, 0 fruit, 0 bread, 3 meat, 1 fat*

0 Carb Choices

Kitchen Tip

To keep lean meats moist, avoid overcooking. If you have a covered grill, use the cover during part or all of the grilling. If your grill does not have a cover, improvise by covering the food with a large, disposable foil roasting pan.

192 Calories

Lovely Barbecue Chicken

Elizabeth Templeton, Ancaster, Ontario, Canada

"This recipe provides you with a flavorful marinade that's already mixed and lower in calories than commercial marinades."

Prep time: 5 minutes; Cook time: 25 minutes
Marinate time: 24 hours

- **¼ cup low-fat vinaigrette dressing, such as sun-dried tomato**
- **2 tablespoons Worcestershire sauce**
- **2 tablespoons spicy barbecue sauce**
- **12 skinless, boneless chicken thighs, trimmed of visible fat (about 3 pounds)**

In a small bowl, combine the dressing, Worcestershire sauce, and barbecue sauce. Place the chicken in a large, shallow dish and pour the marinade on top, turning to coat. Cover and refrigerate for up to 24 hours.

Preheat the grill to high. Grill the chicken pieces, turning often, for 20 to 25 minutes, or until a thermometer inserted in the thickest portion registers 170°F, the juices run clear, and the chicken is golden on all sides.

Makes 6 servings

Per serving: *192 calories, 27 g protein, 5 g carbohydrate, 6 g fat, 115 mg cholesterol, 289 mg sodium, 0 g fiber*

Diet Exchanges: *0 milk, 0 vegetable, 0 fruit, ½ bread, 4 meat, 1 fat*

½ Carb Choice

Kitchen Tip

This chicken makes a great entrée, or it can be cut up as a salad topper.

Balsamic Chicken

Barb Neri, Syracuse, New York

"Having a quick meal makes it easier to stay on a program and avoid buying takeout. This chicken is great as a main course or as an addition to a spinach salad."

Prep time: 5 minutes; Cook time: 15 minutes

- **1 tablespoon olive oil**
- **1 pound boneless, skinless chicken tenders**
- **¼ teaspoon garlic salt**
- **2 tablespoons balsamic vinegar**

Warm the oil in a large skillet over medium-high heat. Season the tenders with the garlic salt and cook for 3 to 4 minutes, or until browned on both sides. Add the vinegar, toss to coat, and cook for about 10 minutes longer, or until no longer pink and the juices run clear.

Makes 4 servings

Per serving: *140 calories, 26 g protein, 1 g carbohydrate, 4 g fat, 66 mg cholesterol, 160 mg sodium, 0 g fiber*

Diet Exchanges: *0 milk, 0 vegetable, 0 fruit, 0 bread, 3½ meat, 0 fat*

0 Carb Choices

SECRETS OF WEIGHT-LOSS WINNERS

• Drink a full glass of water before each meal. It helps you on your way to eight glasses a day and fills you up slightly, so you eat less.

—Barbara Ragusa, Pompano Beach, Florida

• My staff of seven and I all purchased exercise balls, which we keep under our desks. We sit on the balls as chairs when we're not in meetings. The simple act of balancing on the balls while working, plus a regime of discreet exercises, helps build muscles.

—Candice McDonald, Radium Springs, New Mexico

• At a buffet, eating a little of everything guarantees high calories. Decide on three or four things, only one of which is high in calories. Save that for last so there's less chance of overeating.

—Prevention.com

Pizza Pizzazz Chicken

Rene Collins, Clute, Texas

"This family favorite is a low-carb, low-fat, and low-calorie main dish packed with flavor!"

Prep time: 8 minutes; Cook time: 15 minutes

4 small boneless, skinless chicken breast halves (about 1 pound)
Salt
Ground black pepper
1 teaspoon olive oil
½ cup marinara sauce
1 can (4 ounces) mushrooms
1 clove garlic, minced
¼ teaspoon dried oregano
4 slices part-skim mozzarella cheese (about 4 ounces)
12 slices turkey pepperoni
6 black olives, sliced
2 tablespoons grated Parmesan cheese

Place each chicken breast between 2 sheets of plastic wrap and pound lightly with a meat mallet to flatten. Season with a little salt and pepper and set aside.

Warm the oil in a large nonstick skillet over medium-high heat. When hot, add the chicken and cook for about 4 minutes per side, or until a thermometer inserted in the thickest portion registers 160°F and the juices run clear. Transfer to a plate and set aside.

In the same skillet, combine the marinara sauce, mushrooms, garlic, and oregano. Season with salt and pepper to taste. Bring to a gentle boil, cover, reduce the heat, and simmer for 5 minutes.

Arrange the chicken on top of the sauce and lay 1 slice of mozzarella on each breast, topped with 3 slices of pepperoni and a few olive slices. Cover and let stand until the cheese is melted. Sprinkle with Parmesan cheese and serve.

Makes 4 servings

Per serving: *320 calories, 42 g protein, 6 g carbohydrate, 13 g fat, 110 mg cholesterol, 860 mg sodium, 1 g fiber*

Diet Exchanges: *0 milk, 0 vegetable, 0 fruit, ½ bread, 6 meat, 1 fat*

½ Carb Choice

Italian Chicken and Vegetables

Sharon Elzinga, Tinley Park, Illinois

"Because both my husband and I work full-time, I needed a healthy recipe that could be prepared in less than half an hour or I'd find myself 'grazing' while preparing dinner. I always strive to keep meals as colorful as possible, and to use only meats that cook up quickly."

Prep time: 10 minutes; Cook time: 25 minutes

- **1 tablespoon vegetable oil**
- **1 pound small boneless, skinless chicken breasts**
- **2 medium sweet potatoes, peeled and cubed**
- **3 tablespoons water**
- **2 small zucchini, sliced**
- **2 small yellow squash, sliced**
- **1 cup asparagus tips, cut into 1" pieces**
- **1½ teaspoons dried Italian seasoning**
- **Salt**

Warm the oil in a large skillet over medium-high heat. When hot, add the chicken and cook for about 5 minutes per side, or until brown. Reduce the heat and add the sweet potatoes and 2 tablespoons of the water. Cover and simmer for 10 minutes. Add the zucchini, squash, and asparagus, then sprinkle with the Italian seasoning and salt. Add the remaining 1 tablespoon of water, cover, and cook for 5 minutes longer, or until the vegetables are fork-tender.

Makes 4 servings

Per serving: *260 calories, 30 g protein, 23 g carbohydrate, 5 g fat, 65 mg cholesterol, 250 mg sodium, 4 g fiber*

Diet Exchanges: *0 milk, 1 vegetable, 0 fruit, 1 bread, 4 meat, 1 fat*

1½ Carb Choices

382 Calories

Chicken Milano

Lori Witmer, Spring Grove, Pennsylvania

"This meal has become 'comfort food' for our whole family, especially on cold winter days. I usually make a triple batch so I can take it to work for lunch."

Prep time: 5 minutes; Cook time: 30 minutes

- **1 cup rice**
- **1 teaspoon olive oil**
- **1 pound boneless, skinless chicken breasts, cut into bite-size pieces**
- **1 medium onion, sliced**
- **1 small clove garlic, minced**
- **1 can ($10\frac{3}{4}$ ounces) tomato soup**
- **1 jar (4 ounces) mushrooms, drained**
- **2 medium zucchini, sliced**
- **$\frac{1}{2}$ teaspoon dried basil**
- **$\frac{1}{8}$ teaspoon red-pepper flakes**

Cook the rice according to package directions.

Meanwhile, warm the oil in a large skillet over medium-high heat. When hot, add the chicken and cook for about 5 minutes per side, or until a thermometer inserted in the thickest portion registers 160°F and the juices run clear. Transfer to a plate and set aside.

In the same skillet, combine the onion, garlic, tomato soup, mushrooms, zucchini, basil, and red-pepper flakes and bring to a boil, stirring occasionally. Immediately reduce the heat to low, cover, and simmer for about 15 minutes, or until the vegetables are tender. Add the chicken and heat until warmed through.

Spoon the chicken and vegetables over the rice and serve.

Makes 4 servings

Per serving: *382 calories, 34 g protein, 50 g carbohydrate, 5 g fat, 71 mg cholesterol, 430 mg sodium, 5 g fiber*

Diet Exchanges: *0 milk, 2 vegetable, 0 fruit, $2\frac{1}{2}$ bread, $3\frac{1}{2}$ meat, $\frac{1}{2}$ fat*

3 Carb Choices

Kitchen Tip

To reduce splatter when cooking boneless, skinless chicken breasts, pat them dry with paper towels and lightly coat with unbleached or all-purpose flour before adding to the preheated pan with a pair of tongs.

Lemon Chicken

Wilmer Myers, Broadway, Virginia

Prep time: 10 minutes; Cook time: 15 minutes
Stand time: 5 minutes

- **1 tablespoon olive oil**
- **1 pound boneless, skinless chicken breasts, cut into strips**
- **2 cloves garlic, minced**
- **½ cup onion, chopped**
- **1 carrot, grated**
- **Zest of 1 lemon, grated**
- **1 can (14½ ounces) chicken broth**
- **1 tablespoon parsley**
- **2 tablespoons sliced black olives**
- **2 cups quick-cooking white rice**

Warm the oil in a large skillet over medium-high heat. When hot, add the chicken and cook for 5 to 10 minutes, or until no longer pink and the juices run clear. During the last few minutes of cooking, add the garlic and onion.

When the chicken is done, stir in the carrot, lemon zest, broth, parsley, olives, and rice. Bring to a boil, then remove from the heat, cover, and let stand for 5 minutes. Fluff with a fork before serving.

Makes 4 servings

Per serving: *368 calories, 31 g protein, 40 g carbohydrate, 8 g fat, 66 mg cholesterol, 540 mg sodium, 1 g fiber*

Diet Exchanges: *0 milk, 1 vegetable, 0 fruit, 2½ bread, 4 meat, 1 fat*

3 Carb Choices

Ron's Mediterranean Chicken

Rosemary Noe, Swampscott, Massachusetts

Prep time: 7 minutes; Cook time: 30 minutes

- **2 tablespoons olive oil**
- **3 cloves garlic, minced**
- **1½ pounds chicken tenders**
- **½ cup Marsala wine**
- **2 tablespoons balsamic vinegar**
- **2 tablespoons dark raisins**
- **2 tablespoons pitted and chopped kalamata olives**
- **2 sprigs fresh rosemary, chopped**
- **½ teaspoon dried oregano**

Preheat the oven to 350°F. Coat a 13" × 9" baking dish with cooking spray.

Warm the oil in a large skillet over medium-high heat. When hot, add the garlic and cook for about 1 minute, or until fragrant. Add the chicken and cook for 3 to 4 minutes, or until lightly browned. Transfer the chicken to the prepared baking dish.

Using the same skillet, reduce the heat to medium-low and add the wine, vinegar, raisins, olives, rosemary, and oregano. Cook, stirring constantly, until the mixture comes to a boil. Pour over the chicken.

Bake, uncovered, for about 20 minutes until a thermometer inserted in the thickest part of the chicken registers 160°F and the juices run clear.

Makes 4 servings

Per serving: *327 calories, 40 g protein, 11 g carbohydrate, 9 g fat, 99 mg cholesterol, 146 mg sodium, 0 g fiber*

Diet Exchanges: *0 milk, 0 vegetable, ½ fruit, 0 bread, 6 meat, 1½ fat*

1 Carb Choice

American Mandarin Chicken

Tammy Kuettel, Portland, Oregon

Prep time: 7 minutes; Cook time: 45 minutes

- **1 tablespoon olive oil**
- **4 boneless, skinless chicken breast halves (about 1 pound)**
- **1 box (6 ounces) rice pilaf mix**
- **1 clove garlic, minced**
- **2½ cups reduced-sodium chicken broth**
- **1 can (6 ounces) mandarin oranges, drained**
- **2 scallions, sliced**
- **1 tablespoon chopped fresh cilantro**

Warm the oil in a large skillet over medium to high heat. When hot, add the chicken and cook for about 5 minutes per side, or until lightly golden. Add the rice mix and garlic and continue cooking until the grains turn golden. Add the broth and heat just until boiling, then cover the skillet and reduce the heat to low.

Simmer for 25 to 30 minutes, or until the rice is tender and a thermometer inserted in the thickest part of the chicken registers 160°F and the juices run clear. Remove from the heat and add the oranges, tossing gently. Top with the scallions and cilantro and serve.

Makes 4 servings

Per serving: *360 calories, 39 g protein, 36 g carbohydrate, 7 g fat, 85 mg cholesterol, 730 mg sodium, 2 g fiber*

Diet Exchanges: *0 milk, 0 vegetable, 0 fruit, 2 bread, 5 meat, 1 fat*

3 Carb Choices

Kitchen Tip

When thawing frozen chicken in the refrigerator, make sure the package is on a plate. That way, as the chicken thaws, you'll catch any juices that seep through the packaging and reduce the risk of spreading any harmful bacteria that might be present.

Thai Chicken Stir-Fry

Kristine Hibbs, Goulds, Newfoundland and Labrador, Canada

"I eat lots of fresh vegetables, but I needed to come up with ways to add flavor and variety so I wouldn't feel like I was eating the same old thing. This recipe was one of the many I made up to make food more interesting, and also to get myself to eat healthy and lose weight."

Prep time: 10 minutes; Cook time: 17 minutes

1 tablespoon olive or vegetable oil
½ pound boneless, skinless chicken breast, cut into bite-size pieces
½ cup sliced celery
½ cup sliced red bell pepper
½ cup sliced green bell pepper
½ cup sliced onion
½ cup sliced white mushrooms
1 cup broccoli florets
2 tablespoons Thai curry paste (see Kitchen Tip)
¼ cup light coconut milk

Warm the oil in a large skillet over medium to high heat. When hot, add the chicken and cook for about 4 minutes, or until no longer pink and the juices run clear. Transfer to a plate and set aside.

In the same skillet, combine the celery, bell peppers, onion, mushrooms, and broccoli and cook for about 5 minutes.

Meanwhile, in a small bowl, stir the curry paste and coconut milk until thoroughly combined. Add to the skillet along with the chicken. Cover and cook for about 7 minutes, or until the vegetables are tender and the flavors blend.

Makes 2 servings

Per serving: *260 calories, 29 g protein, 12 g carbohydrate, 10 g fat, 66 mg cholesterol, 390 mg sodium, 2 g fiber*

Diet Exchanges: *0 milk, 1½ vegetable, 0 fruit, 0 bread, 4 meat, 1½ fat*

1 Carb Choice

Kitchen Tip

Thai curry paste is a distinct blend of spices and peppers that usually has a hint of lemongrass in the mix. It is available in the Asian food section of most grocery stores.

Arroz con Pollo

Marisa Martino, Mahopac, New York

"Brown rice is rich in fiber and chicken breasts are low in fat. By adding vegetables, you get three food groups in one low-fat, hearty meal in one pot."

Prep time: 10 minutes; Cook time: 1 hour

- **1 tablespoon olive oil**
- **½ medium onion, finely chopped**
- **2 cloves garlic, minced**
- **4 split chicken breasts, skin removed**
- **1 cup tomato sauce**
- **1 cup water**
- **1 can (14½ ounces) chicken broth**
- **2 bay leaves**
- **2 teaspoons dried oregano**
- **Salt**
- **Ground black pepper**
- **1¼ cups brown rice**
- **2 cups frozen vegetable mix of your choice (optional)**

Warm the oil in a large skillet over medium to high heat. When hot, add the onion and garlic and cook for 2 to 3 minutes, or until just golden. Add the chicken and cook for 5 minutes per side, or until lightly browned. Transfer to a plate and set aside.

In the same skillet, combine the tomato sauce, water, broth, bay leaves, and oregano and stir well. Season with salt and pepper to taste and bring to a boil. Add the rice, reduce the heat to low, and simmer for about 10 minutes. Add the chicken, cover, and simmer for about 45 minutes longer. During the last 15 minutes of cooking, add the frozen vegetables and stir well. Fluff the rice before serving.

Makes 4 servings

Per serving: *463 calories, 35 g protein, 62 g carbohydrate, 8 g fat, 68 mg cholesterol, 892 mg sodium, 4 g fiber*

Diet Exchanges: *0 milk, 1½ vegetable, 0 fruit, 3½ bread, 4 meat, 1 fat*

4 Carb Choices

SHOPPING SAVVY

Rice, Nice and Easy

Uncle Ben's has decided to make it even more convenient for you to eat your grains. Check out Ready Rice—prepared rice that comes in a microwaveable pouch. Ready Rice goes from your pantry to steaming hot in just 90 seconds. Each 8.8-ounce pouch serves about two. We especially liked the brown rice and the long-grain and wild-rice mix. Available in grocery stores nationwide.

Photo courtesy of Uncle Ben's

Angel Hair Pasta with Chicken and Vegetables

Cindy Ferguson, Hampton, Prince Edward Island, Canada

Prep time: 15 minutes; Cook time: 20 minutes

- ½ pound angel hair pasta
- 2 boneless, skinless chicken breasts, cut into thin strips
- 1 tablespoon olive oil
- 1 cup snow peas
- 1 cup thinly sliced white mushrooms
- 2–3 carrots, cut into matchsticks (about 1 cup)
- ½ red bell pepper, cut into matchsticks (about ½ cup)
- 2 cloves garlic, minced
- ¼ cup mild oyster sauce
- 2 scallions, thinly sliced

In a large pot, cook the pasta according to package directions. Drain and set aside.

Meanwhile, coat a large skillet with cooking spray and set over medium heat. Add the chicken and cook, stirring constantly, for 3 to 4 minutes, or until the chicken is no longer pink and the juices run clear. Transfer to a medium bowl and set aside.

Wipe out the skillet with a paper towel and increase the heat to medium-high. Add the oil and heat for about 1 minute, then add the snow peas, mushrooms, carrots, and bell pepper. Cook, stirring constantly, for about 5 minutes, or until the vegetables brighten in color and become slightly tender.

Add the garlic and chicken for the last minute or two of cooking and heat through. Add the cooked pasta, oyster sauce, and scallions and toss until thoroughly coated. Serve immediately.

Makes 4 servings

Per serving: *380 calories, 29 g protein, 52 g carbohydrate, 5 g fat, 50 mg cholesterol, 190 mg sodium, 3 g fiber*

Diet Exchanges: *0 milk, 1½ vegetable, 0 fruit, 3 bread, 3 meat, 1 fat*

2 Carb Choices

Kitchen Tip

This dish makes great leftovers. Add some chicken bouillon to hot water, pour over the leftovers in a large saucepan, and reheat.

Chicken Penne

Mary Cancela, Tampa, Florida

"I eat one serving of this with a salad after a brisk 3-mile walk, waving hello to all of my neighbors."

Marinate: 2–24 hours; Prep time: 5 minutes
Cook time: 20 minutes

- **1 pound boneless, skinless chicken breasts, cut into bite-size pieces**
- **½ cup fat-free Italian dressing**
- **8 ounces mini penne**
- **1 tablespoon olive oil**
- **1 cup thinly sliced onion**
- **2 cloves garlic, crushed**
- **2 cups mixed sliced red, yellow, and green bell peppers**
- **1 pint grape tomatoes, halved**
- **Freshly grated Parmesan cheese**

In a medium bowl, combine the chicken and ¼ cup of the dressing. Cover and refrigerate for at least 2 hours.

Cook the penne according to the package directions. Reserve ½ cup of the pasta water, drain the rest, and set the pasta aside.

Meanwhile, warm the oil in a large skillet over medium-high heat. When hot, add the chicken and cook for 3 to 4 minutes, or until the chicken is no longer pink and the juices run clear. Transfer to a large bowl and set aside.

In the same skillet, combine the onion, garlic, and bell peppers and cook for 3 to 4 minutes, or until the vegetables soften. Remove from the heat and add the tomatoes. Pour the vegetable mixture over the chicken, followed by the pasta and remaining dressing. If the pasta needs to be loosened up a bit, add some of the reserved pasta water.

Toss gently until thoroughly blended, top with cheese, and serve.

Makes 4 servings

Per serving: *409 calories, 36 g protein, 54 g carbohydrate, 6 g fat, 67 mg cholesterol, 400 mg sodium, 4 g fiber*

Diet Exchanges: *0 milk, 1½ vegetable, 0 fruit, 3 bread, 4 meat, 0 fat*

3½ Carb Choices

Creamy Chicken and Veggies

Christine Walsh, Guysborough County, Nova Scotia, Canada

"This meal is so tasty and filling!"

Prep time: 15 minutes; Cook time: 65 minutes

- **¾ cup instant brown rice**
- **1 cup diced or sliced frozen carrots**
- **1 cup frozen green beans**
- **½ cup frozen pearl onions**
- **1 can (10¾ ounces) low-fat cream soup of your choice**
- **1 can (14½ ounces) reduced-sodium chicken broth**
- **½ teaspoon dried thyme**
- **Salt**
- **Ground black pepper**
- **½ pound boneless, skinless chicken breasts, cut into bite-size pieces**

Preheat the oven to 375°F. Coat a 2½-quart baking dish with cooking spray.

In a medium bowl, combine the rice, carrots, green beans, onions, cream soup, broth, and thyme. Mix well and season with salt and pepper to taste. Arrange the chicken in the baking dish and top with the rice-vegetable mixture.

Bake, covered, for 45 minutes, then uncover and bake for 20 to 25 minutes longer, or until bubbling.

Makes 2 servings

Per serving: *440 calories, 37 g protein, 57 g carbohydrate, 8 g fat, 75 mg cholesterol, 980 mg sodium, 4 g fiber*

Diet Exchanges: *0 milk, 3 vegetable, 0 fruit, 2½ bread, 4½ meat, ½ fat*

4 Carb Choices

Turkey-Stuffed Shells

JoAnn Hering, Andover, Ohio

"I love Italian food, and this dish is a good alternative to the beef-and-pork-stuffed shells I usually make."

Prep time: 25 minutes; Cook time: 1 hour 25 minutes; Stand time: 5–10 minutes

16 ounces jumbo pasta shells
1 pound lean ground turkey breast
½ cup liquid egg substitute
⅔ cup chopped onion
1 clove garlic, minced
¾ teaspoon dried oregano
¾ teaspoon salt
¼ teaspoon ground black pepper
1½ cups (6 ounces) shredded part-skim mozzarella cheese
½ cup chopped fresh spinach
1 jar (26 ounces) marinara sauce
¼ cup grated Parmesan cheese

Preheat the oven to 350°F. Coat a 13" × 9" baking dish with cooking spray.

In a large pot of boiling salted water, cook the pasta for 8 minutes, drain, and set aside.

In a large skillet over medium-high heat, cook the turkey for 5 to 10 minutes, or until no longer pink, breaking it up with the back of a spoon. Set aside.

In a large bowl, combine the egg substitute, onion, garlic, oregano, salt, pepper, and ½ cup of the mozzarella and mix well. Add the cooked turkey and spinach and mix well.

Spread the bottom of the prepared baking dish with a layer of marinara sauce. Fill the shells with equal portions of the turkey mixture, arranging them in the baking dish as you go. When all the shells are filled, cover with the remaining marinara sauce and mozzarella. Sprinkle the Parmesan cheese on top.

Bake, covered, for 45 minutes, then uncover and bake for 15 minutes longer. Let stand for 5 to 10 minutes before serving.

Makes 8 servings

Per serving: *443 calories, 27 g protein, 53 g carbohydrate, 13 g fat, 59 mg cholesterol, 835 mg sodium, 3 g fiber*

Diet Exchanges: *0 milk, ½ vegetable, 0 fruit, 3½ bread, 2½ meat, 1½ fat*

4 Carb Choices

Kitchen Tip

When preparing pasta for casseroles and soups, you can reduce the cooking time by about one-third as was done in the recipe above. The pasta will finish cooking while baking or simmering in the dish.

267 Calories

Sweet and Sour Meat Loaf

Julie Cohn, Anthem, Arizona

"By eliminating the beef from my meat loaf recipes, I have cut my fat intake considerably. We use ground turkey for almost everything now and don't even like the taste of ground beef anymore!"

Prep time: 10 minutes; Cook time: 1 hour 15 minutes; Stand time: 5 minutes

MEAT LOAF

- 1½ pounds skinless ground turkey breast
- 1 egg
- ½ cup seasoned dry bread crumbs
- ¼ cup 1% milk
- 2 tablespoons Worcestershire sauce
- ¼ cup grated Parmesan cheese
- ¼ cup shredded reduced-fat Cheddar cheese

SAUCE

- ¼ cup tomato sauce
- 1½ tablespoons cider vinegar
- 1½ tablespoons packed brown sugar

Preheat the oven to 350°F.

To make the meat loaf: In a large bowl, combine the turkey, egg, bread crumbs, milk, Worcestershire sauce, and cheeses. With clean hands, mix well and shape into a loaf. Place in a nonstick 9" × 5" loaf pan and bake for 45 minutes.

To make the sauce: Meanwhile, in a small saucepan over high heat, combine the tomato sauce, vinegar, and brown sugar. Bring to a boil, then reduce the heat to low. Simmer for about 2 to 3 minutes, or until slightly thickened.

About 20 minutes after the meat loaf has begun to bake, brush the top with the sauce and bake for 20 to 25 minutes longer, brushing one more time if desired. Let stand for 5 minutes before slicing.

Makes 6 servings

Per serving: *267 calories, 25 g protein, 13 g carbohydrate, 12 g fat, 130 mg cholesterol, 596 mg sodium, 1 g fiber*

Diet Exchanges: *0 milk, 0 vegetable, 0 fruit, 1 bread, 3½ meat, ½ fat*

1 Carb Choice

Creamy Baked Chicken Enchiladas

Melisa Smith, Clinton, Tennessee

Prep time: 15 minutes; Cook time: 40 minutes

- **1 tablespoon olive oil**
- **1 pound boneless, skinless chicken breasts, cut into bite-size pieces**
- **1 cup sliced white mushrooms**
- **1 medium onion, diced**
- **1 teaspoon Worcestershire sauce**
- **8 flour tortillas (8"–10" diameter)**
- **2 cans (10¾ ounces each) reduced-fat cream of mushroom soup**
- **1 cup warm water (105°–115°F)**
- **1 cup (4 ounces) shredded reduced-fat Monterey Jack cheese**
- **Fat-free sour cream (optional)**
- **Salsa (optional)**

Preheat the oven to 350°F. Coat a 13" × 9" baking dish with cooking spray.

Warm the oil in a large skillet over medium-high heat. When hot, add the chicken and cook for 3 to 4 minutes, or until lightly browned on all sides. Add the mushrooms and onion and cook for about 10 minutes longer, or until the chicken is no longer pink, the juices run clear, and the mushrooms and onions have softened. Stir in the Worcestershire sauce, remove from the heat, and set aside.

To assemble the enchiladas, fill the center of each tortilla with equal portions of the chicken mixture and roll up, folding in the ends as you go. Arrange the filled tortillas seam side down in the prepared baking dish.

In a small bowl, combine the soup with the water and whisk until creamy. Pour over the tortillas, cover, and bake for 30 minutes. Uncover and sprinkle with the cheese. Return to the oven and bake for about 5 to 10 minutes longer, or until the cheese is melted.

Serve with sour cream and/or salsa, if desired.

Makes 8 servings

Per serving: *420 calories, 25 g protein, 47 g carbohydrate, 14 g fat, 44 mg cholesterol, 879 mg sodium, 3 g fiber*

Diet Exchanges: *0 milk, ½ vegetable, 0 fruit, 3 bread, 2½ meat, 2 fat*

3 Carb Choices

Beef and Broccoli

Cindy Ferguson, Hampton, Prince Edward Island, Canada

Prep time: 8 minutes; Cook time: 13 minutes

- **2 tablespoons cornstarch**
- **1 can (14½ ounces) beef broth**
- **2 tablespoons light soy sauce**
- **2 tablespoons oyster sauce**
- **1 tablespoon vegetable oil**
- **1 pound boneless sirloin steak, cut into thin strips**
- **4 cups fresh broccoli florets**
- **1 clove garlic, minced**
- **1 medium onion, sliced**

In a small bowl, combine the cornstarch, broth, soy sauce, and oyster sauce and whisk until smooth. Set aside.

Warm the oil in a large skillet or wok over medium-high heat for 1 minute. Add the steak and cook, stirring constantly, for 5 to 7 minutes, or until the beef is browned. Transfer to a covered bowl to keep warm.

Add the broccoli, garlic, and onion to the skillet and cook, stirring constantly, for 1 to 2 minutes, or until the broccoli is bright green and crisp-tender. Add the broth mixture and bring to a boil, stirring. Reduce the heat, add the beef, and simmer for 5 minutes, or until the sauce thickens.

Makes 4 servings

Per serving: *265 calories, 31 g protein, 11 g carbohydrate, 11 g fat, 77 mg cholesterol, 567 mg sodium, 3 g fiber*

Diet Exchanges: *0 milk, 1 vegetable, 0 fruit, ½ bread, 4 meat, 1½ fat*

1 Carb Choice

GREAT LOW-FAT COOKING STYLES: ASIAN

Asian food is one of the world's most healthful and appetizing cuisines.

Asian-Inspired Mix. In a cup, mix 3 tablespoons reduced-sodium soy sauce, 2 crushed garlic cloves, 1½ teaspoons toasted sesame oil, and 1 teaspoon finely grated fresh ginger. Brush over whatever meat, poultry, or fish you're broiling. Coats about 1¼ pounds.

Asian Barbecue Sauce. In a small saucepan, mix ⅓ cup tomato sauce, ¼ cup hoisin sauce, 3 tablespoons rice wine vinegar, 2 tablespoons medium-dry sherry, 3 minced garlic cloves, and 1 tablespoon grated fresh ginger. Bring to a boil over medium-high heat. Cook, stirring often, for about 3 minutes, or until syrupy. Brush over whatever meat or poultry you're grilling during the last 3 minutes. Coats about 1¼ pounds.

Onion-Grilled London Broil

Sally Waggoner, Muncie, Indiana

Prep time: 5 minutes; Marinate time: 2 hours
Stand time: 30 minutes; Cook time: 25 minutes

1 sweet onion, quartered
1 clove garlic
2 tablespoons soy sauce
1 tablespoon Dijon mustard
1 tablespoon honey
1 tablespoon olive oil
1 teaspoon ground black pepper
1 pound London broil

In the workbowl of a food processor, combine the onion, garlic, soy sauce, mustard, honey, oil, and pepper. Pulse until smooth, then transfer to a resealable plastic bag. Add the London broil and refrigerate for at least 2 hours, or preferably overnight.

Let the steak stand at room temperature for about 30 minutes before grilling (cold meat is more likely to stick to a hot grill). Preheat the grill to high.

Remove the steak from the bag and discard the onion mixture. Grill the steak for about 10 minutes per side, or until a thermometer inserted in the center registers 145°F for medium-rare/160°F for medium/165°F for well-done.

Transfer to a cutting board and let stand for 10 minutes, then slice thinly across the grain and serve.

Makes 4 servings

Per serving: *230 calories, 26 g protein, 8 g carbohydrate, 10 g fat, 35 mg cholesterol, 620 mg sodium, 0 g fiber*

Diet Exchanges: *0 milk, ½ vegetable, 0 fruit, ½ bread, 3½ meat, 1½ fat*

½ Carb Choice

Marinated Pork Tenderloin

Gayle Socha, Parma, Ohio

"This quick, easy meal is lean and tasty."

Prep time: 5 minutes; Marinate time: 1 hour
Cook time: 12 minutes

- **¼ cup orange juice concentrate, thawed**
- **2 tablespoons vegetable oil**
- **2–3 cloves garlic, chopped**
- **1 tablespoon light soy sauce**
- **4 pork tenderloin chops (4 ounces each)**

In a shallow baking pan, combine the orange juice, oil, garlic, and soy sauce. Add the pork and turn to coat. Cover and refrigerate for 1 hour or more, turning once or twice.

Preheat the grill to medium-high. Remove the pork from the marinade and pat dry. Grill for about 6 minutes per side, or until a thermometer inserted in the center of a chop registers 160°F and the juices run clear.

Makes 4 servings

Per serving: *180 calories, 20 g protein, 6 g carbohydrate, 8 g fat, 45 mg cholesterol, 380 mg sodium, 0 g fiber*

Diet Exchanges: *0 milk, 0 vegetable, 0 fruit, 0 bread, 5 meat, 1 fat*

0 Carb Choices

SHOPPING SAVVY

Get Grilling

The Lodge Pro-Logic cast-iron 12" grill pan is one serious stove-top griller. It cooks evenly, sears beautifully, and retains heat for a long time (use thick oven mitts). No seasoning necessary for this cast-iron beauty: It's preseasoned. Your job is to maintain the finish. First, rinse the pan with hot water (no soap) and dry. Heat over medium heat for 3 minutes before adding food, and—counter to the instructions—oil the food, not the pan. Don't turn food for at least 1 minute. Afterward, soak the pan in hot water (never soap) and scrub with a stiff brush. Dry completely and oil lightly. Sold at housewares stores.

Photo courtesy of Pro-Logic

Stuffed Lamb Chops

Vasiliy Velichko, Far Rockaway, New York

Prep time: 10 minutes; Cook time: 17 minutes

1½ cups fresh spinach
1 tablespoon pine nuts
1 teaspoon cornstarch
2 tablespoons Italian-style bread crumbs
2 tablespoons feta cheese, crumbled
¼ teaspoon dried thyme
Salt
Ground black pepper
4 loin lamb chops (about 4 ounces each)
1 teaspoon olive oil
2 tablespoons red wine

In a small skillet over low heat, combine the spinach, pine nuts, cornstarch, bread crumbs, and feta cheese. Cook gently until the spinach is bright green and wilted. Remove from the heat, add the thyme, and season with salt and pepper to taste. Let cool. Cut a small pocket into the side of each lamb chop and stuff with equal amounts of the spinach mixture.

Warm the oil in a large skillet over medium heat. When hot, add the stuffed lamb chops and cook for about 4 minutes per side. Add the wine and cook for 2 to 3 minutes longer, or until most of the liquid has evaporated.

Drizzle the lamb chops with any pan sauces and serve.

Makes 4 servings

Per serving: *152 calories, 16 g protein, 5 g carbohydrate, 7 g fat, 47 mg cholesterol, 224 mg sodium, 1 g fiber*

Diet Exchanges: *0 milk, 0 vegetable, 0 fruit, 0 bread, 2 meat, 1 fat*

0 Carb Choices

DESSERTS AND BREAKFAST TREATS

Cookies and Bars

Fruit, Pudding, and Frozen Treats

Cakes and Pies

Muffins and Breads

Smoothies

Breakfasts

Vanilla Crisps

Shirley Hill, Chatham, Ontario, Canada

"These light cookies satisfy my urge for sweets and let me continue to lose weight."

Prep time: 12 minutes; Cook time: 15 minutes
Cool time: 5 minutes

- **2 eggs, separated**
- **½ teaspoon baking powder**
- **⅛ teaspoon salt**
- **¼ cup sugar**
- **2 teaspoons vanilla extract**
- **¼ teaspoon grated lemon zest**
- **⅓ cup all-purpose flour**
- **Confectioners' sugar**

Preheat the oven to 375°F. Line baking sheets with parchment paper.

In a large bowl, with an electric mixer on medium speed, beat the egg whites until foamy. Slowly add the baking powder, salt, and sugar and continue beating on medium speed until stiff peaks form.

In another bowl, combine the egg yolks, vanilla, and lemon zest and beat with a fork until thoroughly mixed. Fold into the beaten egg whites just until combined. Sift the flour over the egg mixture and fold in until the batter is smooth and light. Drop 2 teaspoons of batter per cookie about 2" apart onto the prepared baking sheets.

Bake for 12 to 15 minutes, or until golden. Cool on the sheets for 5 minutes, then remove to racks to cool completely. The cookies will crisp upon cooling. Dust with confectioners' sugar before serving. For best results, store covered.

Makes 24 cookies

Per cookie: *21 calories, 1 g protein, 3 g carbohydrate, 0 g fat, 17 mg cholesterol, 30 mg sodium, 0 g fiber*

Diet Exchanges: *0 milk, 0 vegetable, 0 fruit, 0 bread, 0 meat, 0 fat*

0 Carb Choices

Fruit and Fiber Cookies

Patricia Molinari, Calgary, Alberta, Canada

"These are great when you've had a busy morning and haven't had breakfast."

Prep time: 10 minutes; Cook time: 20 minutes

- **4 medium bananas, mashed**
- **⅓ cup vegetable oil**
- **½ teaspoon almond extract**
- **Grated zest of 1 lemon**
- **1½ cups quick-cooking rolled oats**
- **¾ cup whole wheat flour**
- **½ cup raisins**
- **½ cup chopped apricots**
- **½ cup chopped dates or prunes**
- **½ cup chopped pecans, walnuts, or almonds**

Preheat the oven to 350°F. Lightly coat baking sheets with cooking spray.

In a large bowl, combine the bananas, oil, almond extract, and lemon zest. With an electric mixer on medium speed, beat for 1 minute, or until a smooth batter forms. Add the oats, flour, raisins, apricots, dates, and nuts and stir until just blended. Drop the dough by rounded teaspoons about 2" apart onto the prepared baking sheets. Flatten each cookie by pressing gently with the tines of a fork.

Bake for 15 to 20 minutes, or until lightly browned. Remove to a rack to cool.

Makes 40 cookies

Per cookie: *74 calories, 1 g protein, 11 g carbohydrate, 3 g fat, 0 mg cholesterol, 60 mg sodium, 2 g fiber*

Diet Exchanges: *0 milk, 0 vegetable, ½ fruit, 0 bread, 0 meat, ½ fat*

1 Carb Choice

To bake cookies evenly, rotate the baking sheet halfway through the baking time. If baking more than one sheet of cookies at a time, reverse the baking sheets from top to bottom and front to back.

Caramel-Frosted Banana Drops

Jennifer Foster, Seattle, Washington

Prep time: 10 minutes; Cook time: 20 minutes

COOKIES

- **1 cup packed brown sugar**
- **1 cup trans-free margarine or butter, softened**
- **½ cup mashed banana (about 1 large banana)**
- **2 teaspoons vanilla extract**
- **2⅓ cups all-purpose flour**
- **½ teaspoon salt**
- **¾ cup chopped walnuts or pecans**

FROSTING

- **¼ cup packed brown sugar**
- **2 tablespoons trans-free margarine or butter**
- **⅓ cup confectioners' sugar**
- **¼ teaspoon vanilla extract**
- **2 tablespoons 1% milk**

Preheat the oven to 350°F.

To make the cookies: In a large bowl, combine the brown sugar and margarine or butter. With an electric mixer on medium speed, beat for 2 minutes, or until fluffy. Add the banana and vanilla extract and beat for 30 seconds longer, or until combined. Add the flour and salt and stir until just blended. Stir in the nuts. Drop the dough by heaping teaspoons about 2" apart onto ungreased baking sheets.

Bake for 9 to 14 minutes, or until light golden brown. Remove to a rack to cool.

To make the frosting: In a small saucepan, combine the brown sugar and margarine or butter. Cook over low heat, stirring constantly, for 1 to 2 minutes, or until the sugar is dissolved. Transfer to a medium bowl and allow to cool slightly. With a wire whisk, beat in the confectioners' sugar, vanilla extract, and milk and stir for 3 to 5 minutes, or until smooth and glossy.

Frost the cookies when cool.

Makes about 54 cookies

Per cookie: *80 calories, 1 g protein, 10 g carbohydrate, 4 g fat, 0 mg cholesterol, 55 mg sodium, 0 g fiber*

Diet Exchanges: *0 milk, 0 vegetable, 0 fruit, ½ bread, 0 meat, 1 fat*

½ Carb Choice

Chocolate Chip Cookies

Sally Hines, Encino, California

Prep time: 10 minutes; Cook time: 10 minutes

- **2¼ cups all-purpose flour**
- **¾ teaspoon baking soda**
- **½ teaspoon salt**
- **½ cup trans-free margarine or butter**
- **¾ cup granulated sugar**
- **¾ cup packed brown sugar**
- **2 eggs or equivalent liquid egg substitute**
- **½ cup unsweetened applesauce**
- **1 teaspoon vanilla extract**
- **1 bag (12 ounces) chocolate chips**
- **1 cup nuts of your choice**

Preheat the oven to 375°F. Generously coat baking sheets with cooking spray.

In a medium bowl, combine the flour, baking soda, and salt.

In a large bowl, combine the margarine or butter, granulated sugar, and brown sugar. With an electric mixer on medium speed, beat for 2 minutes, or until fluffy. Add the eggs one at a time, mixing after each addition, for 1 minute, or until thoroughly combined. Add the applesauce and vanilla extract and mix again until thoroughly combined. Working in two or three batches, add the flour mixture, stirring after each addition, until just blended. Stir in the chocolate chips and nuts. Drop the dough by rounded tablespoons 2" apart onto the prepared baking sheets.

Bake for 10 to 12 minutes, or until light golden brown. Remove to a rack to cool.

Makes 36 cookies

Per cookie: *154 calories, 2 g protein, 21 g carbohydrate, 8 g fat, 12 mg cholesterol, 95 mg sodium, 1 g fiber*

Diet Exchanges: *0 milk, 0 vegetable, 0 fruit, 1½ bread, 0 meat, 1½ fat*

1½ Carb Choices

(shown with Sweet 'n' Cool Peanut Bars, opposite page)

Sweet 'n' Cool Peanut Bars

Helen Velichko, Kansas City, Missouri

Prep time: 5 minutes; Cook time: 2 minutes

- **½ cup packed brown sugar**
- **½ cup creamy peanut butter**
- **½ cup light corn syrup**
- **1 teaspoon vanilla extract**
- **1¾ cups rice cereal**
- **1½ cups old-fashioned rolled oats**
- **¼ cup raisins or chocolate chips**

Generously coat a 9" × 9" baking pan with cooking spray.

In a large microwaveable bowl, combine the sugar, peanut butter, and corn syrup. Microwave on high power for 2 minutes, or until boiling, stirring once. Remove from the microwave oven and stir in the vanilla extract, cereal, oats, and raisins or chocolate chips. Mix well, then press firmly and evenly into the prepared baking pan.

Cool in the pan and cut into bars.

Makes 18 bars

Per bar: *131 calories, 3 g protein, 22 g carbohydrate, 4 g fat, 0 mg cholesterol, 47 mg sodium, 1 g fiber*

Diet Exchanges: *0 milk, 0 vegetable, 0 fruit, 1½ bread, 0 meat, 1 fat*

1½ Carb Choices

SECRETS OF WEIGHT-LOSS WINNERS

• Keeping a food journal has helped me stay on track more than anything else. It's amazing how much food I had put into my mouth without even thinking about it.

—Helen Goering, Columbus, Nebraska

• Add applesauce to your cake mix recipes instead of oil for a low-fat and still very yummy alternative.

—Nancy Govero, Olathe, Kansas

• Remember, 10 deep breaths can conquer almost any craving!

—Prevention.com

• I always have a hot cup of tea with a little honey in it prior to breakfast. This takes away any sweet cravings and helps fill my stomach, so I don't want a large, fatty breakfast.

—Faith McArdle, Avon Lake, Ohio

Country Cookies

Kathy Tweed, Cape May Court House, New Jersey

Prep time: 12 minutes; Chill time: 1 hour
Cook time: 12 minutes

2 cups all-purpose flour
2 teaspoons baking powder
½ teaspoon salt
½ teaspoon ground cloves
½ teaspoon ground ginger
1 teaspoon ground cinnamon
¾ cup vegetable oil
¼ cup molasses
1 cup granulated sugar
1 egg
½ cup raisins
Confectioners' sugar

In a large bowl, sift together the flour, baking powder, salt, cloves, ginger, and cinnamon.

In a medium bowl, combine the oil, molasses, sugar, and egg and stir until thoroughly mixed. With an electric mixer on medium speed, add to the flour mixture and beat for 2 to 3 minutes, or until a dough forms. Add the raisins and stir until thoroughly mixed. Roll the dough into a ball, cover with plastic wrap, and refrigerate for 1 hour.

Preheat the oven to 350°F.

Evenly divide the dough into thirty-six 1" balls and set them about 1" apart on a large nonstick baking sheet. Flatten each cookie by pressing gently with the tines of a fork.

Bake for 10 to 12 minutes. Remove to a rack to cool. Dust with confectioners' sugar.

Makes 36 cookies

Per cookie: *103 calories, 1 g protein, 14 g carbohydrate, 5 g fat, 6 mg cholesterol, 58 mg sodium, 2 g fiber*

Diet Exchanges: *0 milk, 0 vegetable, 0 fruit, 1 bread, 0 meat, 1 fat*

1 Carb Choice

Pumpkin Spice Bars

Katie Burrage, Newfields, New Hampshire

"These bar cookies are easy, tasty, and low-fat. It takes only minutes to mix up a batch, and then you have a wonderful dessert!"

Prep time: 15 minutes; Cook time: 30 minutes

1½ cups all-purpose flour
1 cup whole wheat flour
1½ teaspoons baking soda
½ cup sugar
1 tablespoon ground cinnamon
½ teaspoon ground cloves
½ teaspoon ground nutmeg
⅔ cup molasses
2 egg whites
1 cup water
½ cup canned pumpkin
½ cup raisins
¼ cup chopped walnuts

Preheat the oven to 350°F. Coat a 13" × 9" baking pan with cooking spray.

In a large bowl, combine the all-purpose flour, whole wheat flour, baking soda, sugar, cinnamon, cloves, and nutmeg. Add the molasses, egg whites, water, and pumpkin and stir until thoroughly mixed. Stir in the raisins and walnuts. Spread evenly in the prepared baking pan.

Bake for 25 to 30 minutes, or until a wooden pick inserted in the center comes out clean. Cool in the pan and cut into 2" squares.

Makes 24 bars

Per bar: *108 calories, 2 g protein, 23 g carbohydrate, 1 g fat, 0 mg cholesterol, 95 mg sodium, 1 g fiber*

Diet Exchanges: *0 milk, 0 vegetable, 0 fruit, 1½ bread, 0 meat, 0 fat*

1½ Carb Choices

Kitchen Tip

A dollop of fat-free whipped topping makes a tasty and pretty addition.

Lemon Angel Food Cake Squares

Eva Seibert, Allentown, Pennsylvania

Prep time: 15 minutes; Chill time: 1 hour 40 minutes; Cook time: 20 minutes

1¼ cups granulated sugar
¼ cup cornstarch
⅔ cup fresh lemon juice (from about 3 large lemons)
1 large egg yolk
1 cup water
1 tablespoon trans-free margarine or butter
1 box angel food cake mix
1 teaspoon grated lemon zest
¼ teaspoon lemon extract
Confectioners' sugar

In a 2-quart saucepan, whisk together the granulated sugar and cornstarch until combined. Add the lemon juice, egg yolk, and water and whisk until well blended. Whisking constantly, cook the lemon mixture over medium heat for about 2 to 3 minutes, or until just boiling. Reduce the heat to low and simmer, whisking constantly for 1 to 2 minutes longer, or until thick enough to coat the back of a spoon. Remove from the heat and stir in the margarine or butter. Pour into a medium bowl and cover with plastic wrap. Refrigerate this lemon curd for about 1½ hours, or until cool.

Preheat the oven to 350°F. Coat a 15½" × 10½" jelly-roll pan with cooking spray and line the bottom with parchment paper.

Prepare the angel food cake according to package directions. Add the lemon zest and lemon extract while beating. Spread the batter evenly into the prepared jelly-roll pan.

Bake for 20 minutes, or until the cake is golden and the top springs back when touched. Cool in the pan on a rack for 10 minutes, then invert onto the rack. Carefully remove the parchment and allow the cake to cool completely, then cut horizontally into thirds. Cut each third through the middle and spread one-third of the cooled lemon curd over 3 of the halves. Top each with the remaining halves and cut each piece into 5 equal portions. Sprinkle with confectioners' sugar and serve.

Makes 15 servings

Per serving: *188 calories, 3 g protein, 43 g carbohydrate, 1 g fat, 15 mg cholesterol, 211 mg sodium, 0 g fiber*

Diet Exchanges: *0 milk, 0 vegetable, 0 fruit, 2½ bread, 0 meat, ½ fat*

1 Carb Choice

Peach Crisp

Kathy Tweed, Cape May Court House, New Jersey

Prep time: 15 minutes; Cook time: 45 minutes

6 cups sliced peaches
¼ cup granulated sugar
1 teaspoon cornstarch
½ teaspoon grated lemon zest
½ cup all-purpose flour
¼ cup packed brown sugar
Dash of ground cinnamon
Dash of ground nutmeg
Dash of ground allspice
⅛ teaspoon salt
⅓ cup trans-free margarine or butter, softened
¼ cup old-fashioned rolled oats

Preheat the oven to 375°F. Lightly coat a 9" round baking pan or a 9" glass pie plate with cooking spray.

In a medium bowl, combine the peaches, granulated sugar, cornstarch, and lemon zest. Transfer to the prepared baking pan.

In the same bowl, with a pastry cutter, combine the flour, brown sugar, cinnamon, nutmeg, allspice, salt, and margarine or butter until crumbles form. Add the oats and stir until combined. Sprinkle evenly over the peach filling.

Bake for 45 minutes, or until the filling is bubbling and the top is browned. Serve warm or at room temperature.

Makes 6 servings

Per serving: *282 calories, 3 g protein, 47 g carbohydrate, 11 g fat, 11 mg cholesterol, 178 mg sodium, 4 g fiber*

Diet Exchanges: *0 milk, 0 vegetable, 1½ fruit, 1½ bread, 0 meat, 2 fat*

3 Carb Choices

Kitchen Tip

This recipe works great with any fruit that's been left to get too soft to eat whole.

Apple Clafouti

Shirley Hill, Chatham, Ontario, Canada

"This recipe gives me the sweet pleasure I occasionally need without blowing my diet. A small wedge of clafouti once every couple of weeks satisfies me without the guilt."

Prep time: 15 minutes; Cook time: 40 minutes

- **1 large McIntosh or Granny Smith apple, peeled, cored, and thinly sliced**
- **¼ cup fresh or frozen cranberries**
- **3 tablespoons honey**
- **½ teaspoon ground cinnamon**
- **1 can (12 ounces) fat-free evaporated milk**
- **1 tablespoon olive oil**
- **3 large eggs, lightly beaten**
- **1 teaspoon vanilla extract**
- **⅔ cup all-purpose flour**
- **¼ cup sugar**

Preheat the oven to 375°F. Spray a 9" glass pie plate with cooking spray.

Layer the apples in the bottom of the prepared pie plate to form a concentric circle (overlapping, if necessary). Strew the cranberries on top, then drizzle with the honey and sprinkle with ¼ teaspoon of the cinnamon.

In a food processor or blender, combine the milk, oil, eggs, vanilla extract, flour, sugar, and the remaining cinnamon. Blend until smooth and pour over the apples.

Bake for 40 minutes, or until puffy and golden. Serve warm or at room temperature.

Makes 8 servings

Per serving: *180 calories, 7 g protein, 30 g carbohydrate, 4 g fat, 80 mg cholesterol, 75 mg sodium, 1 g fiber*

Diet Exchanges: *½ milk, 0 vegetable, ½ fruit, 1½ bread, ½ meat, ½ fat*

2 Carb Choices

Trail-Mix Fruit Bake

Vasiliy Velichko, Far Rockaway, New York

Prep time: 10 minutes; Cook time: 30 minutes

- **6 apples or pears**
- **½ cup raisins**
- **1 cup coarsely chopped walnuts or pecans**
- **½ teaspoon vanilla extract**
- **¼ teaspoon ground cinnamon**
- **Apple juice**

Preheat the oven to 375°F.

Halve each piece of fruit lengthwise. With a melon baller or serrated knife, scoop out enough of the insides to remove the seeds and create a small "bowl." Arrange the fruit cut side up in a 13" × 9" baking dish. In a small bowl, combine the raisins, nuts, vanilla extract, and cinnamon with just enough apple juice to moisten. Spoon the mixture into the center of each fruit bowl. Pour additional juice into the baking dish to a depth of about ½" and cover with foil.

Bake for 30 minutes, or until the fruit is tender.

Makes 12 servings

Per serving: *127 calories, 2 g protein, 18 g carbohydrate, 7 g fat, 0 mg cholesterol, 1 mg sodium, 4 g fiber*

Diet Exchanges: *0 milk, 0 vegetable, 1 fruit, 0 bread, 0 meat, 1 fat*

1 Carb Choice

190 Calories

Fruit Pizza

Shirley Hill, Chatham, Ontario, Canada

"This dish satisfies the occasional urge for pizza with a lot more fiber but without the fat. Enjoying this pizza instead of the traditional kind has helped me to lose weight steadily without falling off the wagon!"

Prep time: 22 minutes; Cook time: 13 minutes

- **1 package (10 ounces) refrigerated pizza dough**
- **1 cup part-skim ricotta cheese**
- **1 teaspoon grated lime zest**
- **1½ tablespoons sugar**
- **2 heaping tablespoons sliced almonds**
- **¼ teaspoon ground cinnamon**
- **2 cups (8 ounces) shredded part-skim mozzarella cheese**
- **½ cup dried apricots (or other dried fruit)**
- **½ cup halved seedless red grapes**
- **2 large, ripe kiwifruit, thinly sliced**

Preheat the oven to 450°F. Lightly coat a 15" × 10" baking sheet with cooking spray.

Unroll the pizza dough and press into the baking sheet to fill it entirely. Bake for 7 to 8 minutes, or until golden.

Meanwhile, in a small bowl, combine the ricotta cheese and lime zest. In another small bowl, combine the sugar, almonds, and cinnamon.

When the dough has finished baking, remove it from the oven and place on a heatproof surface. Carefully spread the ricotta mixture on top, then sprinkle with the mozzarella. Arrange the apricots, grapes, and kiwifruit on top and sprinkle with the sugar and almond mixture.

Return the pizza to the oven and bake for about 5 minutes, or until the fruit is hot and cheese is melted.

Makes 12 servings

Per serving: *190 calories, 10 g protein, 24 g carbohydrate, 6 g fat, 15 mg cholesterol, 270 mg sodium, 2 g fiber*

Diet Exchanges: *0 milk, 0 vegetable, ½ fruit, 1 bread, 1 meat, ½ fat*

1½ Carb Choices

It Worked for Me!

Karyn Barczewski

VITAL STATS

Weight lost: 35 pounds

Time to goal: 5 years

Quick tip: Add 2 tablespoons of peanut butter to your diet every day.

Karyn never equated eating with weight gain—for her, a good meal was just good fun. But the pounds caught up with her and so did a fear of developing diabetes. Losing weight through customized diet changes made all the difference.

"My inspiration to lose weight came from one of the crime novels that I love to read. Five years ago, I was enjoying a story about a murdered woman who was my height and weight. In the book, a medical examiner described her as having 'classic mild obesity.' That was all it took for me to realize that, at 137 pounds, I was too heavy for my height of just 5 feet 2 inches.

"The first thing I did was go to Weight Watchers. They were just initiating the point system, and it worked for me: I lost 7 pounds right away. After I lost those first few pounds, however, I noticed that I was having low blood sugar attacks every day after breakfast and then later in the afternoon. I realized that I was eating a lot less fat, but not enough protein. I also found that I was indulging in too many low-fat foods that were mostly processed carbohydrates.

"Around this time, *Prevention* magazine came out with the Peanut Butter Diet, so I tried it. I added one slice of light whole wheat bread and 2 tablespoons of peanut butter to my breakfasts. Amazingly, the peanut butter prevented me from getting the mid-morning shakes, and I wasn't hungry for lunch until around 1:00 P.M. Even when I did feel ready for lunch, I wasn't ravenous, so I could be satisfied with a salad or veggies and meat. I also started limiting my refined carbs and eating more fresh fruits and whole grains.

"I believe that the peanut butter 'trick' helped me stabilize my blood sugar. Over the past 5 years, my eating plan has evolved from the classic Weight Watchers diet to my own blend of good fats, lean protein, and smart carbs. The variety keeps me from getting bored, and I never feel hungry. In addition, even though I'm in my late forties and have a family history of diabetes, my blood sugar tests have all been good."

Fruit Salad

Barbara Eitel, Cambridge, Ontario, Canada

"This soft dessert is a nice alternative to firmer gelatin desserts."

Prep time: 5 minutes; Chill time: 3 hours

- **2 cups fat-free or low-fat cottage cheese**
- **1 package (4-serving size) sugar-free gelatin, any flavor**
- **2 cups fat-free frozen whipped topping, thawed**
- **1 can (8 ounces) crushed pineapple**

In a blender or food processor, whip the cottage cheese with the gelatin until smooth. Transfer to a large bowl and add the whipped topping and pineapple (with juice). Mix thoroughly, cover, and refrigerate for at least 3 hours, or until thoroughly chilled.

Makes 4 servings

Per serving: *279 calories, 24 g protein, 24 g carbohydrate, 2 g fat, 9 mg cholesterol, 1036 mg sodium, 0 g fiber*

Diet Exchanges: *0 milk, 0 vegetable, ½ fruit, 1 bread, 2½ meat, ½ fat*

1½ Carb Choices

SHOPPING SAVVY

We All Scream

What's your pleasure? Ice cream or frozen yogurt? Breyers has both, and both come in scrumptious 98 percent fat-free—and, therefore, guilt-free—versions. Ice cream flavors include vanilla (flecked with vanilla bean) and Chocolate Fudge Brownie. Per ½-cup serving: 90 calories, 1.5 grams of fat.

Frozen yogurt flavors are vanilla and a three-flavor tub of vanilla, chocolate, and strawberry. Per ½-cup serving: 120 calories, 1.5 grams of fat. Sold in stores nationally.

Looking for a favorite or obscure ice cream flavor? Locate it at icecreamusa.com.

Photos courtesy of Breyers

Pink Stuff

Mona McKinley, Dundee, Florida

"This dish allows me to enjoy a great-looking and tasty treat with very few calories."

Prep time: 10 minutes; Chill time: overnight

- **1 can (21 ounces) light cherry pie filling**
- **1 can (14 ounces) low-fat sweetened condensed milk**
- **1 can (20 ounces) crushed pineapple, drained**
- **1½ cups fat-free frozen whipped topping, thawed**
- **½ cup chopped pecans**

In a large bowl, mix the pie filling, milk, and pineapple. Fold in the whipped topping. Add the pecans and mix well. Cover and refrigerate overnight.

Makes 16 servings

Per serving: *170 calories, 3 g protein, 30 g carbohydrate, 3½ g fat, 5 mg cholesterol, 40 mg sodium, 1 g fiber*

Diet Exchanges: *0 milk, 0 vegetable, 1 fruit, 2 bread, 0 meat, 1 fat*

2 Carb Choices

SIMPLE WAYS TO EAT MORE FRUIT

Eating enough fruit may often seem like a chore, but it really can be easy, and fun. Try these ideas to increase your fruit intake, and add a tasty and healthful touch to favorite dishes.

Add orange, clementine, or tangerine sections along with a teaspoon of grated citrus zest to your next beef or chicken stir-fry. Stir diced apple and some raisins into a curry dish, or into the rice you're serving the curry over.

Add halved grapes, chopped apple, or sliced nectarines to turkey or chicken salad.

Fold pineapple chunks into chicken or tuna salad. For kids (or adults), cut up chunks of watermelon, cantaloupe, and papaya and serve in plastic to-go cups. It's finger food at its most healthful.

An oldie but goodie: Accompany a scoop of low-fat or fat-free cottage cheese with juice-packed canned peaches or pears for an easy lunch.

Layer thinly sliced pears on a roast beef or turkey sandwich—honey mustard adds a wonderful accent.

Top low-fat ice cream or frozen yogurt with mashed fresh berries mixed with a little sugar.

For a tropical effect, spoon a mix of finely chopped mango, pineapple, and kiwifruit over spicy grilled chicken or shrimp. It's great with jerk-seasoned stuff.

Use fruit juice instead of wine in savory sauces.

Stir chopped berries into light cream cheese or part-skim ricotta before spreading on a bagel.

Stir chopped fresh fruit into yogurt instead of buying the fruit-flavored kind. Want it sweeter? Stir in some sugar-free fruit spread or syrup.

Add apple or pear slices to a spinach salad along with a handful of toasted walnuts or pecans.

Homemade Vanilla Pudding with Fresh Berries

270 Calories

Elizabeth Martlock, Jim Thorpe, Pennsylvania

Prep time: 5 minutes; Cook time: 15 minutes
Chill time: overnight

½ cup cornstarch
1 cup sugar
½ teaspoon salt
3 eggs
4 cups fat-free half-and-half
1 teaspoon vanilla extract
2 cups fresh berries of your choice

In a medium bowl, combine the cornstarch, sugar, salt, and eggs and whisk until smooth.

In a large saucepan over medium heat, bring the half-and-half almost to a boil. With a ladle, transfer about 1½ cups at a time into the egg mixture, whisking quickly after each addition. (This will bring the eggs up to the temperature of the cream without scrambling them.) When all of the half-and-half has been added to the eggs, transfer the entire mixture back to the saucepan and return it to the stove over medium heat.

To prevent scorching, stir constantly with a wooden spoon. Be sure to scrape the entire bottom of the pot as the cream returns to a boil. Continue stirring vigorously as the mixture thickens (it will appear chunky at this stage). Once the entire mixture is completely chunky and is spurting air, it is done.

Remove the saucepan from the heat and whisk in the vanilla extract. Transfer the pudding to a heatproof bowl and whisk periodically as it cools. Cover and refrigerate overnight. (For faster cooling, place in a bowl over another bowl filled with ice water and whisk periodically.)

Just before serving, whisk once more, then fold in fresh berries.

Makes 8 servings

Per serving: *270 calories, 7 g protein, 53 g carbohydrate, 2 g fat, 80 mg cholesterol, 270 mg sodium, 0 g fiber*

Diet Exchanges: *1 milk, 0 vegetable, ½ fruit, 2 bread, ½ meat, ½ fat*

3½ Carb Choices

Kitchen Tip

You can experiment with many different variations of this recipe. To make a mocha pudding, omit the berries and add instant coffee to the cream mixture; whisk in melted chocolate at the end. To make raspberry pudding, whisk in raspberry liqueur at the end and serve with fresh raspberries. To make lemon pudding, replace the vanilla extract with lemon extract and add 1 tablespoon of grated lemon zest at the end.

Peanut Butter Pudding

Eva Seibert, Allentown, Pennsylvania

Prep time: 7 minutes; Cook time: 7 minutes
Chill time: 4 hours

- **1 package (0.3 ounces) unflavored gelatin**
- **3 tablespoons water**
- **1 cup fat-free milk**
- **1⅓ cups fat-free evaporated milk**
- **⅓ cup smooth peanut butter**
- **¾ cup packed brown sugar**
- **1 tablespoon vanilla extract**

In a small bowl, add the gelatin to the water. Let soften for about 5 minutes.

Meanwhile, in a medium saucepan, combine the milk, evaporated milk, peanut butter, and sugar. Cook over medium heat, whisking constantly, until just before boiling. Add the vanilla extract and gelatin mixture and mix thoroughly. Let cool to room temperature, then evenly divide into 8 custard cups and refrigerate for 4 hours or overnight.

Makes 8 servings

Per serving: *196 calories, 8 g protein, 28 g carbohydrate, 6 g fat, 4 mg cholesterol, 123 mg sodium, 0 g fiber*

Diet Exchanges: *½ milk, 0 vegetable, 0 fruit, 1 bread, 0 meat, 1½ fat*

1½ Carb Choices

It Worked for Me!

Elise Paone

VITAL STATS

Weight lost: 50 pounds

Time to goal: 10 months

Quick tip: Stay focused during the week and give yourself a "diet break" on weekends.

Elise had been heavy off and on since childhood, and then had a bout with an eating disorder. As an adult, she took on the challenge of finding a healthy, balanced way to lose weight and keep it off.

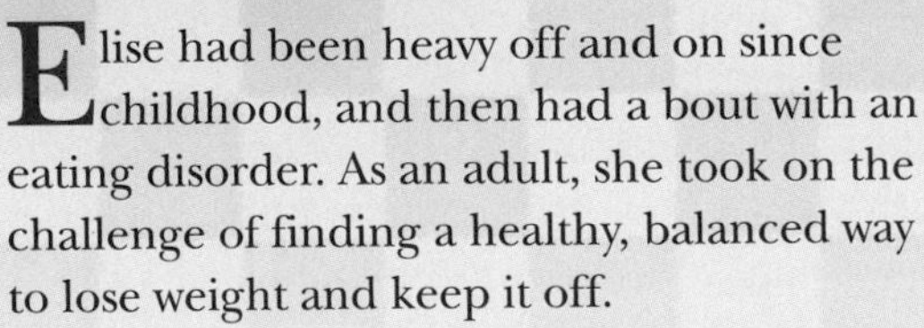

"One of the gifts I received for Christmas in 2002 was a photo of my mother, my sister, and me. I looked at that picture and instead of feeling joy, I was repulsed—of the three of us, my face was hidden in rolls of fat, and I knew without a doubt that I had a weight problem.

"I had been on Weight Watchers before and found it was too complicated for me. The Atkins diet made me feel ill, and I thought it was weird not to have any carbohydrates at all. So I followed a combination of both approaches. I used the basic Weight Watchers formula: Keep the fat low but boost the fiber grams. At the same time, I also eliminated almost all refined carbohydrates from my diet.

"I have to admit that I tended to eat the same 'safe' foods over and over again; as someone with a history of bingeing, this helped me feel in control of how much I ate. I also kept a food log for about 4 or 5 months, which held me accountable for my food choices and made me stop snacking so much. I also measured or weighed everything I ate—no picking from the serving pan or cooking pot.

"I did not exercise initially, and I guess I thought that when the weight came off, I would automatically look great. But I realized that I had lost so much that I needed to tone up. Until then, I wasn't aware that muscle tone was such an important part of looking physically fit—I had thought it was simply pounds.

"My eating habits are really very healthy now. I eliminated a lot of carbs, but I haven't cut them out completely. In the past I would either skip breakfast or grab a bagel; now my first meal of the day is mostly protein, which helps me feel satisfied. The rest of the day is a balance of protein and good carbs, like an open-face cheese sandwich on whole grain bread or fat-free chicken and some rice crackers."

Frozen Strawberry Mousse

Nancy Silverman, New Haven, Connecticut

Prep time: 15 minutes; Chill time: overnight

- **1 cup graham cracker crumbs (from about 9 squares)**
- **1 quart very ripe strawberries, hulled and sliced + additional for garnish**
- **3 egg whites, at room temperature**
- **⅓ cup sugar**
- **1 container (8 ounces) fat-free frozen whipped topping, thawed + additional for garnish**

Coat a 9" springform pan with cooking spray. Press the graham cracker crumbs into the bottom of the pan. Puree the strawberries in a food processor.

In a large bowl, with an electric mixer on high speed, whip the egg whites and sugar for about 5 minutes, or until glossy peaks form.

In another large bowl, fold the strawberry puree into the whipped topping, then fold the strawberry mixture into the beaten egg whites. Pour into the springform pan and freeze overnight.

To unmold, dip a knife in warm water, run it around the edge of the pan, then release the ring. Garnish with extra berries, mint leaves, and whipped topping and serve immediately.

Makes 8 servings

Per serving: *160 calories, 3 g protein, 32 g carbohydrate, 1.5 g fat, 0 mg cholesterol, 100 mg sodium, 2 g fiber*

Diet Exchanges: *0 milk, 0 vegetable, ½ fruit, 2 bread, 0 meat, 0 fat*

2 Carb Choices

Kitchen Tip

Children and pregnant women should not consume dishes prepared with raw eggs due to the risk of salmonella contamination.

Summer Berry Cake

Dawn Fiore, Bethlehem, Pennsylvania

"This beautiful cake is perfect for company. The natural sweetness of the fruit adds to the overall flavor, and the yogurt keeps the cake incredibly moist."

Prep time: 15 minutes; Cook time: 1 hour

CAKE

- **2 cups all-purpose flour**
- **2½ teaspoons baking powder**
- **¼ teaspoon salt**
- **6 tablespoons trans-free margarine or butter, softened**
- **½ cup granulated sugar**
- **1 egg**
- **1 egg white**
- **¾ cup + 2 tablespoons fat-free vanilla yogurt**
- **1 cup fresh strawberries, hulled and sliced**
- **1 cup fresh blueberries**

TOPPING

- **¼ cup trans-free margarine or butter, softened**
- **⅓ cup packed brown sugar**
- **½ cup all-purpose flour**
- **¾ teaspoon ground cinnamon**
- **Confectioners' sugar (optional)**

Preheat the oven to 350°F. Generously coat a springform pan with cooking spray and lightly dust with flour.

To make the cake: In a medium bowl, combine the flour, baking powder, and salt.

In a large bowl, with an electric mixer on medium speed, beat the margarine or butter and granulated sugar for 1 minute, or until fluffy. Beat in the whole egg and egg white until thoroughly combined. With the mixer on low speed, add the flour mixture, 1 cup at a time, alternating with the yogurt and beating well after each addition. Spread the batter in the springform pan and layer the berries on top.

To make the topping: In a medium bowl, combine the margarine or butter, brown sugar, flour, and cinnamon until the mixture resembles coarse crumbs. Sprinkle evenly over the berries.

Bake for 50 minutes to 1 hour, or until the top is light brown and a wooden pick inserted in the center comes out almost clean. Cool completely in the pan, then run a knife around the outside edge and release the ring. Dust with confectioners' sugar, if desired, and serve.

Makes 10 servings

Per serving: *324 calories, 6 g protein, 48 g carbohydrate, 12 g fat, 34 mg cholesterol, 297 mg sodium, 2 g fiber*

Diet Exchanges: *0 milk, 0 vegetable, ½ fruit, 2½ bread, 0 meat, 2½ fat*

3 Carb Choices

Kitchen Tip

Be sure to rinse the strawberries before hulling them, as hulled berries absorb water like a sponge.

Healthy Cheesecake

Lori Nogler, Leominster, Massachusetts

"Enjoy without the guilt!"

Prep time: 10 minutes; Cook time: 55 minutes
Chill time: 4 hours

CRUST

- **⅔ cup reduced-fat graham cracker crumbs (from about 4 large crackers)**
- **3 tablespoons trans-free margarine or butter, melted**

FILLING

- **1 package (8 ounces) fat-free cream cheese**
- **1 package (8 ounces) reduced-fat cream cheese**
- **1 cup reduced-fat sour cream**
- **2 eggs**
- **2 egg whites**
- **¼ cup Splenda**
- **¼ cup granulated sugar**
- **¼ cup all-purpose flour**
- **1 teaspoon vanilla extract**

Preheat the oven to 350°F.

To make the crust: In a medium bowl, combine the graham cracker crumbs and butter or margarine. Press into the bottom of a 9" springform pan and bake for 7 to 10 minutes.

To make the filling: In a large bowl, combine the cream cheeses, sour cream, eggs, egg whites, Splenda, granulated sugar, flour, and vanilla extract. With an electric mixer on medium speed, beat for 2 minutes, or until smooth. Pour into the prepared crust.

Bake for 45 minutes, or until the center is set. Let cool completely in the pan, then cover and refrigerate for at least 4 hours before serving. When ready to serve, run a knife around the outside edge and release the ring.

Makes 8 servings

Per serving: *260 calories, 12 g protein, 20 g carbohydrate, 15 g fat, 87 mg cholesterol, 350 mg sodium, 0 g fiber*

Diet Exchanges: *½ milk, 0 vegetable, 0 fruit, 1 bread, 1½ meat, 2½ fat*

1½ Carb Choices

Raspberry Cheesecake

JoAnn Hering, Andover, Ohio

Prep time: 20 minutes; Cook time: 1 hour 20 minutes; Chill time: 4 hours

CRUST

1¼ cups reduced-fat graham cracker crumbs
4 tablespoons cinnamon applesauce
2 tablespoons Splenda

FILLING

1 package (8 ounces) fat-free cream cheese
2 packages (8 ounces each) reduced-fat cream cheese
½ cup Splenda
1 cup granulated sugar
2 tablespoons all-purpose flour
1 teaspoon vanilla extract
2 eggs
2 egg whites
2 cups fresh raspberries, pureed and strained to remove the seeds + additional for garnish (optional)

Preheat the oven to 400°F.

To make the crust: In a medium bowl, combine the graham cracker crumbs, applesauce, and Splenda. Press into the bottom of a 9" springform pan.

To make the filling: In a large bowl, combine the cream cheeses, Splenda, granulated sugar, flour, and vanilla extract. With an electric mixer or food processor on medium speed, beat until smooth. Add the whole eggs and egg whites and beat until thoroughly incorporated. Spoon into the prepared crust. Drop the raspberry puree by tablespoons on top and draw a knife through it to create a marbled effect. Place on a baking sheet and immediately reduce the oven temperature to 350°F.

Bake for about 1 hour, or until the center is set. Turn off the oven, prop open the door about an inch, and let the cake finish until the oven is cool.

Cover and refrigerate for 4 hours before serving. When ready to serve, run a knife around the outside edge and release the ring. Top with fresh raspberries, if desired.

Makes 16 servings

Per serving: *138 calories, 7 g protein, 13 g carbohydrate, 7 g fat, 44 mg cholesterol, 216 mg sodium, 1 g fiber*

Diet Exchanges: *0 milk, 0 vegetable, 0 fruit, 1 bread, 1 meat, 1 fat*

1 Carb Choice

Applesauce Spice Cake

Teresa Mattson, Ormond Beach, Florida

"This spice cake helps satisfy my family's sweet tooth."

Prep time: 10 minutes; Cook time: 40 minutes

- **1 cup all-purpose flour**
- **1 cup whole wheat flour**
- **1 cup packed brown sugar**
- **1 tablespoon cornstarch**
- **2 teaspoons baking soda**
- **½ teaspoon salt**
- **½ teaspoon ground cinnamon**
- **¼ teaspoon ground ginger**
- **⅛ teaspoon ground cloves**
- **¼ teaspoon ground mace**
- **2½ cups unsweetened applesauce**
- **½ cup raisins**

Preheat the oven to 325°F. Generously coat a 13" × 9" baking pan with cooking spray and lightly dust with flour.

In a large bowl, mix the all-purpose flour, whole wheat flour, sugar, cornstarch, baking soda, salt, cinnamon, ginger, cloves, and mace. Add the applesauce and raisins and stir well. Pour into the prepared baking pan.

Bake for 35 to 40 minutes, or until a wooden pick inserted in the center comes out clean.

Makes 12 servings

Per serving: *180 calories, 3 g protein, 43 g carbohydrate, 0 g fat, 0 mg cholesterol, 320 mg sodium, 3 g fiber*

Diet Exchanges: *0 milk, 0 vegetable, 1 fruit, 2½ bread, 0 meat, 0 fat*

3½ Carb Choices

SHOPPING SAVVY

Just My Size

Earthbound Farm has an adorable way for you to eat more fruit. Their yummy Thompson seedless organic raisins come in single-serving, simple-to-tote 1.5-ounce snack boxes or 0.5-ounce mini boxes. Tuck one into a briefcase or purse or a child's backpack or lunch box for extreme portion control. A 1.5-ounce snack box contains ¼ cup of raisins, which equals 1 fruit serving. Found at most supermarkets.

Photos courtesy of Earthbound Farm

Light and Easy Cherry Cheesecake

Donna Sheets, Mocksville, North Carolina

"This recipe gave me a snack that I could indulge in without the guilt or the consequences."

Prep time: 10 minutes; Cook time: 8 minutes
Chill time: 4 hours

CRUST

- **1½ cups graham cracker crumbs**
- **¼ cup light trans-free margarine or butter**
- **3 tablespoons sugar**

FILLING

- **1 package (8 ounces) fat-free cream cheese, softened**
- **½ cup sugar**
- **1 egg**
- **1 teaspoon vanilla extract**

TOPPING

- **10 ounces cherry pie filling**

To make the crust: In a 9" glass pie plate, combine the graham cracker crumbs, margarine or butter, and sugar. Press firmly into the bottom of the pie plate to form a crust. Microwave on medium to high power for 1½ minutes, rotating the dish once during cooking.

To make the filling: Place the cream cheese in a medium microwaveable bowl and stir until smooth. Add the sugar, egg, and vanilla extract and mix thoroughly. Microwave on medium to high power for 2 minutes. With a wire whisk, stir until smooth. Return the bowl to the microwave oven and heat for 2 minutes longer. Stir the mixture again and pour into the crust.

Microwave the cheesecake on medium to high power for 2 minutes, or until the center is set, rotating the dish once during cooking. Let cool, then chill in the refrigerator for at least 4 hours before serving. Top with the cherry pie filling.

Makes 8 servings

Per serving: *263 calories, 6 g protein, 41 g carbohydrate, 8 g fat, 29 mg cholesterol, 330 mg sodium, 1 g fiber*

Diet Exchanges: *0 milk, 0 vegetable, ½ fruit, 2 bread, 1 meat, 1½ fat*

3 Carb Choices

Kitchen Tip

To make this recipe even lighter, substitute light cherry pie filling for the regular filling.

Lemon Pudding Cake

Eva Seibert, Allentown, Pennsylvania

"This cake has a soft, puddinglike texture and should be served with a spoon, rather than in slices."

Prep time: 15 minutes; Cook time: 50 minutes

- **¾ cup sugar**
- **¼ cup all-purpose flour**
- **¼ teaspoon salt**
- **3 egg yolks**
- **3 tablespoons trans-free margarine or butter, softened**
- **1 teaspoon grated lemon zest**
- **¾ cup lemon juice**
- **1½ cups 1% milk**
- **3 egg whites, at room temperature**

Preheat the oven to 350°F. Coat an 8" × 8" baking pan with cooking spray.

In a small bowl, sift together the sugar, flour, and salt. Set aside.

In a large bowl, whisk the egg yolks for about 1 minute, or until smooth. Stir in the margarine, lemon zest, lemon juice, and milk. Add flour mixture and combine.

In another large bowl, with an electric mixer on medium speed, beat the egg whites until stiff peaks form. Whisk into the egg yolk mixture until combined and no visible lumps remain. Pour into the prepared baking pan and place that in a larger pan. Fill the outer pan with hot water about 1" up the sides.

Bake for 45 to 50 minutes, or until set. Serve warm or chilled.

Makes 8 servings

Per serving: *173 calories, 4 g protein, 24 g carbohydrate, 7 g fat, 86 mg cholesterol, 167 mg sodium, 0 g fiber*

Diet Exchanges: *0 milk, 0 vegetable, 0 fruit, 1½ bread, ½ meat, 1½ fat*

1½ Carb Choices

Fudge Pudding Cake

Eva Seibert, Allentown, Pennsylvania

Prep time: 15 minutes; Cook time: 45 minutes
Cool time: 15 minutes

- **1 ½ cups all-purpose flour**
- **¾ cup granulated sugar**
- **½ teaspoon baking soda**
- **½ teaspoon salt**
- **3 squares (1 ounce each) unsweetened chocolate**
- **2 tablespoons trans-free margarine**
- **¾ cup low-fat buttermilk**
- **½ teaspoon vanilla extract**
- **¾ cup packed brown sugar**
- **1½ cups boiling water**

Preheat the oven to 350°F. Generously coat an 8" × 8" glass baking pan with cooking spray.

In a small bowl, sift together the flour, granulated sugar, baking soda, and salt.

In a medium heatproof bowl, place 1 chocolate square and the margarine. In a small saucepan over medium heat, warm the buttermilk until tiny bubbles form at the edge(do not let it come to a boil). Immediately pour over the chocolate and margarine. Let stand for about 1 minute, then whisk until the chocolate and butter are completely melted. Add the vanilla extract and stir, then add the flour mixture and stir until well combined.

Pour the batter into the prepared baking pan and sprinkle the brown sugar on top. In a medium heatproof bowl, combine the boiling water with the remaining chocolate squares and stir until the chocolate is melted. Pour evenly over the brown sugar topping.

Bake for 40 to 45 minutes, or until the cake is set. Cool in the pan for 10 to 15 minutes. Serve warm.

Makes 8 servings

Per serving: *320 calories, 5 g protein, 61 g carbohydrate, 8 g fat, 0 mg cholesterol, 280 mg sodium, 2 g fiber*

Diet Exchanges: *0 milk, 0 vegetable, 0 fruit, 3½ bread, 0 meat, 1 fat*

4 Carb Choices

Apple Soufflé Cake

Eva Seibert, Allentown, Pennsylvania

Prep time: 20 minutes; Cook time: 50 minutes

- **1¼ cup all-purpose flour**
- **¼ teaspoon baking powder**
- **3 medium Granny Smith apples, peeled, cored, and thinly sliced**
- **2 teaspoons ground cinnamon**
- **1 cup sugar**
- **⅓ cup trans-free margarine or butter, softened**
- **1 egg**
- **½ cup 1% milk**

Preheat the oven to 350°F. Lightly coat a 9" springform pan with cooking spray.

In a small bowl, combine the flour and baking powder.

In a medium bowl, toss the apples with the cinnamon and ¼ cup of the sugar. Spread evenly in the prepared springform pan.

In a large bowl, with an electric mixer on medium speed, blend the margarine or butter with the remaining ¾ cup sugar for 2 minutes, or until fluffy. Add the egg and mix until thoroughly combined. Add the flour mixture, alternating with the milk. Pour the batter over the apples.

Bake for 45 to 50 minutes, or until golden brown. Cool in the pan for 10 minutes, then release the ring and carefully invert onto a serving plate. Serve warm or chilled.

Makes 8 servings

Per serving: *284 calories, 3 g protein, 49 g carbohydrate, 9 g fat, 36 mg cholesterol, 113 mg sodium, 3 g fiber*

Diet Exchanges: *0 milk, ½ vegetable, 0 fruit, 2½ bread, 0 meat, 1½ fat*

3 Carb Choices

Kitchen Tip

To peel apples, first remove the stem, then, using a vegetable peeler (a knife takes too much of the fruit with the peel), start at the stem end and begin turning the apple into the blade. Angle the peeler at about 60 degrees so that each rotation moves you farther along the circumference of the apple, resulting in a spiral of apple peel.

Walnut-Pumpkin Pie

Kathy Tweed, Cape May Court House, New Jersey

Prep time: 15 minutes; Cook time: 50 minutes

FILLING

- 1 can (16 ounces) pumpkin
- 1 can (12 ounces) evaporated milk
- 2 eggs
- ½ cup packed brown sugar
- ¼ cup Splenda
- 1½ teaspoons ground cinnamon
- ½ teaspoon ground cloves
- ½ teaspoon ground ginger
- ½ teaspoon ground nutmeg
- ¼ teaspoon salt

CRUST

- 1 reduced-fat graham cracker crust (9" diameter)

WALNUT TOPPING

- 1 tablespoon trans-free margarine or butter
- ¼ cup finely chopped walnuts
- ¼ cup packed brown sugar

WHIPPED TOPPING

- 2 cups frozen fat-free whipped topping, thawed
- 2 tablespoons maple syrup

Preheat the oven to 375°F.

To make the filling: In a large bowl, combine the pumpkin, evaporated milk, eggs, brown sugar, Splenda, cinnamon, cloves, ginger, nutmeg, and salt. With an electric mixer on medium speed, beat for 2 to 3 minutes, or until smooth. Fill the pie crust, leaving a ½" border at the top.

Bake for 35 to 40 minutes, or until the top is set and beginning to brown.

To make the walnut topping: While the pie is baking, in a small saucepan, combine the margarine or butter, walnuts, and sugar. Cook over medium heat, stirring constantly, for 2 to 3 minutes, or until the butter and sugar are melted. Remove the pie from the oven and spread the walnut topping evenly over the top. Return to the oven and bake for 10 minutes longer.

To make the whipped topping: A few hours before serving, place the whipped topping in a medium bowl, then fold in the maple syrup. Chill until ready to use.

Makes 8 servings

Per serving: *304 calories, 6 g protein, 50 g carbohydrate, 9 g fat, 70 mg cholesterol, 245 mg sodium, 2 g fiber*

Diet Exchanges: *½ milk, 0 vegetable, 0 fruit, 3 bread, ½ meat, 1½ fat*

3½ Carb Choices

Banana Cream Pie

Stacy Petrovich, Allentown, Pennsylvania

Prep time: 15 minutes; Cook time: 10 minutes
Chill time: overnight

CRUST

- 1¼ cups reduced-fat graham cracker crumbs
- 3 tablespoons trans-free margarine or butter, melted
- 2 tablespoons sugar
- ¼ cup mini chocolate chips

FILLING

- 1 cup fat-free sour cream
- ½ cup fat-free milk
- 1 package (3.4 ounces) instant French vanilla pudding mix
- 12 ounces light frozen whipped topping, thawed
- 3 large bananas, sliced
- 2 teaspoons lemon juice
- 2 tablespoons mini chocolate chips

Preheat the oven to 350°F. Lightly coat a 9"springform pan with cooking spray.

To make the crust: In a medium bowl, combine the graham cracker crumbs, margarine or butter, and sugar, then press into the prepared springform pan.

Bake for 10 minutes. Remove from the oven and sprinkle with the chocolate chips.

To make the filling: While the crust cools, in a large bowl, whisk the sour cream and milk until blended. Add the pudding mix and whisk until dissolved, then add the whipped topping and blend. Spread half of the filling over the prepared crust. Place the bananas in a small bowl and drizzle with the lemon juice, then layer the bananas over the filling. Spread the remaining filling over the bananas and sprinkle the chocolate chips on top. Cover and refrigerate overnight.

Makes 10 servings

Per serving: *282 calories, 3 g protein, 43 g carbohydrate, 10 g fat, 5 mg cholesterol, 288 mg sodium, 2 g fiber*

Diet Exchanges: *½ milk, 0 vegetable, ½ fruit, 2 bread, 0 meat, 2 fat*

3 Carb Choices

Kitchen Tip

To speed the ripening of your bananas, store them in a brown paper bag. To delay ripening, keep them in the refrigerator. The peels will turn black, but the bananas will not ripen any further.

Peaches and Cream Pie

Chris Detris, Breinigsville, Pennsylvania

Prep time: 15 minutes; Cook time: 35 minutes

- **¾ cup all-purpose flour**
- **1 package (3.4 ounces) instant vanilla pudding mix**
- **½ cup + 3 tablespoons 1% milk**
- **1 egg**
- **1 teaspoon baking powder**
- **½ teaspoon salt**
- **1 can (20 ounces) sliced peaches, drained**
- **1 package (8 ounces) fat-free cream cheese, softened**
- **½ cup + 2 teaspoons sugar**
- **½ teaspoon ground cinnamon**

Preheat the oven to 350°F. Coat a 9" glass pie plate with cooking spray.

In a medium bowl, combine the flour, pudding mix, ½ cup of the milk, the egg, baking powder, and salt and stir until blended. Pour into the prepared pie plate and arrange the peaches on top.

In a small bowl, combine the cream cheese, ½ cup of the sugar, and the remaining 3 tablespoons of milk and stir until thoroughly combined. Pour over the peaches and sprinkle with the cinnamon and remaining sugar.

Bake for 35 minutes, or until set. Serve warm or cold.

Makes 8 servings

Per serving: *203 calories, 7 g protein, 42 g carbohydrate, 1 g fat, 29 mg cholesterol, 441 mg sodium, 2 g fiber*

Diet Exchanges: *0 milk, 0 vegetable, ½ fruit, 2 bread, ½ meat, 0 fat*

3 Carb Choices

Kitchen Tip

To make clean pie slices, wipe the knife clean after each slice. This is particularly important with cream pies.

Key Lime Pie

Melissa Dapkewicz, Fogelsville, Pennsylvania

Prep time: 7 minutes; Cook time: 5 minutes
Chill time: 4 hours

- **2 tablespoons cornstarch**
- **⅔ cup Splenda**
- **1 can (12 ounces) evaporated milk**
- **½ cup key lime juice**
- **2 drops green food coloring (optional)**
- **2 cups regular or light frozen whipped topping, thawed**
- **1 reduced-fat graham cracker crust (9" diameter)**
- **Lime slices (optional)**
- **Chocolate shavings (optional)**

In a medium saucepan, whisk together the cornstarch and Splenda, then gradually whisk in the evaporated milk and lime juice. Set over medium heat and cook, stirring constantly, for 5 minutes, or until thick and smooth. Remove from the heat and let cool slightly. Transfer to a large bowl, cover with plastic wrap, and refrigerate for at least 4 hours.

When chilled, add the food coloring (if desired), fold in the whipped topping, and spread into the prepared crust. Garnish with lime slices and chocolate shavings, if desired. Chill until ready to serve.

Makes 8 servings

Per serving: *245 calories, 4 g protein, 28 g carbohydrate, 12 g fat, 12 mg cholesterol, 165 mg sodium, 0 g fiber*

Diet Exchanges: *½ milk, 0 vegetable, 0 fruit, 2 bread, 0 meat, 2½ fat*

2 Carb Choices

Pumpkin Pie

Melissa Dapkewicz, Fogelsville, Pennsylvania

Prep time: 10 minutes; Cook time: 50 minutes
Chill time: 4 hours

- **¾ cup Splenda**
- **1 tablespoon cornstarch**
- **1 tablespoon ground cinnamon**
- **½ teaspoon ground allspice**
- **¼ teaspoon salt**
- **1 can (16 ounces) pumpkin**
- **½ cup reduced-fat sour cream**
- **¾ cup low-fat evaporated milk**
- **¾ cup liquid egg substitute**
- **1 reduced-fat graham cracker crust (9" diameter)**

Preheat the oven to 350°F.

In a large bowl, stir together the Splenda, cornstarch, cinnamon, allspice, and salt. With an electric mixer on medium speed, add the pumpkin, sour cream, evaporated milk, and egg substitute and beat until thoroughly blended. Pour into the prepared crust.

Bake for 45 to 50 minutes, or until set. Cool on a rack, cover, and chill until ready to serve.

Makes 8 servings

Per serving: *294 calories, 7 g protein, 43 g carbohydrate, 11 g fat, 9 mg cholesterol, 399 mg sodium, 2 g fiber*

Diet Exchanges: *½ milk, 0 vegetable, 0 fruit, 2½ bread, ½ meat, 1½ fat*

3 Carb Choices

Zucchini Muffins

Renae Worsley, Clearfield, Utah

"I switched from fattening store-bought muffins to making my own, and I've lost 10 pounds in a year."

Prep time: 12 minutes; Cook time: 20 minutes
Cool time: 10 minutes

- **2 cups whole wheat flour**
- **1 tablespoon baking powder**
- **½ teaspoon salt**
- **1 teaspoon ground cinnamon**
- **¾ cup fat-free milk**
- **2 egg whites, lightly beaten**
- **¼ cup vegetable oil**
- **¼ cup honey**
- **1 cup shredded zucchini**
- **½ cup raisins (optional)**

Preheat the oven to 375°F. Coat a 12-cup muffin pan with cooking spray.

In a large bowl, combine the flour, baking powder, salt, and cinnamon.

In another large bowl, combine the milk, egg whites, oil, honey, and zucchini. Add to the flour mixture and stir until just combined. Do not overmix (the batter is supposed to be a little lumpy). Stir in raisins, if desired. Evenly divide the batter among the prepared muffin cups.

Bake for 20 minutes, or until a wooden pick inserted in the center of a muffin comes out clean. Cool on a rack for 10 minutes before serving.

Makes 12 muffins

Per muffin: *121 calories, 4 g protein, 16 g carbohydrate, 5 g fat, 1 mg cholesterol, 215 mg sodium, 3 g fiber*

Diet Exchanges: *0 milk, 0 vegetable, 0 fruit, 1 bread, 0 meat, 1 fat*

1 Carb Choice

Whole Wheat Cranberry-Orange Muffins

Teresa Mattson, Ormond Beach, Florida

"These muffins are really filling and help stave off holiday nibbling when I'm spending a lot of time in the kitchen."

Prep time: 15 minutes; Cook time: 25 minutes
Cool time: 10 minutes

- **1 tablespoon trans-free margarine or butter, melted**
- **½ cup packed brown sugar**
- **½ teaspoon ground cinnamon**
- **2 cups whole wheat flour or whole grain pastry flour**
- **2 teaspoons baking powder**
- **¼ teaspoon baking soda**
- **1 teaspoon salt**
- **½ cup granulated sugar**
- **3 tablespoons grated orange zest**
- **1 cup orange juice**
- **½ cup unsweetened applesauce**
- **2 eggs, lightly beaten**
- **1 cup fresh cranberries, chopped**
- **½ cup finely chopped walnuts (optional)**

Preheat the oven to 350°F. Generously coat a 12-cup muffin pan with cooking spray.

In a small bowl, combine the margarine or butter, brown sugar, and cinnamon.

In a large bowl, combine the flour, baking powder, baking soda, salt, granulated sugar, and orange zest. In another large bowl, mix the orange juice, applesauce, eggs, cranberries, and nuts, if desired. Add to the flour mixture and stir until just combined. Do not overmix. Evenly divide the batter among the prepared muffin cups. Sprinkle each muffin with the sugar-cinnamon mixture.

Bake for 20 to 25 minutes, or until a wooden pick inserted in the center of a muffin comes out clean. Cool on a rack for 10 minutes before serving.

Makes 12 muffins

Per muffin: *178 calories, 4 g protein, 37 g carbohydrate, 2 g fat, 36 mg cholesterol, 315 mg sodium, 3 g fiber*

Diet Exchanges: *0 milk, 0 vegetable, ½ fruit, 2 bread, 0 meat, ½ fat*

2½ Carb Choices

Kitchen Tip

To make use of stale muffins, crumble them and lightly toast in a 350°F oven for about 15 minutes. Use the toasted crumbs to top desserts such as crisps, cobblers, betties, buckles, and crumb cakes.

Carrot Cake Muffins

Elizabeth Martlock, Jim Thorpe, Pennsylvania

Prep time: 10 minutes; Cook time: 25 minutes
Cool time: 10 minutes

1⅔ cups whole wheat flour
2 teaspoons ground cinnamon
1¼ teaspoons baking soda
½ teaspoon salt
⅔ cup sugar
½ cup vegetable oil
4 eggs
2 cups grated carrots
¼ cup walnuts, chopped (optional)

Preheat the oven to 325°F. Coat a 12-cup muffin pan with cooking spray and dust with flour.

In a medium bowl, sift together the flour, cinnamon, baking soda, and salt.

In a large bowl, combine the sugar and vegetable oil. With an electric mixer on medium speed, beat for 30 seconds, or until thoroughly combined. Add the eggs one at a time, beating for 30 seconds after each addition. Reduce the mixer speed to low and slowly add the flour mixture until thoroughly combined. Add the carrots and walnuts (if desired) and stir until well incorporated. Evenly divide the batter among the prepared muffin cups.

Bake for 25 minutes, or until a wooden pick inserted in the center of a muffin comes out clean. Cool on a rack for 10 minutes before serving.

Makes 12 muffins

Per muffin: *219 calories, 4 g protein, 26 g carbohydrate, 12 g fat, 35 mg cholesterol, 246 mg sodium, 3 g fiber*

Diet Exchanges: *0 milk, ½ vegetable, 0 fruit, 1½ bread, 0 meat, 2½ fat*

2 Carb Choices

Kitchen Tip

Cream cheese icing makes a great topper for these delicious carrot cake treats.

Banana-Honey Muffins

Charlene Bry, Reedsport, Oregon

Prep time: 12 minutes; Cook time: 18 minutes
Cool time: 10 minutes

- **1 cup whole wheat flour or whole grain pastry flour**
- **½ cup all-purpose flour**
- **1 teaspoon baking soda**
- **¼ teaspoon salt**
- **Dash of ground nutmeg**
- **2 eggs, lightly beaten**
- **1 cup mashed banana (about 2 bananas)**
- **½ cup unsweetened applesauce**
- **⅓ cup honey**
- **½ cup dark raisins or chopped walnuts**

Preheat the oven to 375°F. Generously coat a 12-cup muffin pan with cooking spray.

In a large bowl, combine the whole wheat flour, all-purpose flour, baking soda, salt, and nutmeg.

In another large bowl, combine the eggs, banana, applesauce, and honey. With an electric mixer on medium speed, beat for about 1 minute, or until smooth. Add the flour mixture and stir until just moistened. Do not overmix. Fold in the raisins or walnuts, then evenly divide the batter among the prepared muffin cups.

Bake for 15 to 18 minutes, or until a wooden pick inserted in the center of a muffin comes out clean. Cool on a rack for 10 minutes before serving.

Makes 12 muffins

Per muffin: *134 calories, 3 g protein, 30 g carbohydrate, 1 g fat, 35 mg cholesterol, 166 mg sodium, 2 g fiber*

Diet Exchanges: *0 milk, 0 vegetable, 1 fruit, 1 bread, 0 meat, 0 fat*

2 Carb Choices

Kitchen Tip

To make muffins with evenly rounded tops, fill standard-size muffins cups no more than two-thirds full. If using large or jumbo muffin cups, fill each cup three-quarters full.

Honey-Oatmeal Whole Wheat Rolls

Elizabeth Martlock, Jim Thorpe, Pennsylvania

"This is my favorite bread, and it's good for you, too!"

Prep time: 25 minutes; Cook time: 15 minutes
Rise time: 1 hour 15 minutes

4–4½ cups whole wheat flour
¼ cup packed brown sugar
½ cup rolled oats + 1 tablespoon
1 package dry yeast
2 cups warm water (105°–115°F)
1½ tablespoons honey
1 tablespoon molasses
4 tablespoons vegetable oil
½ teaspoon salt
1 egg
1 tablespoon water

Brush the inside of a large bowl with vegetable oil.

In another large bowl, combine the flour and sugar.

Cook ½ cup oats as directed on the package and set aside to cool.

In a small bowl, whisk the yeast into 1 cup of the warm water. Add the honey and set aside for 5 minutes. When foamy, add to the flour and sugar mixture along with the molasses, oil, salt, and remaining 1 cup of warm water. With an electric mixer fitted with a dough hook and set on low speed, beat until combined. Add the cooked oatmeal. Increase the mixer speed to medium and beat for 5 minutes longer, or until the dough becomes smooth, even in color, and has gained a more elastic look. (If kneading by hand, flour a board and work until smooth and elastic.)

Transfer the dough to a large bowl, cover with plastic wrap and a towel, and let rest in a warm, draft-free place for about 1 hour, or until doubled in size.

Preheat the oven to 450°F. Coat baking sheets with cooking spray.

Once the dough has doubled, roll to ½" thickness and cut into rolls. Transfer to the prepared baking sheets and let rise for about 15 minutes, or until the rolls double in size.

Bake for about 12 minutes. While the rolls are baking, lightly beat the egg and the 1 tablespoon of water to create an egg wash. Remove the rolls from the oven, coat with the egg wash, and dust with the dry oats. Bake for 3 minutes longer. Immediately remove the rolls from the pan. Cool slightly on a rack before serving.

Makes 36 rolls

Per roll: *77 calories, 2 g protein, 13 g carbohydrate, 2 g fat, 12 mg cholesterol, 37 mg sodium, 2 g fiber*

Diet Exchanges: *0 milk, 0 vegetable, 0 fruit, 1 bread, 0 meat, ½ fat*

1 Carb Choice

Spiced Pumpkin-Raisin Bread

Elizabeth Martlock, Jim Thorpe, Pennsylvania

Prep time: 30 minutes; Cook time: 1 hour

- **1 cup raisins**
- **½ cup hot water**
- **2 cups whole wheat flour**
- **¾ teaspoon baking soda**
- **1 teaspoon baking powder**
- **1 teaspoon salt**
- **½ teaspoon ground cloves**
- **½ teaspoon ground nutmeg**
- **½ teaspoon ground cinnamon**
- **1 cup canned pumpkin**
- **¾ cup sugar**
- **2 eggs**
- **½ cup vegetable oil**

Preheat the oven to 350°F. Coat a 9" × 5" loaf pan with cooking spray.

Soak the raisins in the hot water for at least 30 minutes.

Meanwhile, in a large bowl, sift together the flour, baking soda, baking powder, salt, cloves, nutmeg, and cinnamon. In another large bowl, combine the pumpkin, sugar, and eggs. With an electric mixer on medium speed, beat for 1 minute, or until thoroughly combined. Gradually add the oil in a steady stream and beat until smooth. Add the flour mixture and mix well. Add the raisins and their soaking liquid and stir gently until smooth. Pour the batter into the prepared loaf pan.

Bake for 1 hour, or until a wooden pick inserted in the center comes out clean. Immediately remove from the pan and cool on a wire rack.

Makes 10 servings

Per serving: *308 calories, 5 g protein, 47 g carbohydrate, 13 g fat, 43 mg cholesterol, 384 mg sodium, 4 g fiber*

Diet Exchanges: *0 milk, ½ vegetable, 1 fruit, 2 bread, 0 meat, 2½ fat*

3 Carb Choices

Tea Frosty

Sandy Umber, Springdale, Arizona

"This recipe satisfies my craving for junk food."

Prep time: 5 minutes

3 or 4 ice cubes
1 cup brewed black or green tea
1 cup low-fat vanilla ice cream or ice milk

In a blender, combine the ice cubes, tea, and ice cream. Blend until smooth.

Makes 2 servings

Per serving: *92 calories, 3 g protein, 15 g carbohydrate, 3 g fat, 9 mg cholesterol, 56 mg sodium, 0 g fiber*

Diet Exchanges: *0 milk, 0 vegetable, 0 fruit, 1 bread, 0 meat, ½ fat*

1 Carb Choice

Kitchen Tip

You can add a little Splenda to this recipe if it's not sweet enough for you.

SHOPPING SAVVY

Super Quenchers

After a hard workout, or a tough day at the computer, refresh yourself with one of Odwalla's Super Quencher juice drinks. AntioxiDance is a mix of cherry, orange, passionfruit, and wild berry concentrate, supplying a superdose of antioxidants. B Berrier is a tart-sweet combo of cranberry, lime, and raspberry, fortified with B vitamins. Each 15.2-fluid-ounce bottle provides 2 servings. Found in natural foods stores and grocery stores nationwide.

Photo courtesy of Odwalla

Mango Freeze

Emilie Toomarian, La Canyada, California

"This has been breakfast for the last two weeks, and I love it! It's full of zing, it's filling, and it fulfills my fruit quotient. I've lost 3 pounds already!"

Prep time: 5 minutes

½ cup vanilla soy milk
¼ cup cold water
1 cup frozen mango
½ banana
½ cup fresh or frozen blueberries

In a blender, combine the soy milk, water, mango, banana, and blueberries. Blend for 1 minute, then stir. Repeat once or twice, depending on the density of the frozen mango.

Makes 2 servings

Per serving: *122 calories, 3 g protein, 28 g carbohydrate, 2 g fat, 0 mg cholesterol, 11 mg sodium, 4 g fiber*

Diet Exchanges: *0 milk, 0 vegetable, 2 fruit, 0 bread, 0 meat, ½ fat*

2 Carb Choices

Pineapple Smoothie

R. E. Dawson, Arlington Heights, Virginia

"This decadently thick drink satisfies my desire for ice cream. Sometimes I vary it by adding coconut flavoring or chunks of strawberries."

Prep time: 5 minutes

1 cup low-fat or light vanilla yogurt
4–6 ice cubes
1 cup pineapple chunks

In a blender, combine the yogurt and ice cubes. Blend, pulsing as needed, until the ice is in large chunks. Add the pineapple and blend at "whip" speed until smooth.

Makes 1 serving

Per serving: *284 calories, 13 g protein, 53 g carbohydrate, 4 g fat, 12 mg cholesterol, 163 mg sodium, 2 g fiber*

Diet Exchanges: *0 milk, 0 vegetable, 1½ fruit, 2½ bread, 0 meat, 1 fat*

4 Carb Choices

Ahoy Soy!

228 Calories

Robin Whitehurst, Annapolis, Maryland

"I drink this shake slowly for breakfast. It's filling and healthy and keeps me from snacking midmorning."

Prep time: 3 minutes

- **1 cup vanilla soy milk**
- **1 tablespoon creamy peanut butter**
- **½ banana**
- **½ teaspoon cinnamon**
- **4–6 Ice cubes**

In a blender, combine the soy milk, peanut butter, banana, cinnamon, and ice cubes. Blend until smooth.

Makes 1 serving

Per serving: *228 calories, 11 g protein, 23 g carbohydrate, 13 g fat, 0 mg cholesterol, 102 mg sodium, 7 g fiber*

Diet Exchanges: *1 milk, 0 vegetable, ½ fruit, 0 bread, ½ meat, 2½ fat*

1½ Carb Choices

Fruity Health Smoothie

Cindy Merrill, South Portland, Maine

"This delicious smoothie takes the place of dessert or an afternoon snack."

Prep time: 7 minutes

- **1 bag (16 ounces) frozen peach slices**
- **1 can (16 ounces) mandarin oranges, drained**
- **1 can (16 ounces) apricots, drained**
- **¼ cup oat bran**
- **Pinch of nutmeg**
- **1 cup light coconut milk**

In a blender, combine the peaches, oranges, apricots, oat bran, and nutmeg.

Blend until smooth. Add the coconut milk and blend until combined. Serve over ice.

Makes 4 servings

Per serving: *330 calories, 5 g protein, 56 g carbohydrate, 13 g fat, 0 mg cholesterol, 17 mg sodium, 9 g fiber*

Diet Exchanges: *0 milk, 0 vegetable, 3½ fruit, ½ bread, 0 meat, 2½ fat*

4 Carb Choices

Austrian Anytime Scramble

Agnes Forras, Seattle, Washington

"This tasty recipe provides variety on a low-carb weight-loss program."

Prep time: 2 minutes; Cook time: 5 minutes

- **4 eggs**
- **2 tablespoons finely chopped fresh parsley**
- **¼ cup (about 1 ounce) shredded Asiago cheese**
- **Salt**
- **Ground black pepper**
- **Tomato slices (optional)**

Coat a medium skillet with cooking spray.

In a medium bowl, beat the eggs, then add the parsley and cheese. Season with salt and pepper. Set the skillet over medium-high heat and add the egg mixture. Scramble until set and serve with fresh tomato slices, if desired.

Makes 2 servings

Per serving: *205 calories, 15 g protein, 2 g carbohydrate, 15 g fat, 437 mg cholesterol, 263 mg sodium, 0 g fiber*

Diet Exchanges: *0 milk, 0 vegetable, 0 fruit, 0 bread, 2½ meat, 2 fat*

0 Carb Choices

SECRETS OF WEIGHT-LOSS WINNERS

• Think outside the box! Breakfast doesn't have to be selected from only a few types of foods. What I do for breakfast sometimes is stir-fry some tasty veggies in a tablespoon of light, heart-healthy canola oil, then add a small splash of stir-fry sauce. I plate the veggies and then sprinkle either feta cheese (low-fat) or thin slices of low-fat turkey breast on top. I get a healthy, filling start to the day that includes protein, "good" carbs, and lots of vitamins.

—Donna Ladouceur, Markham, Ontario, Canada

• Make eating purposeful, not mindless. Whenever you put food in your mouth, peel it, unwrap it, plate it, and sit. Engage all of the senses in the pleasure of nourishing your body.

—Prevention.com

• Remember, *eat* before you meet. Have this small meal before you go to any parties: a hard-cooked egg, an apple, and a thirst-quencher, such as water, seltzer, diet soda, or tea.

—Prevention.com

Spinach Omelet

Shirley Hill, Chatham, Ontario, Canada

"This satisfying omelet is an appetizing alternative to boring salads at lunchtime."

Prep time: 5 minutes; Cook time: 7 minutes

- **4 large eggs**
- **4 egg whites**
- **1 tablespoon 1% milk**
- **1 teaspoon trans-free margarine or butter**
- **1½ cups loosely packed baby spinach**
- **¼ cup (about 1 ounce) shredded part-skim mozzarella or reduced-fat Cheddar cheese**
- **Salt**
- **Ground black pepper**

In a medium bowl, beat the whole eggs, egg whites, and milk. In a large skillet over medium heat, melt the margarine. Add the beaten egg mixture and cook until it begins to set. Sprinkle the spinach and cheese on top, cook for 1 or 2 minutes longer, then gently fold into an omelet. Cook until the spinach appears wilted and the eggs are completely set. Season with salt and pepper to taste and serve immediately.

Makes 2 servings

Per serving: *249 calories, 23 g protein, 4 g carbohydrate, 15 g fat, 438 mg cholesterol, 368 mg sodium, 1 g fiber*

Diet Exchanges: *0 milk, ½ vegetable, 0 fruit, 0 bread, 3 meat, 2 fat*

0 Carb Choices

Kitchen Tip

To prevent your omelet from getting tough and chewy, bring the eggs to room temperature before adding them to the pan. Cold eggs take longer to cook through.

Also, make sure the pan is well-heated before adding the eggs.

Fruit Omelet

Kim Champion, Phoenix, Arizona

Prep time: 5 minutes; Cook time: 7 minutes

- **1 cup liquid egg substitute**
- **½ cup part-skim ricotta cheese**
- **1 cup sliced strawberries**
- **Confectioners' sugar**

Coat a large skillet with cooking spray and warm over medium heat. When hot, add the egg substitute and cook until almost set. Top half of the egg mixture with the ricotta cheese. Gently fold the other half over the ricotta and continue cooking until the ricotta begins to ooze out the sides of the omelet. Remove to a large plate and top with the berries. Sprinkle with the confectioners' sugar and serve immediately.

Makes 2 servings

Per serving: *216 calories, 23 g protein, 10 g carbohydrate, 9 g fat, 20 mg cholesterol, 300 mg sodium, 2 g fiber*

Diet Exchanges: *0 milk, 0 vegetable, ½ fruit, 0 bread, 3 meat, 1 fat*

½ Carb Choice

SHOPPING SAVVY

It's Pronounced "Keen-*wa*"

Need a new way to start your day? Instead of oatmeal, have a bowl of Alti-Plano Gold instant hot cereal made with quinoa. It's ready in 1 minute; all you add is boiling water. Sold in a variety pack of individual serving pouches, it's high in fiber and protein, and it's gluten-free. Flavors include Chai Almond, Oaxacan Chocolate, and Spiced Apple Raisin. Sold at some natural foods stores or on the Web at altiplanogold.com or from the gluten-free pantry at glutenfree.net.

Photo courtesy of AltiPlano Gold

298 Calories

Baked Apple Oatmeal

Anastasia Buyanova, Washington, D.C.

"This oatmeal recipe is great because it has no added sugar like a lot of the prepackaged instant oatmeals. The apple adds sweetness and makes it delicious."

Prep time: 5 minutes; Cook time: 20 minutes

1 medium cooking apple, cored and chopped
½ cup old-fashioned rolled oats
2 tablespoons raisins
½ teaspoon cinnamon
Pinch of salt
1 cup water

Preheat the oven to 350°F.

In a small baking dish, combine the apple, oats, raisins, cinnamon, salt, and water and stir well.

Bake, uncovered, stirring once or twice, for 15 to 20 minutes, or until the mixture becomes thick and the apple pieces are fork-tender.

Makes 1 serving

Per serving: *298 calories, 7 g protein, 66 g carbohydrate, 3 g fat, 0 mg cholesterol, 4 mg sodium, 11 g fiber*

Diet Exchanges: *0 milk, 0 vegetable, 2½ fruit, 2 bread, 0 meat, 0 fat*

SHOPPING SAVVY

Dreamy Yogurt

Fage Total Greek Yogurt is milder and creamier than most yogurts because it's produced in the Greek yogurt tradition. They strain off the whey, making a thicker, less tart, and very delicious yogurt. Choose your fat content: The fat-free comes in a 5.3-ounce container, the 2% fat in a 7-ounce container. A paper inner liner under the foil top keeps the yogurt really fresh. Available in most supermarkets, plus some Trader Joe's and Whole Foods markets.

Photo courtesy of Fage USA

126 Calories

Breakfast Cookies

Jennifer Maslowski, New York, New York

"I was feeling really deprived until I finally worked out this delicious butter-free cookie recipe. Since it's got less fat and sugar and more nutrition than many packaged breakfast products, I've found that having two in place of breakfast on my 'low' days really gives me a morale boost. Of course, one or two make a great snack, too."

Prep time: 15 minutes; Cook time: 13 minutes
Cool time: 10 minutes

- **1½ cups whole wheat flour or whole grain pastry flour**
- **1 teaspoon baking soda**
- **1 teaspoon salt**
- **¾ cup olive oil**
- **½ cup sugar**
- **½ cup honey**
- **2 eggs, lightly beaten**
- **2 tablespoons fat-free milk**
- **1½ tablespoons vanilla extract**
- **2¼ cups quick-cooking oats**
- **1 cup golden raisins**
- **¼ cup mini chocolate morsels (or a dark chocolate bar broken into bits)**

Preheat the oven to 350°F.

In a large bowl, combine the flour, baking soda, and salt.

In another large bowl, whisk together the oil, sugar, and honey until creamy. Add the eggs and stir until thoroughly combined. Add the milk and vanilla extract and stir again. Add the flour mixture and stir until just combined, then fold in the oats, raisins, and mini morsels. Drop the dough by tablespoons onto an ungreased baking sheet.

Bake for 9 to 13 minutes, or until slightly browned but still very soft. Cool on the baking sheet for several minutes, then carefully transfer to a rack.

When completely cooled, store in an airtight container.

Makes 36 cookies

Per cookie: *126 calories, 2 g protein, 18 g carbohydrate, 5 g fat, 12 mg cholesterol, 106 mg sodium, 1 g fiber*

Diet Exchanges: *0 milk, 0 vegetable, 0 fruit, 1 bread, 0 meat, 1 fat*

1 Carb Choice

Photography Credits

Front Cover
Mitch Mandel/Rodale Images

Back Cover
Courtesy of Elise Paone (before and after)

Mitch Mandel/Rodale Images (Sun-Dried-Tomato Salmon, Summer Berry Cake, Meatball Souvlaki)

Interior
All recipe photos by Mitch Mandel/Rodale Images

© Light and Healthy Foods/Brand X Pictures: pages 3, 39

© Food Icons/Brand X Pictures: pages 4, 7, 25, 28, 34

© Food Perspectives/Digital Stock: pages 8, 13, 17, 19, 24, 26, 32

© Naughty but Nice/Digital Vision: pages 21, 30, 38

© Mealtimes/BananaStock: page 36

Courtesy of Nancy Silverman: page 57

Courtesy of Janice Saeger: page 67

Courtesy of James Hoffmann: page 93

Courtesy of Dawn D'Andria: page 117

Courtesy of Ena Bogdanowicz: page 135

Courtesy of Craig Downey: page 169

Courtesy of Karyn Barczewski: page 212

Courtesy of Elise Paone: page 219

Index

Underscored page references indicate boxed text. **Boldfaced** page references indicate photographs.

C

D

E

F

G

M

Q

R

S

T

Conversion Chart

These equivalents have been slightly rounded to make measuring easier.

VOLUME MEASUREMENTS

U.S.	*Imperial*	*Metric*
¼ tsp	–	1 ml
½ tsp	–	2 ml
1 tsp	–	5 ml
1 Tbsp	–	15 ml
2 Tbsp (1 oz)	1 fl oz	30 ml
¼ cup (2 oz)	2 fl oz	60 ml
⅓ cup (3 oz)	3 fl oz	80 ml
½ cup (4 oz)	4 fl oz	120 ml
⅔ cup (5 oz)	5 fl oz	160 ml
¾ cup (6 oz)	6 fl oz	180 ml
1 cup (8 oz)	8 fl oz	240 ml

WEIGHT MEASUREMENTS

U.S.	*Metric*
1 oz	30 g
2 oz	60 g
4 oz (¼ lb)	115 g
5 oz (⅓ lb)	145 g
6 oz	170 g
7 oz	200 g
8 oz (½ lb)	230 g
10 oz	285 g
12 oz (¾ lb)	340 g
14 oz	400 g
16 oz (1 lb)	455 g
2.2 lb	1 kg

LENGTH MEASUREMENTS

U.S.	*Metric*
¼"	0.6 cm
½"	1.25 cm
1"	2.5 cm
2"	5 cm
4"	11 cm
6"	15 cm
8"	20 cm
10"	25 cm
12" (1')	30 cm

PAN SIZES

U.S.	*Metric*
8" cake pan	20 × 4 cm sandwich or cake tin
9" cake pan	23 × 3.5 cm sandwich or cake tin
11" × 7" baking pan	28 × 18 cm baking tin
13" × 9" baking pan	32.5 × 23 cm baking tin
15" × 10" baking pan	38 × 25.5 cm baking tin (Swiss roll tin)
1½ qt baking dish	1.5 liter baking dish
2 qt baking dish	2 liter baking dish
2 qt rectangular baking dish	30 × 19 cm baking dish
9" pie plate	22 × 4 or 23 × 4 cm pie plate
7" or 8" springform pan	18 or 20 cm springform or loose-bottom cake tin
9" × 5" loaf pan	23 × 13 cm or 2 lb narrow loaf tin or pâté tin

TEMPERATURES

Fahrenheit	*Centigrade*	*Gas*
140°	60°	–
160°	70°	–
180°	80°	–
225°	105°	¼
250°	120°	½
275°	135°	1
300°	150°	2
325°	160°	3
350°	180°	4
375°	190°	5
400°	200°	6
425°	220°	7
450°	230°	8
475°	245°	9
500°	260°	–